LORD SIVA
AND HIS WORSHIP

Sri Swami Sivananda

Published by
THE DIVINE LIFE SOCIETY
P.O. SHIVANANDANAGAR—249 192
Distt. Tehri-Garhwal, Uttaranchal, Himalayas, India

Price]   2004   [Rs. 90/-

First Edition:	1945	Second Edition:	1961
Third Edition:	1978	Fourth Edition:	1981
Fifth Edition:	1984	Sixth Edition:	1987
Seventh Edition:	1992	Eighth Edition:	1996
Ninth Edition:	2000	**Tenth Edition:**	**2004**

(3,000 Copies)

©The Divine Life Trust Society

ISBN 81-7052-025-8

Published by Swami Vimalananda for The Divine Life Society, Shivanandanagar, and printed by him at the Yoga-Vedanta Forest Academy Press, P.O. Shivanandanagar, Distt. Tehri-Garhwal, Uttaranchal, Himalayas, India

Dedicated to
LORD SIVA
The Consort of Uma,
Gauri or Parvati,
The Bestower of Eternal Bliss,
Knowledge and Immortality

ॐ

Blessed Aspirants,

Lord Siva is the God of Love. His Grace is boundless. He is the Saviour and Guru. He is the Beloved of Uma. He is Satyam, Sivam, Subham, Sundaram, Kantam. He is the Supreme Light that shines in your heart.

Meditate on His Form. Hear His Lilas. Repeat His Mantra 'Om Namah Sivaya'. Study Siva Purana. Do His worship daily. Behold Him in all names and forms. He will bless you with His Vision.

Swami Sivananda

PUBLISHERS' NOTE

This is a most valuable and instructive book for the aspirants, particularly for the devotees of Lord Siva. It contains fifteen chapters. It is full of instructions on practical Sadhana for attaining Siva-Tattva or God-realisation. The chapters will speak for themselves. The secrets of Siva-Tandava, Sakti-Yoga, Siva-Tattva, etc., are very nicely presented. The translation of the Saiva Upanishads is a beautiful addition. The lives of Siva Acharyas, the Bhaktas and the Nayanars are inspiring and soul-stirring. A study of their lives will make one's life sublime and holy.

Up to this time, there has been no such presentation on this subject. The philosophical portion is highly illuminating and helpful to the readers. The book contains the essence of all Saiva Puranas, such as Periya Puranam, Linga Puranam, Siva Parakrama and Tiruvilayadal Puranam. Its value is enhanced by the addition of some important Siva-Stotras with English translation.

The book is written in a most lucid and clear style. It must be studied by all religious-minded persons, as it is of solid worth from the spiritual point of view.

—THE DIVINE LIFE SOCIETY

CONTENTS

Publishers' Note . . . . (7)

Chapter I
SIVA MANTRAS AND STOTRAS

Siva Mantras	17
Siva-Panchakshara-Stotram	18
Siva-Shadakshara-Stotram	19
Linga-Ashtakam	20
Ardhanari-Natesvara-Stotram	23
Siva-Kavacham	24
Sarvalinga Stava	31
Attributes of Siva	34
The Sublime Vision	37
Song of Lord Nataraja	40
Glory of Lord Siva	40

Chapter II
SIVA TATTVA

Sadasiva	48
Ardhanarisvara	50
World-Teacher	51
Pasupata Yoga	51

Chapter III
THE SAIVA SIDDHANTA PHILOSOPHY

Siva and Tattvas	52
Pati-Pasu-Pasa	54
Sadhana	56
Ashtamurti	58
Suddha Saiva	59

Chapter IV
PHILOSOPHY OF SYMBOLS

Philosophy of Symbols	61
Snake on the Body of Siva	62
Significance of Bhasma, Nandi, etc.	63
Philosophy of Abhisheka	65
Fruit of Abhisheka and Rudra Japa in Siva's Temple	67

Chapter V
PHILOSOPHY OF SIVA TANDAVA

Lord Nataraja — The Great Dancer	75
Dance of Siva	76

Chapter VI
SAKTI YOGA PHILOSOPHY

Siva and Sakti	87
Siva and Parvati	90
The Divine Mother	92

Sakti Energises the Trimurtis 94
Mother Ganga 95
Tripura Rahasya 98
Kamakshi and the Dumb Poet 102
Hymn for Forgiveness to Mother 103

Chapter VII
VIRASAIVISM AND KASHMIR SAIVISM

Virasaivism 105
Kashmir Saivism 106

Chapter VIII
LORD SIVA AND HIS LILAS

Tripurari 109
Siva Jyoti 109
Nilakantha 110
Ravana and Siva 110
Hari and Siva 110
Brahma's Boon 110
Birth of Subrahmanya 111
Lord Siva and Daksha 111
Dakshinamurti 112
Tripura Samhara 113
Lord Siva Curses and Pardons Nakirar . . 114
Know Your Guru 116
Lord Siva Drinks Poison 119

Lord Siva Rides on the Bull	120
Lord Siva Wears the Ganga on His Head	121
Lord Siva's Lila of Begging	121
Lord Siva Wears Trident, Deer, Etc.	122
Lord Siva Has Uma on His Left	123
Lord Siva Wears Elephant's Skin	124
Lord Siva the Fuel-Seller	124
The Twenty-five Lilas of Lord Siva	127

Chapter IX

SIVA YOGA SADHANA

Secret of Panchakshara	128
Meditation on Lord Siva	130
Worship of Siva	132
Siva Manasa Puja	134
Panchakshara Mantra Writing	135
Siva Jnanam	135
Worship of Siva Linga	138
Siva Linga Is Chinmaya	140
Way to Attain Lord Siva	142
Greatness of the Prasad	144
Benefit of Pilgrimage	145
Benefits of Parikrama	147
Real Flower and Arati	149

Chapter X
THE SAIVA UPANISHADS

Rudra of the Upanishads	152
Rudraksha Jabala Upanishad	154
Bhasma Jabala Upanishad	158
Tripura-Tapini-Upanishad	163
Rudra Upanishad	171

Chapter XI
THE SAIVA ACHARYAS

Appar or Tirunavukarasar	176
Tirujnana Sambandhar	181
Sundaramurti	187
Manickavasagar	191
Tirumular	195
Basavanna	196

Chapter XII
SIVA BHAKTAS

Saints and Sages	198
Markandeya	200
The Story of Rishabha Yogi	201
Pushpadanta	205
Kannappa Nayanar	206
Sirutonda Nayanar	210
Lord Siva's Mother	211

The Sixty-three Nayanar Saints 214

Chapter XII
FESTIVALS

Lighting Festival at Arunachala 220
Vijaya Dasami 222
Dassera 225
Vasanta Navaratri 227
Gauri Puja 229

Chapter XIV
SIVA YOGA MAALA

Books on Saivism 230
Chidambara Rahasya 232
Siva and Vishnu Are One 234
Sivaratri Mahima 237
The Twelve Jyotirlingas 241
Siva Nama Kirtan 242

SIVA STOTRAM

Sri Siva-ashtottara-sata Namavali 247
Sri Devi-ashtottara-sata Namavali 249
Sivanirajanam 251
Sivadhyanavali 253
Sivapushpanjali 254
Bilvashtakam 254
Sivamahimnah Stotram 255

Sivastuti	263
Vedasara-Sivastava	263
Sri Siva-manasa-puja	265
Sri Rudram and Chamakam	267
Jagadisa Arati	284
Siva Arati	285

LORD SIVA
AND HIS WORSHIP

Chapter I
SIVA MANTRAS AND STOTRAS

SIVA MANTRAS

१. ॐ नमः शिवाय

Om Namah Sivaya.

Om is Sat-Chit-Ananda Para-Brahman. 'Namah Sivaya' means 'Prostration to Lord Siva.' This is the five-lettered formula or the Panchakshara-Mantra of Lord Siva. This is a very powerful Mantra which will bestow on the chanter the Highest Bliss of Existence.

२. ॐ तत्पुरुषाय विद्महे महादेवाय धीमहि।
    तन्नो रुद्रः प्रचोदयात्॥

Om tatpurushaya vidmahe mahadevaya dheemahi;
Tanno rudrah prachodayat.

We comprehend (realise) that Celebrated Supreme Being (Purusha), and meditate upon that Great God, Mahadeva; may that Rudra impel us to do so. This is the Rudra Gayatri Mantra.

३. ॐ त्र्यंबकं यजामहे सुगन्धि पुष्टिवर्धनम्।
    उर्वारुकमिव बन्धनान्मृत्योर्मुक्षीय माऽमृतात्॥

Om tryambakam yajamahe sugandhim pushtivardhanam;
Urvarukamiva bandhananmrityormukshiya mamritat.

I bow down to that three-eyed Lord Siva, who is full of sweet fragrance, who nourishes the human beings. May He free me from the bondage of Samsara and death, just as a ripe cucumber fruit is separated from the creeper. May I be fixed in Immortality! This is the Maha-Mrityunjaya Mantra.

SIVA-PANCHAKSHARA-STOTRAM

नागेन्द्रहाराय त्रिलोचनाय भस्माङ्गरागाय महेश्वराय ।
नित्याय शुद्धाय दिगम्बराय तस्मै नकाराय नमः शिवाय ॥१

Salutations to the ashes-clad, three-eyed Lord, embodied as the first letter Na, who is pure, nude and eternal and whose garland is the lord of serpents.

मन्दाकिनीसलिलचन्दनचर्चिताय नन्दीश्वरप्रमथनाथमहेश्वराय ।
मन्दारपुष्पबहुपुष्पसुपूजिताय तस्मै मकाराय नमः शिवाय ॥२

I bow to Him, embodied as Makara, who is adorned with innumerable divine flowers as Mandara and the like, who is the Sovereign King of the Pramatha Ganas and whose body is anointed with the holy waters of the celestial Ganga.

शिवाय गौरीवदनारविन्दसूर्याय दक्षाऽध्वरनाशकाय ।
श्री नीलकण्ठाय वृषध्वजाय तस्मै शिकाराय नमः शिवाय ॥३

To the blue-necked Lord, embodied as the letter Si, the destroyer of Daksha's sacrifice and the resplendent Sun of Gauri's lotus-face, whose banner bears the emblem of a bull, may our salutations be.

वसिष्ठकुम्भोद्भवगौतमार्यमुनीन्द्रदेवाऽर्चितशेखराय ।
चन्द्रार्कवैश्वानरलोचनाय तस्मै वकाराय नमः शिवाय ॥४

I prostrate before the God of gods, embodied as Vakara, whose eyes are sun, moon and the fire and whom the gods and the great sages like Vasishtha, Agastya and Gautama, ever pray and worship.

यक्षस्वरूपाय जटाधराय पिनाकहस्ताय सनातनाय ।
दिव्याय देवाय दिगम्बराय तस्मै यकाराय नमः शिवाय ॥५

Prostrations to that Ancient Naked God, embodied as the letter Ya, the Yaksha incarnate, whose hairs are long and matted and who holds Pinaka in His hand.

पञ्चाक्षरमिदं पुण्यं यः पठेच्छिवसन्निधौ ।
शिवलोकमवाप्नोति शिवेन सह मोदते ॥६

Whoever repeats this prayer, composed with the five holy letters before Lord Siva, attains that supreme abode of His and enjoys there with Him in eternal bliss.

SIVA-SHADAKSHARA-STOTRAM

ॐकारं बिन्दुसंयुक्तं नित्यं ध्यायन्ति योगिनः ।
कामदं मोक्षदं चैव ॐकाराय नमो नमः ॥१

May our salutations ever be unto Omkara upon which the Yogins fix their minds constantly in deep meditations and which satiates all desires and sanctions eternal salvation.

नमन्ति ऋषयो देवा नमन्त्यप्सरसां गणाः ।
नरा नमन्ति देवेशं नकाराय नमो नमः ॥२

The mortals and the sages, the gods and the bands of Apsaras bow to the Supreme Lord, who embodied as Nakara, we salute again.

महादेवं महात्मानं महाध्यानं परायणम् ।
महापापहरं देवं मकाराय नमो नमः ॥३

To that Great Effulgent Being, embodied as Makara, who is the Transcendent Self, the destroyer of multifarious

SIVA MANTRAS AND STOTRAS 19

sins and the Supreme Object of worship and meditation, we salute ever and ever again.

शिवं शान्तं जगन्नाथं लोकानुग्रहकारकम्।
शिवमेकपदं नित्यं शिकाराय नमो नमः ॥४

To the all-auspicious and all-powerful Lord of the universe, embodied as the letter Si, who bestows peace and prosperity upon the world and who is One and Eternal, may our salutations always be.

वाहनं वृषभो यस्य वासुकिः कण्ठभूषणम्।
वामे शक्तिधरं देवं वकाराय नमो नमः ॥५

Who wears Sakti on the left hand and who has a bull to ride on and the serpent king Vasuki to garland, to Him embodied as Vakara we salute again and again.

यत्र यत्र स्थितो देवः सर्वव्यापी महेश्वरः।
यो गुरुः सर्वदेवानां यकाराय नमो नमः ॥६

To the all-pervading Mahesvara, embodied as the letter Ya, God with a form and without, who is the preceptor of the shining ones, wherever He may be, may our salutations be.

षडक्षरमिदं स्तोत्रं यः पठेच्छिवसंनिधौ।
शिवलोकमवाप्नोति शिवेन सह मोदते ॥७

Whoever repeats this prayer, composed with the five letters, 'Namah Sivaya' before Lord Siva, enjoys Supreme Bliss in His Eternal Abode.

LINGA-ASHTAKAM

ब्रह्ममुरारिसुरार्चित लिङ्गं निर्मलभाषितशोभितलिङ्गम्।
जन्मजदुःखविनाशकलिङ्गं तत्प्रणमामि सदाशिवलिङ्गम् ॥१

I bow before that Sadasivalinga, which is adored by Brahma, Vishnu and the other gods, which is praised by pure and holy speeches and which destroys the cycle of births and deaths.

देवमुनिप्रवरार्चित लिङ्गं कामदहं करुणाकरलिङ्गम्।
रावणदर्पविनाशनलिङ्गं तत्प्रणमामि सदाशिवलिङ्गम्।।२

I bow before that Sadasivalinga, the destroyer of Cupid, which the Devas and the sages worship, which is infinitely compassionate and which subdued the pride of Ravana.

सर्वसुगन्धिसुलेपितलिङ्गं बुद्धिविवर्धनकारणलिङ्गम्।
सिद्धसुरासुरवन्दितलिङ्गं तत्प्रणमामि सदाशिवलिङ्गम्।।३

l bow before that Sadasivalinga, which is lavishly smeared with variegated perfumes and scents, which elevates the power of thought and enkindles the light of discrimination, and which the Siddhas, the Suras and the Asuras prostrate before.

कनकमहामणिभूषितलिङ्गं फणिपतिवेष्टितशोभितलिङ्गम्।
दक्षसुयज्ञविनाशनलिङ्गं तत्प्रणमामि सदाशिवलिङ्गम्।।४

I bow before that Sadasivalinga, the destroyer of Daksha's sacrifice, which is decorated with various ornaments, studded with different gems and rubies and which glows with the serpent lord coiled around.

कुंकुमचन्दनलेपितलिङ्गं पङ्कजहारसुशोभितलिङ्गम्।
सञ्चितपापविनाशनलिङ्गं तत्प्रणमामि सदाशिवलिङ्गम्।।५

I bow before that Sadasivalinga, which is smeared with saffron and sandal-paste, which is fair with lotus-garlands, and which extirpates the multitude of all accumulated sins.

देवगणार्चितसेवितलिङ्गं भावैर्भक्तिभिरेवच लिङ्गम् ।
दिनकरकोटिप्रभाकरलिङ्गं तत्प्रणमामि सदाशिवलिङ्गम् ॥६॥

I bow before that Sadasivalinga which is worshipped by the multitude of gods with genuine thoughts full of faith and devotion and whose splendour is like that of million suns.

अष्टदलोपरिवेष्टितलिङ्गं सर्वसमुद्भवकारणलिङ्गम् ।
अष्टदरिद्रविनाशितलिङ्गं तत्प्रणमामि सदाशिवलिङ्गम् ॥७॥

I bow before that Sadasivalinga destructive of all poverty in its eight aspects, which is the cause of all creation and which stands on the eight Dalas.

सुरगुरुसुरवरपूजितलिङ्गं सुरवनपुष्पसदार्चितलिङ्गम् ।
परात्परं परमात्मक लिङ्गं तत्प्रणमामि सदाशिवलिङ्गम् ॥८॥

I bow before that Sadasivalinga which is the Transcendent Being and the Supreme Self, worshipped by all Suras with their priest ahead, with innumerable flowers from the celestial gardens.

लिङ्गाष्टकमिदं पुण्यं यः पठेच्छिव सन्निधौ ।
शिवलोकमवाप्नोति शिवेन सहमोदते ॥९॥

Whoever repeats these eight Slokas, praising Sivalinga in the presence of Lord Siva, attains that Supreme Abode of Siva and enjoys there with Him everlasting Bliss and Beatitude.

ARDHANARI-NATESVARA-STOTRAM

चांपेयगौरार्धशरीरकायै कर्पूरगौरार्धशरीरकाय ।
धम्मिल्लकायै च जटाधराय नमः शिवायै च नमः शिवाय ॥१॥

1. To Her whose body shines as bright as polished gold, to Him whose body shines as brilliant as white camphor, to

Her with a fitting head-dress and to Him with matted locks, to Gauri and Lord Siva may our prostrations be.

कस्तूरिकाकुंकुमचर्चितायै चितारजपुञ्जविचर्चिताय ।
कृतस्मरायै विकृतस्मराय नमः शिवायै च नमः शिवाय ॥२॥

2. To Her of body smeared with musk and saffron, to Him of body smeared with ashes of the crematorium, to Her who radiates love through Her beauty, to Him who destroyed the god of love (Kamadeva), to Gauri and Lord Siva may our prostrations be.

चलत्क्वणत्कङ्कणनूपुरायै मिलत्फणाभास्वरनूपुराय ।
हेमाङ्गदायै भुजगाङ्गदाय नमः शिवायै च नमः शिवाय ॥३॥

3. To Her adorned with tinkling beautiful anklets, to Him adorned with snake-anklets circled round His lotus-feet, to Her shining with golden bracelets, and to Him with snake-bracelets, to Gauri and Lord Siva may our prostrations be.

विलोलनीलोत्पललोचनायै विकासिपङ्केरुहलोचनाय ।
समेक्षणायै विषमेक्षणाय नमः शिवायै च नमः शिवाय ॥४॥

4. To Her with eyes as broad as the petals of the blue lotus (Nilotpala), to Him with eyes as broad as the petals of the fully blossomed lotus, to Her with an even number of eyes (two), to Him with an odd number of eyes (three), to Gauri and Lord Siva may our prostrations be.

मन्दारमालाकलितालकायै कपालमालाङ्कितकन्धराय ।
दिव्याम्बरायै च दिगम्बराय नमः शिवायै च नमः शिवाय ॥५॥

5. To Her whose hair is decorated with garlands of sweet-smelling divine flowers, to Him whose neck is adorned with a garland of skulls, to Her decorated with excellent divine garments, to Him clad with eight quarters, to Gauri and Lord Siva may our prostrations be.

अम्भोधरश्यामलकुन्तलायै तडित्प्रभाताम्रजटाधराय ।
गिरीश्वरायै निखिलेश्वराय नमः शिवायै च नमः शिवाय ॥६॥

6. To Her with hair as dark as the fresh rain clouds, to Him with matted hair resembling the colour of lightning, to Her who is the Supreme Goddess of the Mountains (Himalayas), to Him who is the Lord of the entire universe, to Gauri and Lord Siva may our prostrations be.

प्रपञ्चसृष्ट्युन्मुखलास्यकायै समस्तसंहारकताण्डवाय ।
जगज्जनन्यै जगदेकपित्रे नमः शिवायै च नमः शिवाय ॥७॥

7. To Her whose dance marks the creation of the world, to Him whose dance indicates the total destruction of everything in this world, to Her who is the World-Mother and to Him who is the Father of this universe, to Gauri and Siva may our prostrations be.

प्रदीप्तरत्नोज्ज्वलकुण्डलायै स्फुरन्महापन्नगभूषणाय ।
शिवान्वितायै च शिवान्विताय नमः शिवायै च नमः शिवाय ॥

8. To Her with bright shining ear-rings of gems, to Him who wears the great serpent as an ornament, to Her who is ever united with Lord Siva, to Him who is ever in union with Gauri, to Gauri and Lord Siva may our prostrations be.

SIVA-KAVACHAM

Rishi Rishabha spoke to the prince:

Om! My Salutations unto Lord Neelakantha, the Beloved of Uma, the three-eyed and thousand-armed Sambhu, who destroys the enemies by His mighty valour!

I now, for your good, reveal the supreme secret of all penances, possessing which you will be ever successful, redeemed from all sins and pains.

After adoring the Omnipresent Lord, I declare the esoteric truth of Siva-Kavacha, for the weal and welfare of the human beings.

Having seated himself in composure, in a sacred place, one should contemplate upon the Imperishable Siva, with all his senses subdued and Pranas controlled.

He is to meditate upon the Subtle and Infinite, having installed Him in the lotus of the heart, who is all-pervading and beyond the senses.

Having disentangled himself from the bond of actions, by constant meditation and merging wholly in the Supreme Bliss, and with his heart ever intent on the Shadakshara, "Om Namah Sivaya", he is to protect himself thus wearing the armour of Siva (Siva-Kavacha).

May that Supreme Divinity raise me from the dark fathomless well of Samsara, and may His glorious name destroy my sins in their totality.

May He render me free from all fears in all places, who exists in all forms, who is all-blissful, who is smaller than the smallest and is possessed of Mighty Power.

May the eightfold form of Siva who supports the universe as earth, protect me from all earthly ailments, and may He who gives life to humanity as water, remove all my fears from water.

May the Kaala Rudra, who having burnt the worlds at the end of Kalpa, engages Himself in Tandava rescue me from all troubles from wild conflagrations and wind.

May He, the four-headed Trinayana, who is resplendent like lightning and gold, look after me in the East, and He who holds axe, Veda, hook, noose, trident and rosary in His hands, whose colour is dark and glossy as the raining clouds, in the South.

SIVA MANTRAS AND STOTRAS

I adore Him who is pure and spotless as jasmine, moon, conch and crystal, who bears the Vedas and rosary in His hands, as the emblems of bestowing boons and fearlessness, for my safety in the West; and Him who shines like the filament of a blossoming lotus, in the North.

May the five-faced Isvara, who is white and transparent as the crystal, who holds hook, noose, hatchet, skull, drum and trident in His hands and also the Vedas and a rosary as the token of security, protect me above.

I pray to Lord Chandramauli to take care of my head, Phalanetra to look after my forehead, and Him, the destroyer of lust, for the protection of my eyes.

I worship Visvanatha, who is renowned in Vedas and who holds a skull in His hand to keep my nose, ears and skull, safe and sound.

The five-faced Lord, whose tongue is the very Vedas, may protect my face and tongue; the blue-necked One who holds Pinaka in His hands may protect my throat and my hands.

May the Lord, the destroyer of the sacrifice of Daksha, whose arms are the very embodiment of Dharma, guard my chest and arms against all dangers and evils.

May my hip, waist, stomach, navel, be in the care of Dhurjati, the destroyer of Cupid, and who holds the mountain as His bow.

I leave my thighs, knees and feet to His grace who is all graceful.

In the first watch of the day, may Mahesa be my protector; in the second, Vamadeva; Trilochana in the third and Vrishaketu in the fourth.

Sasisekara may keep me from all the evils in the evening, Gangadhara during midnight, Gauripati at dawn and Mrityunjaya at all times.

May Sankara be my protector when I am in, Sthanu, when I am out, Pasupati in the intermediate region and Sadasiva in all places.

May He, who is known by the Vedas, be my saviour when sitting, the Lord of the Pramathas while walking and the Sovereign Ruler of the universe while at rest.

May Nilakantha, the formidable foe of the three cities, dispel my fears and dangers while on the way, and amidst impassable mountainous peaks and valleys.

May the All-powerful Almighty save me from the cruel clutches of the wild animals, while journeying through thick forests.

I offer my hearty prayers to Lord Virabhadra who is as fierce as Yama at the end of Kalpa and whose terrible laughter causes the worlds to tremble, for destroying my fears in crossing the terrible ocean of formidable foes.

I worship the Lord, to destroy the fearful hosts of the enemy armies, arrayed against with the four divisions, infantry, cavalry, chariots and elephants with the sharp and ferocious edge of his sword.

May the blazing fire emitted by the trident of the Lord, reduce the desperadoes to ashes and His bow, Pinaka, frighten the wild beasts such as tigers, lions and bears.

May He protect me from all evils arising from inauspicious dreams and omens, from all mental and bodily agonies, and from all the calamities of different types.

I bow down to that Lord Sadasiva, who is that Supreme Truth, who is the very form of holy hymns and sacred rites, who is beyond all knowledge and truth, who is the incarnation of Brahma and Rudra, whose very eyes are the sun, moon and fire, who has a body smeared with white holy ashes, who wears a crown and artless jewellery, studded with various gems and diamonds, who is the creator, sustainer and destroyer of the whole universe, who destroyed Daksha's sacrifice, who kills the tide of time, who resides alone in Muladhara, who transcends the categories of knowledge, upon whose head the holy Ganga makes her permanent abode, who is immanent in all beings, who possesses the six qualities, who is the truth and essence of philosophy, who is the means to attain the three Vargas (Dharma, Artha and Kama), who is the Lord of the worlds, who wears the eight serpent-kings round His neck and who is the very form of Pranava.

I adore Him who is the embodiment of consciousness, whose form is of ether and the directions, who wears the necklace of stars and planets, who is pure and spotless, who is the preceptor of all the worlds, who is the Supreme Witness of the whole universe, who is the Supreme Secret of all Vedas, who transcends all philosophy, who bestows boons upon all His devotees and who showers mercy upon the poor and ignorant.

I pray to the all-merciful Lord who is ever pure and all-blissful, who is free from all lust, greed and sorrow, who is bereft of all flaws and qualities, who is devoid of desire, disease, ego and attachment, who is all-pervading, endless and eternal, who is beyond the chains of causes and effects, in whom all pains and pleasures, pride, power and pomp, fears and dangers, sins and sufferings sink and die.

I worship Him, who is the embodiment of Pure Consciousness, in whom doubts are dried and actions cease, who is beyond all change, time and destruction, who is full, pure, mute and eternal, who is Satchidananda (Existence-Absolute, Knowledge-Absolute and Bliss-Absolute), who is the incommunicable place personified, who is all-effulgence and effulgence embodied, who is the beneficent One, the radiant vision of Infinite Beauty and Beatitude. O my Lord! Victory on Thee. Thou art the incarnation of Rudra, Raudra and Bhadra. Thou art that Mahabhairava, Kalabhairava. Thy garlands are the necklaces of skulls and Thou holdest the divine weapons Khatvanga, sword, skin (Charma), noose, hook, drum, trident, bow, arrow, club, Sakti (a weapon) and the like in Thy hands. O thousand-faced God! Thou art fearful to look at with Thy terrible teeth and Thy pealing laughter pierces through all the worlds. Serpents are Thy ear-rings, Thy garlands and bracelets. Thou wearest elephant-skin on Thy body. Thou art the conqueror of death, the destroyer of the three cities, O three-eyed God!

Thou art all-existent, Immanence of things, Essence of Peace, and the Supreme Bliss and Silence, O Sambhu! Thou art verily the Brahman of Veda and Vedanta. Thou art all-pervading, ancient and eternal. Save me, my Lord! Dispel my fears from unnatural death and dangers, destroy my enemies, with Thy trident and chop them off with the edge of Thy sword. Frighten the bands of Betala, Kushmanda and the like with the bow and arrows. Save me from falling into the pit of fearful hell and render me free and fearless. Cover me with Thy armour and protect me always. I am poor, meek, humble and helpless. I dedicate all at Thy feet and leave myself at Thy disposal. Thou art my only prop and saviour. O Lord Sadasiva! Mrityunjaya! Tryambaka! Salutations to Thee again and again.

Rishabha spoke: In this manner, I have unfolded the supreme secret of Siva-Kavacha which grants every boon and gratifies all desires and which relieves one from all pains and sufferings.

Always, one clad in this (Armour of Siva), is free from all fears, all dangers and downfall, by His divine Grace.

One, released from chronic diseases and premature death, enjoys long life and Eternal Bliss.

This Armour (of Siva) strikes at the root of evil and elevates one to the lofty heights of peace and prosperity.

One, in the end, redeemed from all sins and obstacles, attains the blissful seat of salvation by its mighty power.

Therefore my boy! Wear this presented by me with full faith, by which you will be very happy.

Suta said: Having spoken thus, sage Rishabha gave the prince a big conch, a mighty sword with which he would be able to conquer his enemies in no time.

Then he sprinkled some holy ashes on his body and gave the magnetic touch which rendered him feel the strength of twelve thousand elephants.

Having obtained such strength, power and courage, the prince shone with the glory of the autumn sun!

The Sage again told him: This sword given by me is purified by sacred Mantras, by whose mere sight, the enemy will become lifeless. Death itself will be terrified and take to his heels.

Hearing the thundering sound of this conch, the enemies will fall down unconscious, with their weapons cast aside.

These are the two Instruments which will destroy the opposing armies and encourage your own.

Clad in Siva's Armour, you will destroy your enemies with these two divine weapons. You will obtain your ancestral kingdom and become the sovereign ruler of this earth.

Consoling him thus, with all his blessings, the Sage after receiving due respects and honours, departed.

SARVALINGA STAVA

O Omkaresvara, Umamahesvara,
Ramesvara, Tryambakesvara,
Mahabalesvara, Mahakalesvara, Muktesvara,
        Om Namah Sivaya.

O Jambukesvara, Kalahastisvara,
Tarakesvara, Paramesvara,
Narmadesvara, Nagesvara, Nanjundesvara,
        Om Namah Sivaya.

O Ardhanarisvara, Kapalisvara,
Brihadisvara, Bhuvanesvara, Kumbhesvara,
Vriddhachalesvara, Ekambaresvara, *Om Namah Sivaya.*

O Kailasapate, Pasupate,
Gauripate, Parvatipate,
Umapate, Sivakamipate,   *Om Namah Sivaya.*

O Visvesa, Tyagesa, Sarvesa,
Sundaresa, Mahesa, Jagadisa,
Ghusrunesa, Matribhutesa,   *Om Namah Sivaya.*

O Kailasanatha, Kashinatha,
Kedaranatha, Muktinatha,
Amaranatha, Pasupatinatha,   *Om Namah Sivaya.*

O Kasi Visvanatha, Kanchinatha,
Somanatha, Baijnatha, Vaidyanatha,
Tunganatha, Trilokinatha,   *Om Namah Sivaya.*

O Kalabhairava, Tripurantaka,
Nilalohita, Haro Hara,
Siva, Sambho, Sankara, Sadasiva, *Om Namah Sivaya.*

O Mahadeva, Mahakala,
Nilakantha, Nataraja, Chandrasekhara,
Chidambaresa, Papavimochaka, *Om Namah Sivaya.*

O Halasyasundara, Minakshisundara,
Kalyanasundara, Kadambavanasundara,
Srisaila-vasa, Virabhadra,   *Om Namah Sivaya.*

O Gauri Sankara, Gangadhara,
Dakshinamurte, Mrityunjaya,
Om Namo Bhagavate Rudraya,   *Om Namah Sivaya.*

O Vaikkatappa, Tiruvoniappa.
Chittambala, Ponnambala,
Chitsabhesa, Chidambaresa,   *Om Namah Sivaya.*

O Kamadahana, Brahmasiraschheda,
Kurma-Matsya-Varaha-Svarupa,
Virabhairava, Vrishabharudha,   *Om Namah Sivaya.*

O Kalantaka, Mallikarjuna,
Arunachala, Nandivahana,
Bhikshadana, Bhaktarakshaka,   *Om Namah Sivaya.*

O Bhimasankara, Bhasmadhara,
Pannagabhushana, Pinakadhari,
Trilochana, Trisulapane,   *Om Namah Sivaya.*

Who can describe Thy glory O Hara!
Even Sruti says Neti Neti,
Thou art Supreme Brahman,
Thou art full of auspicious qualities, *Om Namah Sivaya.*

O Destroyer of Tripuras,
My silent adorations unto Thee,
Thou art Rudra, the destroyer,
Thou art bestower of Immortality, *Om Namah Sivaya.*

Thy vehicle is the bull,
Tiger-skin is Thy garment,
Trident, Damaru, Axe,
Are Thy instruments,   *Om Namah Sivaya.*

Snake is Thy ornament,
You are besmeared with ashes,

Ganga flows from Thy head,
Moon is Thy Chudamani,   *Om Namah Sivay*

You incarnated as Dakshinamurti,
To initiate Sanaka, Sanandana,
Into the mysteries of Brahma Jnana,
Through silence and Chinmudra,   *Om Namah Sivaya.*

Thy form speaks of renunciation,
Thou art embodiment of knowledge,
Thou art famous for Nritya,
Agada Bhum is Thy song,   *Om Namah Sivaya.*

You assumed the form of light,
Brahma and Vishnu failed
To measure Thee,
Thou art Infinity and Eternity,   *Om Namah Sivaya.*

You saved Markandeya, Manikkavasakar,
You blessed Kannappa, Tirunavukkarasu,
Tirujnanasambandhar, Sundarar,
Appar and Pattinathadiyar,   *Om Namah Sivaya.*

Thou art ocean of mercy,
Thou art giver of boons,
You blessed Arjuna and Bana,
You swallowed the poison,
And saved the world.   *Om Namah Sivaya.*

You destroyed the Cupid,
Thou art the Father
Of Ganesa and Subrahmanya,
You cut the head of proud Daksha, *Om Namah Sivaya.*

Tripurasundari, Rajarajesvari,
Gauri, Chandi, Chamundi,
Durga, Annapurna,
Are Thy Saktis,   *Om Namah Sivaya.*

Thy garland is strung of skulls,
Thy matted lock is the abode for Ganga,

SIVA MANTRAS AND STOTRAS

Thou dwellest in the cremation ground,
Thy form is terrible, Thou art Mahakala,
Thou art Death unto death itself,   *Om Namah Sivaya.*
Thou art the greatest Devotee of Hari,
Thou wearest in Thy head the Ganga,
Which flows from Hari's feet,
You initiate the Rarna Taraka Mantra at Banares,
                              Om Namah Sivaya.

Lord Rama worshipped Thee alone at Ramesvar,
You existed in sound as Sadasiva,
In the heart as Atmalinga,
In the Vedas as Pranava,   *Om Namah Sivaya.*

O Hara! O Lord! O Siva!
Prostrations unto Thee again and again,
Let me remember Thee always,
Let me ever dwell in Thee,   *Om Namah Sivaya.*

Make me desireless, fearless and 'I' less,
Let me ever repeat Thy five letters,
Let me behold Thee everywhere,
Let me merge in Thee for ever,   *Om Namah Sivaya.*

He who sings or repeats or hears this Sarvalinga Stava
Morning and evening with faith, devotion and Bhava,
Will be freed from all sins and diseases,
Will attain son, wealth, prosperity,
                              Bhakti, Bhukti, Mukti.

ATTRIBUTES OF SIVA

1. *Advaita, Akhanda, Akarta, Abhokta,*
   Asanga, Asakta, Nirguna, Nirlipta,
   Chidanandarupah Sivoham Sivoham.
   Non-dual, indivisible, non-doer, non-enjoyer,
   Unattached, without qualities,
   I am Siva (auspiciousness),
   I am Siva of the form of knowledge and bliss.

2. *Avyakta, Ananta, Amrita, Ananda,*
   Achala, Amala, Akshara, Avyaya,
   Chidanandarupah Sivoham Sivoham.
   Unmanifested, endless, immortal, bliss,
   Immovable, without impurities, imperishable,
   inexhaustible,
   I am Siva, I am Siva of the form of knowledge and bliss.

3. *Asabda, Asparsa, Arupa, Agandha,*
   Aprana, Amana, Atindriya, Adrisya,
   Chidanandarupah Sivoham Sivoham.
   Soundless, touchless, smell-less, formless,
   Without Prana, without mind, without senses, unseen,
   I am Siva, I am Siva of the form of knowledge and bliss.

4. *Satyam, Sivam, Subham, Sundaram, Kantam,*
   Sat-chit-ananda, Sampurna, Sukha, Santam,
   Chidanandarupah Sivoham Sivoham.
   Truth, auspiciousness, good, beautiful, resplendent,
   Existence-knowledge-bliss, all-full, pure happiness,
   peaceful.
   I am Siva, I am Siva of the form of knowledge and bliss.

5. *Chetana, Chaitanya, Chidghana, Chinmaya,*
   Chidakasa, Chinmatra, Sanmantra, Tanmaya,
   Chidanandarupah Sivoham Sivoham.
   Consciousness, mass of knowledge, full of knowledge,
   All-pervading like ether, consciousness alone, full of That,
   I am Siva, I am Siva of the form of knowledge and bliss.

6. *Amala, Vimala, Nirmala, Achala,*
   Avangmanogochara, Akshara, Nischala,
   Chidanandarupah Sivoham Sivoham.
   Pure, stainless, immovable,
   Beyond the reach of mind and speech,
   imperishable, steady,
   I am Siva, I am Siva of the form of knowledge and bliss.

7. *Nitya, Nirupadhika, Niratisaya Ananda,*
   Nirakara, Hrimkara, Omkara, Kutastha,
   Chidanandarupah Sivoham Sivoham.
   Eternal, without attributes, supreme bliss,
   Without form, Hrim and Om (Pranava), rock-seated Self,
   I am Siva, I am Siva of the form of knowledge and bliss.

8. *Purna, Para Brahma, Prajnana Ananda,*
   Sakshi, Drashta, Turiya, Vijnana Ananda,
   Chidanandarupah Sivoham Sivoham.
   All-full, Paramatman, knowledge and bliss,
   Witness, Seer, the fourth state, Self-knowledge, bliss.
   I am Siva, I am Siva of the form of knowledge and bliss.

9. *Satyam, Jnanam, Anantam, Anandam,*
   Sat-chit-ananda, Svayam Jyoti Prakasam,
   Chidanandarupah Sivoham Sivoham.
   Truth, knowledge, endless, bliss,
   Existence-knowledge-bliss, self-luminous,
   I am Siva, I am Siva of the form of knowledge and bliss.

10. *Kaivalya, Kevala, Kutastha, Brahma,*
    Suddha, Siddha, Buddha, Sat-chit-ananda,
    Chidanandarupah Sivoham Sivoham.
    Immortality, alone, changeless, Self,
    Pure, perfect, illumined, existence-knowledge-bliss,
    I am Siva, I am Siva of the form of knowledge and bliss.

11. *Nirdosha, Nirmala, Vimala, Niranjana,*
    Nitya, Nirakara, Nirguna, Nirvikalpa,
    Chidanandarupah Sivoham Sivoham.
    Without defects, pure, spotless,
    Eternal, formless, without qualities, superconsciousness,
    I am Siva, I am Siva of the form of knowledge and bliss.

12. *Atman, Brahma Svarupa, Chaitanya-Purusha,*
    Tejomaya, Ananda, 'Tat-Tvam-Asi' Lakshya,
    Chidanandarupah Sivoham Sivoham.

Self, Supreme Self, consciousness,
Full of light, bliss, that which is indicated by
'Tat-Tvam-Asi—Thou art That'.
I am Siva, I am Siva of the form of knowledge and bliss.

13. *'Soham', 'Sivoham', 'Aham-Brahma-Asmi' Mahavakya,
Suddha, Sat-chit-ananda, Purna Para Brahma,
Chidanandarupah Sivoham Sivoham.*
'I am He', 'I am Siva', 'I am Brahman',
Pure, existence-knowledge-bliss, all-full Self,
I am Siva, I am Siva of the form of knowledge and bliss.

THE SUBLIME VISION

I

The adorable Lord of all bliss, all love, all mercy,
The supreme light that shines in my heart,
The Lord who fed Sambandhar and Appar,
Him I saw at the abode of Rishis.

The Great Ancient, the Goal of Yogis,
The Supreme Purusha that dwells in the Puri,
The Adi Deva, whom the Vedas sing of,
Him I saw at the abode of Rishis.

The pillar of light which baffled Brahma and Vishnu,
The ocean of mercy who saved Markandeya,
The Lord of Madurai whom the Pandya beat,
Him I saw at the abode of Rishis.

The Supreme Teacher who taught the four,
The Adi Deva who has asssumed the five,
Parama, Vyuha, Vibhava, Archa and Antaryamin,
Him I saw at the abode of Rishis.

The Lord who pervades the universe,
The thread-soul, the Sutratman,
The over-soul, the purport of Srutis,
Him I saw at the abode of Rishis.

The effulgence who is above the Three,
Who exists even after the Pralaya,
Who saved Kannappa and Sundarar,
Him I saw at the abode of Rishis.

He who drank the poison and saved the world,
He who danced at Chidambaram,
He who shines as the Jyotirlinga,
Him I saw at the abode of Rishis.

He who brought the jackal-horses to Pandya,
He who gave pearl-palanquin to Sambandhar,
He who is the essence of Panchakshara,
Him I saw at the abode of Rishis.

He who dwells in Banares and Vedas,
In Ramesvar, Arunachal and Kanchi,
In the hearts of all beings,
Him I saw at the abode of Rishis.

He who pleaded on behalf of Darumi,
He who dwells in Kailas with Uma,
He who restored the eyesight of Sundarar,
Him I saw at the abode of Rishis.

II

The Lord who gave stick to blind Appar,
The Grace who begged alms for Sundarar,
The Marga Bandhu who showed the way to
                      Appayya Dikshitar,
  Him I saw at the abode of Rishis.

The Mercy who took the message to Paravai,
The Love who wrote the poem for Darumi,
The Fire that burnt Nakirar,
Him I saw at the abode of Rishis.

The Lord who became a cooly at Madurai
And carried earth for stopping the floods

For the sake of a little sweetmeat,
Him I saw at the abode of Rishis.

The Lord who created tank and garden for the devotee,
Who became the slave of His devotees,
Who sent the pearl-palanquin to Sambandhar,
Him I saw at the abode of Rishis.

The hunter who quarrelled with Arjuna,
The untouchable who debated with Sankara,
The groom who took the horses to Pandya,
Him I saw at the abode of Rishis.

The Lord who has Uma as His left side,
Who is also Narayana of the milk ocean,
Who is the child sleeping on the banian leaf,
Him I saw at the abode of Rishis.

The Lord who is the Holiest, the Oldest,
Who is Jyoti within the Jyoti,
Who is praised by the Devas and Rishis,
Him I saw at the abode of Rishis.

He who is Ambalam in Chidambaram,
Who is brilliance in Arunachalam,
Who is the great thief hiding in forms,
Him I saw at the abode of Rishis.

The Satguru who reveals in the Chidakasa
Who breaks all the three bonds,
Who leads the aspirants to the land of Moksha,
Him I saw at the abode of Rishis.

The Lord who dwells in the Sahasrara,
Who is the way, the goal and the centre,
Who is the truth in the Mahavakya,
Him I saw at the abode of Rishis.

SONG OF LORD NATARAJA

Sivaya Nama Om Sivaya Namah,
Sivaya Nama Om Namah Sivaya,
O Lord Nataraja of Chidambaram,
King Dancer of Thillai Ambalam,
Beloved consort of Sivakami Sundari,
Bhuvanesvari, Rajarajesvari,
Destroyer of sin, bestower of prosperity,
Remover of suffering, giver of Immortality,
Sivaya Nama Om Sivaya Namah,
Sivaya Nama Om Namah Sivaya.

Holder of Trident, drinker of poison,
Master of Yogis, ruler in the Sun,
Dweller in Kailas, rider of Nandi,
Destroyer of Cupid, Lord of Siddhi,
The three-eyed Lord, the five-faced God,
The blue-necked God, the God of gods,
Sivaya Nama Om Sivaya Namah,
Sivaya Nama Om Namah Sivaya.

Thou art my Guru and sole-refuge,
Salutations unto Thee O Lord of Mercy,
Bless me with Thy shower of Grace,
Let me behold Thy benign face,
Let me merge in Thee for ever,
This is my real fervent prayer.
Sivaya Nama Om Sivaya Namah,
Sivaya Nama Om Namah Sivaya.

GLORY OF LORD SIVA

Om. I bow with folded hands to Lord Siva, who is the Lord of the universe (Jagat-Pati), world's Teacher (Jagad-Guru), who is the destroyer of Tripuras (three cities — egoism, lust and anger), who is the Lord of Uma (Uma Sankar), Gauri (Gauri Sankar), Ganga (Ganga

Sankar), who is full of light (Jyotirmaya), knowledge and bliss (Chidanandamaya), who is the Lord of Yogins (Yogesvara), who is the storehouse of knowledge and who is known by various names as Mahadeva, Sankara, Hara, Sambhu, Sadasiva, Rudra, Sulapani, Bhairava, Uma Mahesvara, Nilakantha, Trilochana (the three-eyed), Tryambaka (the three-eyed), Visvanatha, Chandrasekhara, Ardhanarisvara, Mahesvara, Nila-lohita, Parama Siva, Digambara, Dakshinamurti, etc.

How merciful He is! How loving and kind He is! He even wears the skulls of His devotees as a garland around His neck. He is an embodiment of renunciation, mercy, love and wisdom. It is a mistake to say that He is the destroyer. Lord Siva in reality is the regenerator. Whenever one's physical body becomes unfit for further evolution in this birth either by disease, old age or other causes, He at once removes this rotten physical sheath and gives a new, healthy, vigorous body for further quick evolution. He wants to take all His children to His lotus-feet quickly. He desires to give them His glorious 'Siva-Pada'. It is easier to please Siva than Hari. A little Prem and devotion, a little chanting of His Panchakshara is quite sufficient to infuse delight in Siva. He gives boons to His devotees quite readily. How large is His heart! He gave Pasupatastra to Arjuna without difficulty for his little penance. He gave a precious boon to Bhasmasura. In Kalahasti near Tirupati, He gave Darsan to Kannappanayanar, the devoted hunter who plucked his two eyes to replace the weeping eyes in the Murti. In Chidambaram even the untouchable Pariah saint, Nandan had Darsan of Lord Siva. He ran with tremendous speed to make the boy Markandeya immortal, when he was in the clutches of the God of Death—Yama. Ravana of Lanka pleased Siva with his Sama chantings. He initiated the four virgin youths Sanaka, Sanandana, Sanatana and

Sanatkumara into the mysteries of Jnana in the form of Guru Dakshinamurti. In Madurai, in Southern India, Sundaresvara (Lord Siva) assumed the form of a boy and carried earth on His head for a devoted lady for the sake of Puttu (a kind of sweetmeat) as wages, when an anicut was erected in the Vaigai river. Look at the unbounded mercy for His devotees! When Lord Brahma and Lord Vishnu went to find out the head and feet of Lord Siva, He assumed an infinite, expansive blaze of light (Jyotirmaya-Svarupa). They were baffled in their attempts. How magnanimous and self-effulgent He is! He lived in the house of Pattinattu Swami in Southern India for several years as his adopted son, and disappeared after giving him the small note: "Even a broken needle will not follow you after your death". The reading of this note was the starting point for attainment of Jnana for Pattinattu Swami. Why not you attempt this very second with sincerity to realise God (Lord Siva)?

Hatha Yogins awaken the Kundalini Sakti that is lying dormant in the Muladhara Chakra by Asana, Pranayama, Kumbhaka, Mudra and Bandha, take it above through different Chakras (centres of spiritual energy) — Svadhishthana, Manipura, Anahata, Visuddha and Ajna — and join it with Lord Siva at the Sahasrara, the thousand-petalled lotus at the crown of the head. They drink the nectar of Immortality (Siva-Jnana-Amritam). This is termed Amritasrava. When the Sakti is united with Siva, full illumination comes for the Yogi.

Lord Siva represents the destructive aspect of Brahman. That portion of Brahman that is enveloped by Tamo-Guna-Pradhana-Maya is Lord Siva who is the all-pervading Isvara and who also dwells in Mount Kailas. He is the Bhandar or storehouse of Wisdom. Siva minus Parvati, Kaali or Durga is pure Nirguna Brahman. With

Maya (Parvati) He becomes the Saguna Brahman for the purpose of pious devotion of His devotees. Devotees of Rama must worship Lord Siva also. Rama Himself worshipped Lord Siva at the famous Ramesvaram. Lord Siva is the Lord of Ascetics and Lord of Yogins robed in space (Digambara).

His Trisul (trident) that is held in His right hand represents the three Gunas—Sattva, Rajas and Tamas. That is the emblem of sovereignty. He rules the world through these three Gunas. The Damaru in His left hand represents the Sabda Brahman. It represents OM from which all languages are formed. It is He who formed the Sanskrit language out of the Damaru sound.

The wearing of the crescent moon on His head indicates that He has controlled the mind perfectly. The flow of the Ganga represents the nectar of immortality. Elephant represents symbolically the Vritti pride. Wearing the skin of the elephant denotes that He has controlled pride. Tiger represents lust. His sitting on the tiger's skin indicates that He has conquered lust. His holding deer on one hand indicates that He has removed the Chanchalata (tossing) of the mind. Deer jumps from one place to another swiftly. The mind also jumps from one object to another. His wearing of serpents around the neck denotes wisdom and eternity. Serpents live for a long number of years. He is Trilochana, the three-eyed One, in the centre of whose forehead is the third eye, the eye of wisdom. Nandi, the bull that sits in front of Sivalinga, represents Pranava (Omkara). The Linga represents Advaita. It points out "I am one without a second—*Ekameva Advitiyam.*" Just as a man raises his right hand above his head, pointing out his right index-finger only.

Kailas hills in Tibet are a huge range with a central, beautiful, naturally carved and decorated shining peak, eternally clad with silvery snow, 22,280 feet above sea level. Some take the height to be 22,028 feet. This particular peak is in the form of a natural, huge Siva Linga (Virat form). This is worshipped as the form of Lord Siva from a distance. There is neither a temple, nor a Pujari, nor a daily Puja there. I had the fortune to have Darsana of Kailas through the grace of Lord Siva, on July 22, 1931. I even climbed with panting breath to the foot of Kailas peak where the Indus takes its origin. It is a very picturesque, soul-stirring scenery. You will have to ascend from Didipha Guha, the first halting stage in Parikrama of Kailas. The Indus gushes out as a small streamlet through blocks of ice from behind the back portion of Kailas peak. Though in the pictures of Lord Siva it is shown that the Ganga flows from His head, it is really the Indus (Sindhu) that takes its origin from the head of Siva (Kailas) in the physical plane. Parikrama of Kailas covers 30 miles. It takes three days. On the way comes the famous and sacred Gauri Kund which is eternally covered with snow. You will have to break the snow when you take a bath.

The Name of Lord Siva chanted in any way, correctly or incorrectly, knowingly or unknowingly, carefully or carelessly, is sure to give the desired result. The glory of the Name of Lord Siva cannot be established through reasoning and intellect. It can certainly be experienced or realised only through devotion, faith and constant repetition of the Name and singing His hymns with Bhava. Every Name is filled with countless potencies or Saktis. The power of the Name is ineffable. Its glory is indescribable. The efficiency and inherent Sakti of the Name of Lord Siva are unfathomable.

The mind is purified by constant repetition of Siva-Stotra and Names of Lord Siva. The Stotras are filled with good and pure thoughts. Repetition of the hymns to Siva strengthens the good Samskaras. "As a man thinks, that he becomes". This is the psychological law. The mind of a man who trains himself in thinking good, holy thoughts, develops a tendency to think of good thoughts. His character is moulded and transformed by continued good thought. When the mind thinks of the image of the Lord during singing His hymns, the mental substance actually assumes the form of the image of the Lord. The impression of the object thought of is left in the mind. This is called Samskara. When the act is repeated very often, the Samskaras gain strength by repetition, and a tendency or habit is formed in the mind. He who entertains thoughts of Divinity, becomes transformed actually into the Divinity himself by constant thinking. His Bhava or disposition is purified and divinised. When one sings the hymns of Lord Siva, he is in tune with the Lord. The individual mind melts in the cosmic mind. He who sings the hymns becomes one with Lord Siva.

Just as fire has the natural property of burning inflammable things, so also the Name of Lord Siva has the power of burning the sins, Samskaras and Vasanas and bestowing eternal bliss and everlasting peace on those who repeat the Name of the Lord.

Just as burning quality is natural and inherent in fire, so also the power of destroying sins with their very root and branch and bringing the aspirant into blissful union with the Lord through Bhava Samadhi, is natural and inherent in the Name of God.

O friends! Take refuge in the Name of Siva. Sing His hymns. Nami and Name are inseparable. Sing Lord Siva's hymns incessantly. Remember the Name of the Lord with every incoming and outgoing breath. In this Iron Age, Nama-Smarana or singing the hymns is the easiest, quickest, safest and surest way to reach God and attain Immortality and perennial joy. Glory to Lord Siva! Glory to His Name!!

Ravana propitiated Lord Siva by his hymns. Pushpadanta pleased Lord Siva by his celebrated Stotra—Siva Mahimna Stotra, which is even now sung by all devotees of Siva throughout India, and obtained all Aisvarya or Siddhis and Mukti. The glory of the Stotras of Siva is indescribable. You must all sing the hymns of Lord Siva and obtain His grace and salvation, not in the unknown future, but right now in this very second. You can please Lord Siva easily. Fast on the Sivaratri day. If you cannot do this, take milk and fruits. Keep perfect vigil the whole night and sing His Stotras, and repeat 'Om Namah Sivaya'. May the blessings of Lord Siva be upon you all!

Om Santih! Santih! Santih!

Chapter II
SIVA TATTVA

> In Me the universe had its origin,
> In Me alone the whole subsists;
> In Me it is lost — Siva,
> The Timeless, it is I Myself,
> Sivoham! Sivoham! Sivoham!

Salutations to Lord Siva, the vanquisher of Cupid, the bestower of eternal bliss and immortality, the protector of all beings, destroyer of sins, the Lord of the gods, who wears a tiger-skin, the best among objects of worship, through whose matted hair the Ganga flows.

Lord Siva is the pure, changeless, attributeless, all-pervading transcendental consciousness. He is the inactive (Nishkriya) Purusha. Prakriti is dancing on His breast and performing the creative, preservative and destructive processes.

When there is neither light nor darkness, neither form nor energy, neither sound nor matter, when there is no manifestation of phenomenal existence, Siva alone exists in Himself. He is timeless, spaceless, birthless, deathless, decayless. He is beyond the pairs of opposites. He is the Impersonal Absolute Brahman. He is untouched by pleasure and pain, good and evil. He cannot be seen by the eyes but He can be realised within the heart through devotion and meditation.

Siva is also the Supreme personal God when He is identified with His power. He is then omnipotent, omniscient active God. He dances in supreme joy and creates, sustains and destroys with the rhythm of His dancing movements.

He destroys all bondage, limitation and sorrow of His devotees. He is the giver of Mukti or the final emancipation. He is the universal Self. He is the true Self of all creatures. He is the dweller in the cremation-ground, in the region of the dead, those who are dead to the world.

The Jivas and the world originate from Him, exist in Him, are sustained and rejected by Him and are ultimately merged in Him. He is the support, source and substratum of the whole world. He is an embodiment of Truth, Beauty, Goodness and Bliss. He is Satyam, Sivam, Subham, Sundaram, Kantam.

He is the God of gods, Deva-Deva. He is the Great Deity—Mahadeva. He is the God of manes (Prajapati). He is the most awe-inspiring and terrifying deity, Rudra, with Trisul or trident in His hand. He is the most easily pleased (Asutosha). He is accessible to all. Even the untouchable Chandalas and the illiterate rustics can approach Him.

He is the source of all knowledge and wisdom. He is an ideal Yogi and Muni. He is the ideal head of an ideal family with Uma as His devoted wife, Lord Subrahmanya, the brave general of strength and courage, Lord Ganesa, the remover of all obstacles, as His sons.

SADASIVA

At the end of Pralaya, the Supreme Lord thinks of re-creation of the world. He is then known by the name Sadasiva. He is the root-cause of creation. From Sadasiva creation begins. In Manusmriti He is called Svayambhu. Sadasiva is unmanifested, He destroys the Tamas caused by Pralaya and shines as the self-resplendent light bringing forth the five great elements, etc., into being.

The Siva Purana says that Siva is beyond both Prakriti and Purusha. Siva is Mahesvara. He is the witness, well-wisher and nourisher of all beings. The Gita says: *'Upadrashtanumanta cha bharta bhokta mahesvarah'.*

Mahesvara conducts the work of creation according to His will and pleasure. The Sruti says, *'Mayam tu prakritim viddhi mayinam tu mahesvaram'.* Know Prakriti to be Maya and Mahesvara to be the wielder of Maya or Prakriti. The Sakti of Siva works in two different ways. Mula Prakriti and Daivi Prakriti. Mula Prakriti is Apara Prakriti from which the five elements and other visible objects and the Antahkarana are evolved. Para Prakriti is Chaitanya Sakti which converts the Apara Prakriti and gives name and form to it. Apara Prakriti is Avidya and Para Prakriti is Vidya. The controller and dispenser of these two Prakritis is Lord Siva.

Siva is distinct from Brahma, Vishnu and Rudra.

Lord Siva is the Lord of innumerable crores of Brahmandas or worlds. Isvara united with Maya gives rise to Brahma, Vishnu and Rudra out of Rajas, Sattva and Tamo Gunas respectively, under the command of Lord Siva. Brahma, Vishnu and Rudra are the trinities of the world.

There is no difference among the trinities, Brahma, Vishnu and Rudra. By the command of Mahesvara these three do the creative, preservative and destructive duties of the world. The work of all the three deities is done conjointly. They all have one view and one definite purpose in creating, preserving and destroying the visible universe of names and forms. He who regards the three deities as distinct and different, Siva Purana says, is undoubtedly a devil or evil spirit.

The Lord who is beyond the three Gunas, Mahesvara, has four aspects: Brahma, Kaala, Rudra and Vishnu. Siva is the support for all the four. He is the substratum for Sakti also. Siva is distinct from the Rudra included in the trinities. Rudra is really one though according to the different functions He is considered to have eleven different forms.

The first face of Siva does Krida or play, the second does penance, the third destroys or dissolves the world the fourth protects the people and the fifth, being knowledge, fully covers the entire universe by its power. He is Isana the creator and promoter of all beings, from within.

The first form of Siva is the enjoyer of Prakriti as Kshetrajna Purusha. The second is Tatpurusha resting in Sattva-guna, rooted in Bhogya-Prakriti, the Prakriti-enjoyed. The third is Ghora rooted in the eightfold Buddhi like Dharma, etc. The fourth is Vamadeva rooted in Ahankara and the fifth is Sadyojata, the presiding deity of the mind. The eight forms of Siva are Sarva, Bhava, Rudra, Ugra, Bhima, Pasupati, Isana and Mahadeva, rooted respectively in earth, water, fire, air, ether, Kshetrajna, sun and moon.

ARDHANARISVARA

Brahma was unable to create and bring forth creatures from his mental creation. To know the method of creation he did Tapas. As a result of his Tapas Adyasakti arose in Brahma's mind. Through the help of Adyasakti Brahma meditated upon Tryambakesvara. Pleased by the penance of Brahma, Lord Siva appeared in the form of Ardhanarisvara (half male and half female). Brahma praised Ardhanarisvara. Lord Siva then created from His body a Goddess by name Prama-Sakti. Brahma said to the Goddess: "I was not able to bring forth creatures by my mental creation. Though I created the Devatas yet they could not multiply. Therefore, I wish to bring forth creatures by intercourse. Before Your appearance or till now, I was not able to create the endless female species. Therefore, O Devi, be merciful and take birth as the daughter of my son, Daksha."

WORLD-TEACHER

The most auspicious and useful work beneficial to mankind ever carried out by Lord Siva, is to impart the knowledge of Yoga, Bhakti, Jnana, etc., to the world. He blesses those deserve His grace and who cannot get out of Samsara without His grace. He is not only the World-Teacher but also an ideal example to the Jivanmukta or sage. He teaches by His very actions in His daily life.

PASUPATA YOGA

Uniting the self with the true Siva Tattva by the control of the senses is real wearing of Bhasma, because Lord Siva through His third eye of wisdom burnt passion to ashes. The meditation of Pranava should be done through Japa. One should attain the real Jnana, Yoga and Bhakti by steady practice. In the heart, there is a ten-petalled lotus. It has ten Nadis. It is the Jivatma's abode. This Jivatma lives in a subtle form in the mind and it is Chitta or Purusha itself. One should ascend to the moon by cutting open or transcending the Dasagni Nadi by the regular practice of Yoga as instructed by the Guru and practising dispassion, righteousness and equality. The moon then gradually attains fullness, as it gets itself pleased with the Sadhaka on account of his regular application in Yoga and purification of Nadis. In this state, the Sadhaka overcomes waking and sleeping state and through meditation merges himself in the object meditated upcn in this waking state itself.

Chapter III

THE SAIVA SIDDHANTA PHILOSOPHY

SIVA AND TATTVAS

Satyam Sivam Subham Sundaram Kantam.

The Saiva Siddhanta system is the distilled essence of Vedanta. It prevailed in Southern India even before the Christian era. Tirunelvely and Madurai are the centres of Saiva Siddhanta school. Saivites elaborated a distinctive philosophy called the Saiva Siddhanta about the eleventh century A.D. Even today, Saivism is a very popular creed in South India. It is a rival school of Vaishnavism.

Tirumular's work—Tirumantiram—is the foundation upon which the later structure of Saiva Siddhanta philosophy was built. The twenty-eight Saiva Agamas, the hymns of the Saiva saints form the chief sources of Southern Saivism.

In the books which treat of Saivism, there is a reference to four schools, viz., Nakulisa-pasupata, the Saiva, the Pratyabhijna and Rasesvara.

Lord Siva is the supreme Reality. He is eternal, formless, independent, omnipresent, one without a second, beginningless, causeless, taintless, self-existent, ever free and ever pure. He is not limited by time. He is infinite bliss and infinite intelligence.

Lord Siva pervades the whole world by His Sakti. He works through His Sakti. Sakti is conscious energy of Lord Siva. She is the very body of Lord Siva. The potter is the first cause for the pot. The stick and the wheel are the instrumental causes. The clay is the material cause of the pot. Similarly Lord Siva is the first cause of the world. Sakti is the instrumental cause. Maya is the material cause.

Lord Siva is the God of love. His grace is infinite. He is the saviour and Guru. He is engaged in freeing the souls from the thraldom of matter. He assumes the form of a Guru out of the intense love for mankind. He wishes that all should know Him and attain the blissful Siva-Pada. He watches the activities of the individual souls and helps them in their onward march.

In the Saiva Siddhanta, there are 36 Tattvas of which 24 are known as Atma Tattvas, 7 as Vidya Tattvas, and the remaining 5 as Siva Tattvas. The 24 Atma Tattvas are the 5 elements, ether, air, fire, water and earth; the 5 Tanmatras, sound, touch, form, taste and smell; the 5 sense-organs, ear, skin, eye, palate and nose; the internal organ; the 5 motor organs, speech, hand, foot, anus and the generative organ; and Ahankara, Buddhi and Guna. The 7 Vidya Tattvas are Purusha, Raga (love), Vidya (knowledge), Kala (art), Niyati (order), Kaala (time) and Asuddha (impure) Maya. The 5 Siva Tattvas are Suddha Vidya, Isvara, Sadasiva, Sakti and Siva.

Maya evolves into the subtle principles and then into the gross. The individual soul experiences pleasure and pain through Vidya. Siva Tattva is the basis of all consciousness and action. It is undifferentiated (Nishkala) Suddha. Maya, the Sakti of Siva starts her activities. Then Siva becomes the experiencer. Then He is called Sadasiva known also by the name Sadakhya, who is not really separate from Siva. The Suddhamaya becomes active. Then Siva, the experiencer becomes the Ruler. He is then Isvara, who is not really separate from Sadasiva. Suddhavidya is the cause of true knowledge.

The five activities (Pancha-Krityas) of the Lord are: Srishti (creation), Sthiti (preservation), Samhara (destruction), Tirobhava (veiling) and Anugraha (grace). These, separately considered, are the activities of Brahma, Vishnu, Rudra, Mahesvara and Sadasiva.

In the five-lettered Mantra (Panchakshari) *'Namassivaya'*, 'Na' is the screening power of the Lord that makes the soul to move in the world, 'Ma' is the bond that binds him in the Samsaric wheel of the births and deaths, 'Si' is the symbol for Lord Siva, 'Va' stands for His grace and 'Ya' stands for the soul. If the soul turns towards 'Na' and 'Ma' he will be sunk in worldliness. If he associates himself with 'Va' he will move towards Lord Siva.

Hearing the Lilas of Lord Siva and the significance of Panchakshara, is 'Sravana'. Reflection on the meaning of Panchakshara is 'Manana' or 'Chintana'. To develop love and devotion for Lord Siva and meditate on Him, is 'Sivadhyana'. To become immersed in 'Sivananda', is 'Nishtha' or 'Samadhi'. He who attains this stage is called Jivanmukta.

PATI-PASU-PASA

'Pati' is Lord Siva. It is the object of all the Vedas and the Agamas to explain the concepts of Lord (Pati), bound souls (Pasu) which really means cattle, and bondage (Pasa). Lord Siva is infinite, eternal, one without a second. He is changeless and indivisible. He is the embodiment of knowledge and bliss. He energises the intelligence of all souls. He is beyond the reach of mind and speech. He is the ultimate goal of all. He is smaller than the smallest and greater than the greatest. He is self-luminous, self-existent, self-contained and self-delight.

'Pasus' are the individual souls who are sunk in the quagmire of Samsara. They assume bodies to work out their good and evil actions and are born as lower and higher beings according to their nature of Karma. They do virtuous and vicious actions in the course of experiencing the endless fruits of their Karma and have countless births and deaths. Ultimately they attain the grace of Lord Siva through meritorious acts and their ignorance is dispelled. They attain salvation and become one with Lord Siva.

'Pasa' is bond. The web of bonds is distinguished into Avidya or Anavamala, Karma and Maya. Anavamala is egoism. It is the taint due to the false notion of finiteness which the soul has. The soul imagines itself to be finite and confined to the body and of limited knowledge and power. It erroneously identifies itself with the perishable body and mistakes the body for its reality. It has forgotten its essential divine nature.

'Karma' is the cause of bodies and manifold bodily experiences and births and deaths. It is beginningless. It is the cause of the conjunction of the conscious soul with the unconscious body. It is an auxiliary of Avidya. It is done through thought, word and deed. It takes the form of merit and sin and produces pleasure and pain. It is subtle and unseen (Adrishta). It exists during creation and merges into the substratum of Maya during Pralaya. It cannot be destroyed. It must work out its results.

Maya is the material cause of the world. It is unconscious or unintelligent, omnipresent, imperishable. It is the seed of the world. The four categories, viz., Tanu, Karana, Bhuvana and Bhoga beginning with the bodies, spring up from Maya. It permeates all its developments and causes perversion in the Karmic souls. During Pralaya it is the basic resort of all souls. It is itself a bond for the souls. All these processes in it are due to the energising influence by Lord Siva. Just as the trunk, the leaf and the fruit grow from the seed, so also the universe from Kala to earth, springs from Maya.

The real Nada, the root of sound is evolved from pure Maya by the will of Lord Siva. From Nada, the real Bindu springs up. From it, the real Sadasiva originates and gives birth to Isvara. Suddha Avidya is developed from Isvara. The world originates from Bindu and develops into various forms.

SADHANA

One will develop love and devotion for Lord Siva if he is freed from egoism. Chariyai, Kiriyai, Yoga and Jnana are the four Sadhanas or steps to kill egoism and attain Lord Siva. Erecting temples, cleaning them, making garlands of flowers, singing Lord's praises, burning lamps in the temples, making flower gardens constitute Chariyai. Kiriyai is to perform Puja, Archanas. Yoga is restraint of the senses and contemplation on the internal light. Jnana is to understand the true significance of Pati, Pasu, Pasa and to become one with Siva by constant meditation on Him after removing the three Malas, viz., Anava (egoism), Karma (action) and Maya (illusion).

The worship of the all-pervading, eternal Supreme Being through external forms, is called Chariyai. The requisite initiation for this, is Samaya Diksha. The worship of the cosmic form of the Eternal Ruler of the universe externally and internally, is called Kiriyai. The internal worship of Him as formless, is called Yoga. For Kiriyai and Yoga, the requisite initiation is called Visesha Diksha. The direct realisation of Lord Siva through Jnana Guru, is called Jnana. The initiation that leads to it, is called Nirvana Diksha.

The aspirant should free himself from the three kinds of Mala, viz., Anava, Karma and Maya. Then only he becomes one with Lord Siva and enjoys 'Sivanandam'. He should thoroughly annihilate his egoism, free himself from the bondage of Karma and destroy the Maya which is the basis of all impurities.

Guru or the spiritual preceptor is very essential for attaining the final emancipation. Siva is full of grace. He helps the aspirants. He showers His grace on those who worship Him with faith and devotion and who have childlike trust in Him. Siva Himself is the Guru. The grace of Siva is the road to salvation. Siva lives in the Guru and looks with intense love on the sincere aspirant through the eyes of the Guru. Only if you have love for mankind, you can love God.

If the aspirant establishes a relationship between himself and Lord Siva, he will grow in devotion quickly. He can have the mental attitude or Bhava—Dasya Bhava or the relationship of master and servant which Tirunavukarasar had, or the Vatsalya Bhava wherein Lord Siva is the father and the aspirant is the child of Lord Siva which Tirujnanasambandhar had, or the Sakhya Bhava or the relationship of friend (Lord Siva is regarded as the friend of the aspirant) which Sundarar had, or the Sanmarga wherein Lord Siva is the very life of the aspirant which Manikkavasagar had, which corresponds to the Madhurya Bhava or Atma Nivedana of the Vaishnavites.

The devotee becomes one with Siva, like salt with water, milk with milk, when the three Malas (Pasa) are destroyed, but he cannot do the five functions of creation, etc. God only can perform the five functions.

The liberated soul is called a Jivanmukta. Though he lives in the body, he is one in feeling with the Absolute. He does not perform works which can produce further bodies. As he is free from egoism, work cannot bind him. He will do meritorious acts for the solidarity of the world (Lokasangraha). He lives in the body, until his Prarabdha Karma is exhausted. All his present actions are consumed by the grace of the Lord. The Jivanmukta does all actions on account of the impulsion of the Lord within him. Glory to Lord Siva and His Sakti!

ASHTAMURTI

Siva is spoken of as being in eight forms (Ashtamurti). The eight forms of Siva are the five elements, the sun, the moon and the priest who performs sacrifice.

Vishnu appeared in the Mohini form after the churning of the milk-ocean. Siva embraced Vishnu in that form. Sasta is the offspring of Siva and Mohini. Sasta is called also by the name Hari-Hara-Putra or the son of Hari and Hara.

Appar wanted all Saivas to regard Vishnu as only another aspect of Siva.

According to Appar, there are three aspects of Siva. (1) The lower Siva who dissolves the world and who liberates Jivas from their bondage. (2) The higher form is called Parapara. In this form Siva appears as Siva and Sakti (Ardhanarisvara). It has the name Param-Jyoti. Brahma and Vishnu were not able to comprehend this Jyoti. (3) Beyond these two forms is the Param, or the ultimate being from whom Brahma, Vishnu, Rudra originate. It is purely the Saiva form. It is formless. It is the Sivam of the Saiva Siddhanta. It is Para Brahman of the Upanishads and Vedantins.

The Mahavishnu of Vishnu Purana corresponds to Param of Saiva Siddhantins. Narayana or the higher Vishnu corresponds to the Paramjyoti of Appar or Saiva Siddhantins. The lower Vishnu does the function of preservation. He corresponds to the lower Siva.

What is the inner meaning of all the Saiva allusions about Vishnu worshipping Siva and all the Vaishnava allusions about Siva worshipping Vishnu? The lower Siva must take Narayana, the Parapara or Paramjyoti as his Superior. The lower Vishnu must take Paramjyoti or the Parapara as his Superior. The higher Vishnu and higher Siva are identical. They are inferior to Param, the Highest.

In that highest condition called Siva Mukti, there is no duality. No one can see anything. One merges himself in Sivam or the Highest. If you wish to see, you will have to come to the stage immediately below the Highest.

The Siva Murti or manifestation is inferior to the real 'Sivam' which is formless.

According to the Saiva Siddhanta philosophy, the Tattvas are reckoned as ninety-six. They are as follows:

24 Atma Tattvas, 10 Nadis, 5 Avasthas or conditions. 3 Malas or impurities, 3 Gunas (Sattva, Rajas and Tamas), 3 Mandalas (Surya or the sun, Agni or the fire and Chandra or the moon), 3 humours (Vata, Pitta and Sleshma), 8 Vikaras or modifications (Kama, Krodha, Lobha, Moha, Mada, Matsarya, Dambha and Asuya), 6 Adharas, 7 Dhatus, 10 Vayus, 5 Koshas and 9 doorways. The twenty-four Tattvas are the 5 elements (Bhutas), 5 Tanmatras (Sabda, etc.), 5 Jnana-Indriyas, 5 Karma-Indriyas and 4 Karanas (Manas, Buddhi, Chitta and Ahankara). All these 96 relate to the body. Over and above these 96, there are the 5 Kanchukas or coverings. They are Niyati, Kaala, Kala, Raga and Vidya. The five enter the body and cause weariness to the Tattvas of the body and afflict the body.

SUDDHA SAIVA

The Suddha Saiva does not attain the final emancipation by Kriya (Kiriyai) alone. He attains only Salokya. Jnana in Kriya leads to Salokya, the world of Siva. Jnana in Charya

(Chariyai) leads him to Samipya (proximity to Siva). Jnana in Yoga bestows on him Sarupya (likeness in form). Jnana in Jnana leads him to Sayujya, merging or absorption.

'Ambalam' means 'open space of the heart' or Chidakasa or Chidambaram.

And Lingam is the Visvarupa or the God's form of the Universe.

He who brings about the destruction of the world is Siva or Rudra. That is the reason why He is held superior to Brahma and Vishnu.

The Siddhantis divide Jivas or Pasus into three orders, viz., Vijnana Kalar, Pralaya Kalar and Sakalar. Vijnana Kalar have only the Anava Mala (egoism). Pralaya Kalar have Anava and Maya. Sakalar have all the Malas, Anava, Karma and Maya. The Malas affect only the Jivas and not Siva. Those who are freed from the Malas or impurities become identical with Siva. They are Siddhas or perfected beings.

Chapter IV
PHILOSOPHY OF SYMBOLS

PHILOSOPHY OF SYMBOLS

Lord Siva represents the destructive aspect of Brahman. That portion of Brahman that is enveloped by Tamo-Guna-Pradhana Maya is Lord Siva who is the all-pervading Isvara and who also dwells in Mount Kailas. He is the Bhandara or store-house for wisdom. Siva minus Parvati or Kaali or Durga is Nirguna Brahman Himself. With Maya-Parvati He becomes the Saguna Brahman for the purpose of pious devotion of His devotees. Devotees of Rama must worship Lord Siva for 3 or 6 months before they take to worship of Rama. Rama Himself worshipped Lord Siva at the famous Ramesvaram. Lord Siva is the Lord of Ascetics and Lord of Yogins, robed in space (Digambara).

His Trisul (trident) that is held in His right hand represents the three Gunas—Sattva, Rajas and Tamas. That is the emblem of Sovereignty. He wields the world through these three Gunas. The Damaru in His left hand represents the Sabda Brahman. It represents OM from which all languages are formed. It is He who formed the Sanskrit language out of the Damaru.

The crescent moon indicates that He has controlled the mind perfectly. The flow of the Ganga represents the nectar of Immortality. Elephant represents symbolically pride. His wearing the skin of the elephant denotes that He has controlled pride. Tiger represents lust; His sitting on tiger's skin indicates that He has conquered lust. His holding a deer on one hand indicates that He has removed the Chanchalata (tossing) of the mind. Deer jumps from one place to another swiftly. His wearing of serpents denotes wisdom and eternity. Serpents live for a long number of years. He is Trilochana, the three-eyed One, in the centre of whose forehead is the third eye, the eye of wisdom.

'Hoam' is the Bija Akshara of Lord Siva.

He is Sivam (auspicious, Subham), Sundaram (beautiful), Kantam (effulgent). "Santam Sivam Advaitam" (Mandukya Upanishad).

I bow with folded hands crores of times at the lotus-feet of that Lord Siva who is non-dual, who is the Adhishthana, or support for the world and all minds, who is Sat-Chit-Ananda, who is the Ruler, the Antaryamin, the Sakshi (silent witness) for everything, who is self-effulgent, self-existent and self-contained (Paripurna), who is the remover of the primitive Avidya and who is the Adi-Guru or Parama-Guru or Jagad-Guru.

That Lord Siva I am in essence. Sivoham, Sivoham, Sivoham.

SNAKE ON THE BODY OF SIVA

Serpent is the Jiva or the individual soul which rests upon Siva, the Paramatman or the Supreme Soul. The five hoods mean the five senses or the five Tattvas, viz., earth, water, fire, air and ether. They also represent the five Pranas, which hiss in the body like the serpent. The inhalation and exhalation are like the hissing of the serpent. Lord Siva Himself became the five Tanmatras, the five Jnanendriyas, the five Karmendriyas and other groups of five. The individual soul enjoys the worldly objects through these Tattvas. When the individual attains knowledge through control of the senses and the mind, he finds his eternal resting abode in Lord Siva, the Supreme Soul. This is the esoteric significance of Lord Siva wearing the snake on His body.

Lord Siva is absolutely fearless. Srutis declare, "This Brahman is fearless (Abhayam), Immortal (Amritam)." Worldly people are afraid even at the very sight of a snake but Lord Siva is wearing serpents as ornaments on His body. This indicates that Lord Siva is absolutely fearless and immortal.

Generally serpents live for hundreds of years. Wearing of serpents by Lord Siva signifies that He is Eternal.

SIGNIFICANCE OF BHASMA, NANDI, ETC.

Namassivaya is the Mantra of Lord Siva. 'Na' represents earth and Brahma; 'Ma' represents water and Vishnu; 'Si' fire and Rudra; 'Va' Vayu and Mahesvara; 'Ya' Akasa and Sadasiva and also the Jiva.

Lord Siva has white complexion. What is the significance of white colour? He teaches silently that people should have pure heart and entertain pure thoughts and should be free from crookedness, diplomacy, cunningness, jealousy, hatred, etc.

He wears three white-lined Bhasma or Vibhuti on His forehead. What is the significance of this? He teaches silently that people should destroy the three impurities, viz., Anava (egoism), Karma (action with expectation of fruits), and Maya (illusion), and the three desires or Eshanas, viz., desire for landed property, desire for woman, desire for gold, and the three Vasanas, viz., Lokavasana, Dehavasana and Sastravasana, and then attain Him with a pure heart.

What does the Balipitha or altar which stands in front of the sanctum sanctorum of the Siva's temple represent? People should destroy their egoism and mine-ness

(Ahamta and Mamata) before they attain the Lord. This is the significance.

What does Nandi or the bull which is in front of Sivalinga represent? Nandi is the attendant or doorkeeper of Siva. He is the vehicle of Lord Siva. He represents Satsanga. If you make association with the sages, you are sure to attain God-realisation. Sages will show you the way to reach Him. They will remove pitfalls or snares that lie on your path. They will clear your doubts and instil in your heart dispassion, discrimination and knowledge. There is no other safe boat than Satsanga to reach the other shore of fearlessness and immortality. Even a moment's Satsanga or association with the sages, is a great blessing to the aspirants and the worldly-minded persons. They get firm conviction in the existence of God through Satsanga. The sages remove the worldly Samskaras. The company of sages is a formidable fortress to protect oneself from the temptations of Maya.

Lord Siva represents the destructive aspect of the Godhead. He is seen absorbed on the-mountain peak of Kailas. He is an embodiment of serenity, renunciation and indifference to the world. The third eye in the centre of His forehead represents His destructive energy which when let loose destroys the world. Nandi is His favourite. He is the door-Keeper. He is seen hushing all nature, so that the Lord may not be disturbed in His Samadhi. The Lord has five faces, ten hands, ten eyes, two feet.

Vrishabha or the bull represents Dharma Devata. Lord Siva rides on the bull. Bull is His vehicle. This denotes that Lord Siva is the protector of Dharma, is an embodiment of Dharma or righteousness.

Deer represents the Vedas. Its four legs are the four Vedas. Lord Siva is holding the deer in His hand. This indicates that He is the Lord of the Vedas.

He has sword in one of His hands. This signifies that He is the destroyer of births and deaths. The fire in one of His hands shows that He protects the Jivas by burning all fetters.

PHILOSOPHY OF ABHISHEKA

Salutations and adorations to the blissful Lord Siva, the lover of Uma or Parvati, the Lord of all beings (Pasupati).

"Alankarapriyo Vishnuh, Abhishekapriyah Sivah—Lord Vishnu is very fond of Alankara (fine dress, beautiful ornaments, etc.); Siva is fond of Abhisheka." In Siva temples, a pot made up of copper or brass with a hole in the centre is kept hanging over the image or Linga of Siva, and water is falling on the image throughout day and night. Pouring over the Linga, water, milk, ghee, curd, honey, coconut water, Panchamrita, etc., is Abhisheka. Abhisheka is done for Lord Siva. Rudra is chanted along with the Abhisheka. Lord Siva is propitiated by Abhisheka.

Lord Siva drank the poison that emanated from the ocean and wore the Ganga and moon on His head to cool His head. He has the fiery third eye. Constant Abhisheka cools this eye.

The greatest and the highest Abhisheka is to pour the waters of pure love on the Atmalinga of the lotus of the heart. The external Abhisheka with various objects will help the growth of devotion and adoration for Lord Siva and eventually lead to internal Abhisheka with pure abundant flow of love.

Abhisheka is a part of Siva Puja. Without Abhisheka, worship of Siva is incomplete. During Abhisheka Rudra, Purushasukta, Chamaka, Mahamrityunjaya Japa, etc., are chanted in a particular rhythm and order. Monday is very important day for Lord Siva and the thirteenth day of the fortnight (Pradosha) is very sacred. On these days, devotees of Siva worship Him with special Puja, Abhisheka with Ekadasa-Rudra, Archana, offering plenty of Prasad, and illumination.

In Ekadasa-Rudra Abhisheka, every Rudra is chanted with distinctive articles for Abhisheka. Ganga water, milk, ghee, honey, rose-water, coconut water, sandal paste, Panchamrita, scented oil, sugarcane juice and lime juice are made use of for Abhisheka. After every Abhisheka, pure water is poured over the head of Siva. When Rudra is repeated once, the different articles of Abhisheka are made use of after every stanza of the Rudra. The Abhisheka water or other articles used for Abhisheka are considered very sacred and bestow immense benefits on the devotees who take it as the Lord's Prasad. It purifies the heart and destroys countless sins. You must take it with intense Bhava and faith.

When you do Abhisheka with Bhava and devotion, your mind is concentrated. Your heart is filled with the image of the Lord and divine thoughts. You forget your body and its relation and surroundings. Egoism gradually vanishes. When there is forgetfulness, you begin to enjoy and taste the eternal bliss of Lord Siva. Recitation of Rudra or Om Namassivaya purifies the mind and fills it with Sattva.

If you do Abhisheka with Rudrapatha in the name of a person suffering from any disease he will be soon freed from that disease. Incurable diseases are cured by Abhisheka. Abhisheka bestows health, wealth, prosperity, progeny, etc. Abhisheka on Monday is most auspicious.

By offering Panchamrita, honey, milk, etc., to the Lord, thoughts of your body diminish. Selfishness slowly vanishes. You derive immense joy. You begin to increase your offerings unto the Lord. Therefore, self-sacrifice and self-surrender come in. Naturally, there is an outpouring from your heart, "I am Thine, my Lord. All is Thine, my Lord".

Kannappa Nayanar, a great devotee of Lord Siva, a hunter by profession, did Abhisheka with the water in his mouth for the Linga at Kalahasti in South India and propitiated Lord Siva. Lord Siva is pleased by pure devotion. It is the mental Bhava that counts and not the outward show. Lord Siva said to the temple priest: "This water from the mouth of Kannappa, my beloved devotee, is more pure than the water of the Ganga".

A devotee should be regular in doing Abhisheka for the Lord. He should get by heart Rudra and Chamakam. Ekadasa Rudra is more powerful and effective. In Northern India, every man or woman takes a lota of water and pours it on the image of Siva. This also causes beneficial results and brings about the fulfilment of one's desire. Abhisheka on Sivaratri day is very effective.

May you all recite Rudrapatha which describes the glory of Lord Siva and His manifestations in every living being, in every animate and inanimate being! May you do Abhisheka daily and thus obtain the grace of Lord Siva! May Lord Visvanatha bless you all!

FRUIT OF ABHISHEKA AND RUDRA JAPA IN SIVA'S TEMPLE

Chamaka is divided into eleven sections. Each of these is then combined with Namaka (Rudra) and repeated. This is called Rudra. Eleven such Rudras make one Laghu Rudra. Eleven Laghu Rudras make one Maharudra. Eleven Maharudras make one Atirudra.

Rudra is to be repeated after performing the initial Sankalpa, Puja, Nyasa, Anga, Panchamritasnana and Dhyana. The fruit of Rudra Japa is stated as shown below:

No. of Japa	Fruit of Japa
1 Rudra	Freedom from Bala graha (diseases common to children).
3 Rudras	Freedom from imminent difficulties with which one is faced.
5 Rudras	Freedom from the evil effects of certain planets occupying unfavourable positions.
7 Rudras	Freedom from great fear.
9 Rudras	The fruit of one Vajapeya sacrifice; and also attainment of peace of mind.
11 Rudras	Getting the favour of kings and great wealth.
33 Rudras	Attainment of wishes for objects and having no enemies.
77 Rudras	Enjoyment of great happiness.
99 Rudras	Attainment of son, grandson, wealth, grain, Dharma, Artha, Kama and Moksha and freedom from death.
1 Maharudra	Attainment of the favour of kings and becoming the Lord of great wealth.
3 Maharudras	Fulfilment of impossible tasks.
5 Maharudras	Acquirement of vast lands.
7 Maharudras	Attainment of the seven worlds.
9 Maharudras	Freedom from births and deaths.
1 Atirudra	Becoming God.

Materials for Abhisheka: Pure water, milk, sugar-cane juice, ghee, honey, waters of sacred rivers, sea water.

For getting rain, Abhisheka should be done with pure water. For freedom from diseases, and for begetting a son,

Abhisheka should be done with milk. If Abhisheka is done with milk, even a barren woman begets children. The person also attains plenty of cows. If Abhisheka is done with Kusa water, one becomes free from all diseases. He who desires wealth, should perform Abhisheka with ghee, honey and sugarcane juice. He who desires Moksha, should do Abhisheka with sacred waters.

Chapter V
PHILOSOPHY OF SIVA TANDAVA

I

पादस्याविर्भवन्तीमवनतिमवने रक्षतः स्वैरपातैः
संकोचेनैव दोष्णां मुहुरभिनयतः सर्वलोकातिगानाम् ।
दृष्टि लक्ष्येवु नोग्रज्वलनकणमुचं बध्नतो दाहभीते-
रित्याधारानुरोधात् त्रिपुरविजयिनः पातु वो दुःखनृत्तम् ॥

The Tandava or celestial dance of Lord Siva is extremely thrilling and charming, exquisitely graceful in pose and rhythm and intensely piercing in effect.

Nritya or Tandava is an inseparable, sacred movement of the various limbs of the body in accordance with the inner divine Bhava. Nritya is a divine science. The Adigurus for this celestial Nritya were Lord Siva, Krishna and Mother Kaali. In Nritya, the six Bhavas, viz., Srishti, Samhara, Vidya, Avidya, Gati and Agati are demonstrated.

The dance of Lord Siva is for the welfare of the world. The object of His dance is to free the souls from the fetters of Maya, from the three bonds of Anava, Karma and Maya. He is not the destroyer but He is the regenerator. He is the Mangala Data and Ananda Data, bestower of auspiciousness and bliss. He is more easily pleased than Lord Hari, He grants boons quickly, for a little Tapas or a little recitation of His five letters.

'Aghada Bhum' is His song of dance. When Siva starts His dance Brahma, Vishnu, the Siva Ganas and Kaali with Her bowl of skull, join Him. Have you not seen the picture of Pradosha Nritya? It will give you an idea of the dance of Siva.

Kaali was very proud of Her ability in dancing. Siva started dancing to quell Her pride. He danced very beautifully, very artistically. Kaali had to put Her face down in shame.

Lord Siva wears a deer in the left upper hand. He has trident in the right lower arm. He has fire and Damaru and Malu, a kind of weapon. He wears five serpents as ornaments. He wears a garland of skulls. He is pressing with His feet the demon Muyalaka, a dwarf holding a cobra. He faces south. Panchakshari itself is His body. Lord Siva says: "Control the five senses which are hissing like serpents. The mind is jumping like a deer. Control the mind. Burn it in the fire of meditation. Strike it down with the Trisula of discrimination. You can attain Me". This is the philosophical significance of the picture of Lord Siva.

You can witness the dance of Siva in the rising waves of the ocean, in the oscillation of the mind, in the movements of the senses and the Pranas, in the rotation of the planets and constellations, in cosmic Pralaya, in epidemics of infectious diseases, in huge inundations and volcanic eruptions, in earthquakes, landslips, lightning and thunder, in huge conflagrations and cyclonic storm.

As soon as the Guna Samya Avastha, wherein the three Gunas exist in a state of equilibrium, is disturbed by the will of the Lord, the Gunas manifest and quintuplication of elements takes place. There is vibration of Omkara or Sabda Brahman. There is manifestation of primal energy. This is the dance of Siva. The whole cosmic play or activity or Lila is the dance of Siva. All movements within the cosmos are His dance. He gazes on Prakriti and energises Her. Mind, Prana, matter begin to dance. When He begins to dance, the Sakti Tattva manifests. From Sakti, Nada proceeds and from Nada, Bindu originates. Then the universe of names and forms is projected. The undifferentiated matter, energy and sound become differentiated.

The burning grounds are the abodes of Siva. Rudra is the destructive aspect of the Lord. Lord Siva dances in the crematorium with Kaali, in His ten-armed form. The Siva Ganas also join with Him in the dance.

Nataraja of Chidambaram is the expert dancer. He has four hands. He wears the Ganga and the crescent moon on His matted locks. He holds Damaru in His right hand. He shows Abhaya Mudra to His devotees with His raised left hand. The significance is: "O devotees! Do not be afraid. I shall protect you all." One left hand holds the fire. The other right hand points down on the Asura Muyalaka who is holding a cobra. He has raised the left foot in a beautiful manner.

The sound of the drum invites the individual souls to His feet. It represents Omkara. All the Sanskrit alphabets have come out of the play of the Damaru. Creation arises from Damaru. The hand which shows Abhaya Mudra gives protection. Destruction proceeds from fire. The raised foot indicates Maya or illusion. The hand which points down shows that His feet are the sole refuge of the individual souls. Tiruakshi represents Omkara or Pranava.

Chidambaram is a sacred place of pilgrimage in South India. All the Tamil saints have sung hymns in praise of Nataraja. There is Akasa Linga here which indicates that Lord Siva is formless and attributeless. The popular saying goes: "He who dies in Banares with Ramanam in his lips and heart, attains salvation. He who remembers Arunachalam or Tiruvannamalai attains Mukti. He who gets Darsana of Nataraja attains final emancipation." Real Chidambaram is within the heart. Nataraja dances in the hearts of devotees who have burnt egoism, lust, hatred, pride and jealousy.

He dances quite gently. If He dances vehemently the whole earth will sink down at once. He dances with His eyes closed, because the sparks from His eyes will consume the entire universe. The five activities of the Lord, Panchakriyas, viz., Srishti (creation), Sthiti (preservation), Samhara (destruction), Tirobhava (illusion) and Anugraha (grace), are the dances of Siva.

May you all comprehend the true significance of the dance of Siva. May you all dance in ecstasy in tune with Lord Siva and merge in Him and enjoy the Sivananda, the final beatitude of life!

II

Lord Siva is an embodiment of wisdom. He is the Light of lights. He is Paramjyoti or supreme Light. He is self-luminous or Svayam-Jyoti. The dance of Siva represents the rhythm and movement of the world-spirit. At His dance the evil forces and darkness quiver and vanish.

In the night of Brahma or during Pralaya, Prakriti is inert, motionless. There is Guna-Samya Avastha. The three Gunas are in a state of equilibrium or poise. She cannot dance till Lord Siva wills it. Lord Siva rises from His profound silence and begins to dance. The undifferentiated sound becomes differentiated through the vibration set up by the movements of His Damaru or drum. Sabda Brahman comes into being. The undifferentiated energy also becomes differentiated. The equipoise in the Gunas becomes disturbed. The three Gunas Sattva, Rajas and Tamas manifest. All the spheres, the atoms and the electrons also dance rhythmically and in an orderly manner. Atoms dance in the molecule and molecules dance in all bodies. Stars dance in time and space. Prakriti also begins to dance about Him as His glory or Vibhuti. The Prana begins to operate on Akasa or subtle matter. Various forms manifest. Hiranyagarbha or the golden egg or the cosmic mind also manifests.

When the time comes, Lord Siva destroys all names and forms by fire while dancing. There is stillness again.

This is the symbolism involved in the form of Nataraja. The deer in the hand of Siva represents Asuddha Maya. The axe represents knowledge which destroys ignorance. The drum, the outstretched arm that carries fire, the water (Ganga), the hand with the axe, the foot standing on the Asura Muyalaka, are the formless or Sukshma Panchaksharas.

Srishti (creation) is in the drum; Sthiti (preservation) is in the Abhaya hand; Samhara (destruction) is in the hand that holds the axe; Tirobhava (veiling) is in the pressing foot; and Anugraha (blessing) is in the uplifted foot.

There are various kinds of dances of Siva. There are the Samhara dance, the five dances, the six dances, the eight dances, the Kodu Kotti dance, the Pandam dance, the Kodu dance. The Kodu Kotti is the dance after the destruction of everything. Pandam is the dance after the destruction of the three cities, wearing the ashes of those cities. Kodu or Kapalam is the dance holding Brahma's head in the hand. Samhara is the dance at the time of dissolution or Pralaya.

Srishti, Sthiti, Samhara, Tirobhava and Anugraha, and also Muni-Tandava, Anavarata Tandava and Ananda Tandava constitute the eight dances. Sivananda dance, Sundara dance, the golden city dance, the golden

Chidambaram dance and the wonderful dance form the five dances. The five previous dances and the Ananda dance in the end form the six dances.

Lord Siva is the only dancer. He is the Master or expert dancer. He is the King of dancers. He quelled the pride of Kaali. Lord Siva's destruction is not a single act, but is a series of acts. There is a different kind of dance at every stage.

May Lord Nataraja, the great dancer help you in the attainment of Sivanandam or the eternal bliss of Siva!

LORD NATARAJA—THE GREAT DANCER

'Ya' in Namassivaya represents Jiva or the individual soul. The Panchakshara Namassivaya forms the body of Lord Siva. The hand that wears fire is 'Na'. The foot that presses the demon Muyalaka is 'Ma'. The hand that holds Damaru is 'Si'. The right and left hands that move about are 'Va'. The hand that shows Abhaya is 'Ya'.

Once upon a time, a group of Rishis abandoned their faith in the true Lord and took to the worship of false deities. Lord Siva wanted to teach them a lesson. He stirred in them strange passions. The Rishis became very furious. They created many evils through their power of penance and let them loose upon Siva. Lord Siva overcame them and finally defeated the great Kaali, a creation of the Rishis, by the cosmic dance.

At the time of Sri Nataraja's dance, Patanjali Rishi and Vyaghrapada were witnessing the dance and enjoying it. They were standing on either side of the Lord. Even in paintings and sculpture of the Nataraja's Murti, you will find the figures of Patanjali and Vyaghrapada on either side of Nataraja. The lower part of the body of Vyaghrapada will resemble that of tiger and the corresponding part of Patanjali that of the serpent.

The most wonderful dance of Nataraja is the Urdhva Tandava. In this dance the left leg is lifted up and the toe points to the sky. This is the most difficult form of dance. Nataraja defeated Kaali by this pose in dancing. Kaali successfully competed with Nataraja in all other modes of dance. Nataraja lost His earring while dancing. He succeeded by means of His toe, in this form of dance, in restoring the ornament to its original place without the knowledge of the audience.

Nataraja danced with His right leg lifted upwards. This is the Gajahasta pose in dancing or Nritya. He danced continuously without changing His legs once.

There is another dance pose of Siva on the head of an elephant. In this form, Lord Siva is known as Gajasana Murti. At the foot of Lord Siva, there is the head of an elephant monster. Lord Siva has eight hands. He holds the trident, the drum and the noose in His three right hands. He holds the shield and the skull in His two hands. The third left hand is held in Vismaya pose.

An Asura assumed the form of an elephant to kill the Brahmins who were sitting round the Linga of Visvanath in Banares, absorbed in meditation. Lord Siva came out suddenly from the Linga and killed the elephant-monster and used the skin as His garment.

DANCE OF SIVA

The flood of nineteen-twenty-four
Was horrible in Rishikesh;
It carried away many Mahatmas and Sadhus,
This is the dance of Siva.

The impetuous Chandrabhaga
Turned its course in 1943;
People crossed it with difficulty

With the help of elephant,
This is the dance of Siva.

In the morning of eleventh January 1945
There was fall of snow
On the surrounding Himalayas;
The chill was terrible,
This is the dance of Siva.

Lord Visvanath dwells now
In a place where there was forest.
He pleases the whole world.
He bestows health and long life.
This is the dance of Siva.

Forests become Ashrams,
Islands become an ocean,
Ocean becomes an island,
Cities become deserts,
This is the dance of Siva.

Siva gazes at His Sakti
Then there is the atomic dance,
There is the dance of Prakriti,
Lord Siva merely witnesses,
This is the dance of Siva.

Then Prana vibrates, mind moves,
Senses function,
Buddhi operates,
Heart pumps, lungs breathe,
Stomach digests, intestines excrete,
This is the dance of Siva.

This is a world of change,
A changing thing is perishable;
Know the Imperishable
Which is changeless
And become Immortal.

PHILOSOPHY OF SIVA TANDAVA

Chapter VI

SAKTI YOGA PHILOSOPHY

I

The power or active aspect of the immanent God is Sakti. Sakti is the embodiment of power. She is the supporter of the vast universe. She is the supreme power by which the world is upheld. She is the Universal Mother. She is Durga, Kaali, Chandi, Chamundi, Tripurasundari, Rajesvari. There is no difference between God and His Sakti, just as there is no difference between fire and its burning power.

He who worships Sakti, that is, God in Mother form, as the supreme power which creates, sustains and withdraws the universe, is a Sakta. All women are forms of the Divine Mother.

Siva is the unchanging consciousness: Sakti is His changing power which appears as mind and matter. Saktivada or Saktadarsana is a form of monism or Advaitavada.

A Sakta does Sadhana which helps the union of Siva and Sakti, through the awakening of the forces within the body. He becomes a Siddha in the Sadhana, when he is able to awaken Kundalini and pierce the six Chakras. This is to be done in a perfect practical way under the guidance of a Guru who has become perfect. The Sakti must be awakened by Dhyana, by Bhava, by Japa, by Mantra-Sakti. The Mother, the embodiment of the fifty letters, is present in the various letters in the different Chakras. When the chords of a musical instrument are struck harmoniously, fine music is produced. Even so, when the chords of the letters are struck in their order, the Mother who moves in the six Chakras and who is the very self of the letters, awakens Herself. The Sadhaka attains Siddhi easily when She is roused. It is difficult to say when and how She shows Herself and to what Sadhaka. Sadhana means unfolding, rousing up or awakening of power or Sakti. Mode of Sadhana depends upon the tendencies and capacities of the Sadhaka.

Sakti may be termed as that by which we live and have our being in this universe. In this world all the wants of the child are provided by the mother. The child's growth, development and sustenance are looked after by the mother. Even so, all the necessaries of life and its activities in this world and the energy needed for it, depend upon Sakti or the Universal Mother.

No one can free himself from the thraldom of mind and matter without Mother's grace. The fetters of Maya are too hard to break. If you worship Her as the great Mother, you can very easily go beyond Prakriti through Her benign grace and blessings. She will remove all obstacles in the path and lead you safely into the illimitable domain of eternal bliss and make you free. When She is pleased and bestows Her blessings on you, then alone you can free yourself from the bondage of this formidable Samsara.

The first syllable which a child or a quadruped utters is the name of the beloved mother. Is there any child which does not owe its all to the affection and love of its mother? It is the mother who protects you, consoles you, cheers you and nurses you. She is your friend, philosopher, protector and guide throughout your life. Human mother is a manifestation of the Universal Mother.

The Supreme Lord is represented as Siva and His power is represented as his consort, Sakti or Durga or Kaali. Just as the husband and wife look after the well-being of the family, so also Lord Siva and His Sakti are engaged in looking after the affairs of the world.

Radha, Durga, Lakshmi, Sarasvati and Savitri are the five primary forms of Prakriti or Devi. Durga destroyed Madhu and Kaitabha through Vishnu. As Mahalakshmi, She destroyed the Asura Mahisha and as Sarasvati She destroyed Sumbha and Nisumbha with their companions Dhumralochana, Chanda, Munda and Raktabija.

When Vishnu and Mahadeva destroyed various Asuras, the power of Devi was behind them. Devi took Brahma, Vishnu and Rudra and gave them necessary Sakti to proceed with the work of creation, preservation and destruction. She is at the centre of the universe. She is in Muladhara Chakra in our bodies. She vitalises the body through the Sushumna. She vitalises the universe from the summit of Mount Meru.

In this system of Sakti philosophy, Siva is omnipresent, impersonal, inactive. He is pure consciousness. Sakti is dynamic. Siva and Sakti are related as Prakasa and Vimarsa. Sakti or Vimarsa is the power that is latent in the pure consciousness. Vimarsa gives rise to the world of distinctions. Siva is Chit. Sakti is Chidrupini. Brahma, Vishnu and Siva do their functions of creation, preservation and destruction in obedience to Sakti. Sakti is endowed with Iccha (will), Jnana (knowledge) and Kriya (action). Siva and Sakti are one. Sakti Tattva and Siva Tattva are inseparable. Siva is always with Sakti. There are thirty-six Tattvas, in Sakti philosophy. Sakti is in Sakti Tattva, Nada in Sadakhya Tattva, Bindu in Isvara Tattva. The creative aspect of the Supreme Siva is called Siva

Tattva. Siva Tattva is the first creative movement. Sakti Tattva is the will of Siva. It is the seed and womb of the entire world.

The first manifestation is called the Sadakhya or Sadasiva Tattva. In this Tattva there is the beginning of formation of ideas. There is Nada Sakti in this Tattva. Next comes Isvara Tattva. This Tattva is called Bindu. The fourth Tattva is Vidya or Suddhavidya. Then Prakriti modifies into the Tattvas of mind, senses and the matter which constitutes the world.

Nada, Bindu are all names for different aspects of Sakti. Nada is really Siva Sakti. Siva has two aspects. In one aspect, He is the supreme changeless one who is Satchidananda. This is Para Samvit. In the other aspect, He changes as the world. The cause of the change is Siva Tattva. This Siva Tattva and Sakti Tattva are inseparable. Sakti Tattva is the first dynamic aspect of Brahman.

Nishkala Siva is Nirguna Siva. He is not connected with the creative Sakti. Sakala Siva is associated with the creative Sakti. Maya or Prakriti is within the womb of Sakti. Maya is the matrix of the world. Maya is potential in the state of dissolution. She is dynamic in creation. Maya evolves into the several material elements and other physical parts of all sentient creatures under the direction of Sakti. There are thirty-six Tattvas in Sakti philosophy. In Sakti philosophy we have Brahman, Sakti, Nada, Bindu and Suddhamaya. In Saiva Siddhanta philosophy we have Siva, Sakti, Sadakhya and the Suddhamaya. The rest of the evolution in Sakti philosophy is the same as in Saiva Siddhanta philosophy.

Knowledge of Sakti leads to salvation. *"Saktijnanam vina devi nirvanam naiva jayate* — O Devi! Without the knowledge of Sakti, Mukti cannot be attained" (Isvara says to Devi). The Jiva or the individual soul thinks when he is under the influence of Maya that he is the doer and the enjoyer and identifies himself with the body. Through the grace of Sakti and through Sadhana or self-culture, the individual soul frees himself from all fetters, attains spiritual insight and merges himself in the Supreme.

There is in reality nothing but the One Self. The experienced is nothing but the experiencer. Brahman appears as the world through the mirror of mind or Maya. An object is nothing but the One Self appearing through Maya as non-self, to itself as subject. Triputi or knower, knowledge and knowable vanishes in Nirvikalpa Samadhi. Supreme Siva or Brahman alone exists.

In the Kenopanishad, it is said that the gods became puffed up with a victory over the Asuras. They wrongly took the success to be the result of their own valour and prowess. The Lord wanted to teach them a lesson. He appeared before them in the form of a Yaksha, a huge form, the beginning and end of which were not visible. The Devas wanted to find out the identity of this form and sent Agni for this purpose. The Yaksha asked Agni: "What is your name and power?" Agni replied: "I am Agni (Jatavedas). I can burn up the whole universe in a minute." The Yaksha placed before Agni a dry blade of grass and asked him to burn it. Agni was not able to burn it. He ran away from the Yaksha in shame. The gods then sent Vayu to enquire who the Yaksha was. Vayu approached the Yaksha. The Yaksha said to Vayu: "Who are you? What is your power?" Vayu said: "I am wind-god. I can blow up the whole world in a minute." The Yaksha then placed a blade of grass before Vayu and told him to blow that away. Vayu could not make it move an inch from its place. He left the place in shame. Last of all came Indra himself. When Indra reached the place, he found that the Yaksha had vanished.

Then Uma appeared before Indra and revealed to him the real identity of the Yaksha. She said to Indra: "It is the power of the Divine Mother and not that of the gods that crowned the gods with victory. It is the Sakti or Uma or Haimavati, sister of Krishna, that is the source of the strength of all the gods." Sakti is the great teacher of Jnana. She sheds wisdom on her devotees.

May you all obtain the grace of Sakti or the Universal Mother and enjoy the supreme bliss of the final emancipation.

II

Sakti is Chidrupini. She is pure, blissful Consciousness. She is the Mother of Nature. She is Nature itself. She is power of Lord Siva or Brahman. She runs this world-show. She maintains the sportive play or Lila of the Lord. She is Jagat-Janani (creator of the world), Mahishasuramardini (destroyer of Mahishasura) Bhrantinasini (destroyer of illusion or Avidya), and Daridryanasini (destroyer of poverty).

Devi is Sakti of Lord Siva. She is Jada Sakti and Chit Sakti. She is Iccha Sakti, Kriya Sakti and Jnana Sakti. She is Maya Sakti. Sakti is Prakriti, Maya, Mahamaya, Sri Vidya. Sakti is Brahman itself. She is Lalita, Kundalini, Rajesvari, Tripurasundari, Sati and Parvati. Sati manifested to Lord Siva in the ten forms as the Dasa Maha Vidyas, viz., Kaali, Bagalamukhi, Chinnamasta, Bhuvanesvari, Matangi, Shodasi, Dhumavati, Tripurasundari, Tara and Bhairavi.

Worship of Sakti or Saktism is one of the oldest and most widespread religions in the world. Everybody in this world wants power, loves to possess power. He is elated by power. He wants to domineer over others through power. War is the outcome of greed for power. Scientists are followers of Saktism. He who wishes to develop will-power and charming personality, is a follower of Saktism. In reality, every man in this world is a follower of Saktism.

Scientists say now that everything is energy only and that energy is the physical ultimate of all forms of matter. The followers of the Sakta school of philosophy have said the same thing, long ago. They further say that this energy is only a limited manifestation of the Infinite Supreme Power of Maha Sakti.

Sakti is always with Siva. They are inseparable like fire and heat. Sakti evolves Nada and Nada Bindu. The world is a manifestation of Sakti. Suddha Maya is Chit Sakti. Prakriti is Jada Sakti. Nada, Bindu and the rest are only names for different aspects of Sakti.

The countless universes are only dust of Divine Mother's holy feet. Her glory is ineffable. Her splendour is indescribable. Her greatness is unfathomable. She showers Her grace on Her sincere devotees. She leads the individual soul from Chakra to Chakra, from plane to plane and unifies him with Lord Siva in the Sahasrara.

The body is Sakti. The needs of the body are the needs of Sakti. When a man enjoys, it is Sakti who enjoys through him. His eyes, ears, hands and feet are Hers. She sees through his eyes, hears through his ears. Body, mind, Prana, egoism, intellect, organs and all the other functions are Her manifestations.

Saktism speaks of personal and the impersonal aspects of Godhead. Brahman is Nishkala or without Prakriti and Sakala or with Prakriti. The Vedantin speaks of Nirupadhika Brahman (Pure Nirguna Brahman without Maya) and Sopadhika Brahman (with Upadhi or Maya) or Saguna Brahman. It is all the same. Names only are different. It is a play of words or Sabda Jalam. People fight on word only, carry on lingual warfare, hairsplitting, logical chopping and intellectual gymnastics. In reality the essence is one. Clay is the truth. All the modifications such as pot, etc., are in name only. In Nirguna Brahman, Sakti is potential, whereas in Saguna Brahman, it is kinetic or dynamic.

The basis of Saktism is the Veda. Saktism upholds that the only source and authority (Pramana) regarding transcendental or supersensual matters such as the nature of Brahman, etc., is Veda. Saktism is only Vedanta. The Saktas have the same spiritual experience as that of a Vedantin.

The Devi-Sukta of the Rig-Veda, the Sri-Sukta, Durga-Sukta, Bhu-Sukta and Nila-Sukta, and the specific Sakta Upanishads such as Tripuratapini Upanishad, Sitopanishad, Devi Upanishad, Saubhagya-Upanishad, Sarasvati Upanishad, Bhavanopanishad, Bhavrichopanishad, etc., emphatically declare about the Mother-aspect of God. The Kena Upanishad also speaks of Uma (Haimavati) who imparted wisdom of the Self to Indra and the Devas.

Divine Mother is everywhere triple. She is endowed with the three Gunas, viz., Sattva, Rajas and Tamas. She manifests as Will (Iccha Sakti). Action (Kriya Sakti) and Knowledge (Jnana Sakti). She is Brahma Sakti (Sarasvati) in conjunction with Brahma, Vishnu Sakti (Lakshmi) in conjunction with Lord Vishnu, and Siva Sakti (Gauri) in conjunction with Lord Siva. Hence She is called Tripurasundari.

The abode of Tripurasundari, the Divine Mother is called Sri Nagara. This magnificent abode is surrounded by twenty-five ramparts, which represent the twenty-five Tattvas. The resplendent Chintamani palace is in the middle. The Divine Mother sits in the Bindu Pitha in Sri

Chakra in that wonderful palace. There is a similar abode for Her in the body of man also. The whole world is Her body. Mountains are Her bones. Rivers are Her veins. Ocean is Her bladder. Sun and moon are Her eyes. Wind is Her breath. Agni is Her mouth.

The Sakti enjoys Bhukti (enjoyment in the world) and Mukti (liberation from all worlds). Siva is an embodiment of Bliss and Knowledge. Siva Himself appears in the form of man with a life—mixture of pleasure and pain. If you remember this point always, all dualism, all hatred, jealousy, pride will vanish. You must consider every human function as worship or a religious act. Answering calls of nature, talking, eating, walking, seeing, hearing, become worship of Lord, if you develop the right attitude. It is Siva who works in and through man. Where then is egoism or individuality? All human actions are divine actions. One universal life throbs in the hearts of all, sees in the eyes of all, works in the hands of all, hears in the ears of all. What a magnificent experience it is, if one can feel this by crushing this little 'I'! The old Samskaras, the old Vasanas, the old habits of thinking, stand in the way of your realising this experience—Whole.

The aspirant thinks that the world is identical with the Divine Mother. He moves about thinking his own form to be the form of the Divine Mother and thus beholds oneness everywhere. He also feels that the Divine Mother is identical with Para Brahman.

The advanced Sadhaka feels: "I am the Devi and the Devi is in me". He worships himself as Devi instead of adoring any external object. He says: *"Sa-aham*—I am She (Devi)".

Saktism is not a mere theory or philosophy. It prescribes systematic Sadhana of Yoga, regular discipline, according to the temperament, capacity and degree of evolution of the Sadhaka. It helps the aspirant to arouse the Kundalini and unite Her with Lord Siva and enjoy the Supreme Bliss or Nirvikalpa Samadhi. When Kundalini sleeps, man is awake to the world. He has objective consciousness. When She awakes, he sleeps. He loses all consciousness of the world and becomes one with the Lord. In Samadhi, the body is maintained by the nectar which flows from the union of Siva and Sakti with Sahasrara.

Guru is indispensable for the practice of Sakti Yoga Sadhana. He initiates the aspirant and transmits the divine Sakti.

Physical contact with a female is gross Maithuna. This is due to Pasu Bhava or animal disposition or brutal instinct. Mother Kundalini Sakti unites with Lord Siva in Sahasrara during Nirvikalpa Samadhi. This is real Maithuna or blissful union. This is due to Divya Bhava or divine disposition. You must rise from Pasu Bhava to Divya Bhava, through Satsanga, service of Guru, renunciation and dispassion, discrimination, Japa and meditation.

Worship of the Divine Mother with intense faith and perfect devotion and self-surrender will help you to attain Her grace. Through Her grace alone, you can attain knowledge of the Imperishable.

Glory to Tripurasundari, the World-Mother, who is also Raja-Rajesvari and Lalita Devi. May Her blessings be upon you all!

SIVA AND SAKTI

Sakti Tattva is really the negative aspect of the Siva Tattva. Though they are spoken of separately they are really one. Sakti Tattva is the will of Siva.

Ambal, Ambika, Gauri, Jnanambika, Durga, Kaali, Rajesvari, Tripurasundari are all other names for Sakti.

Sakti is Herself pure, blissful consciousness and is nature itself born of the creative play of Her thought. This Sakti cult is the conception of God as the Universal Mother.

Sakti is spoken of as Mother, because that is the aspect of the Supreme in which She is regarded as the genetrix and nourisher of the universe. But God is neither male nor female. He is named according to the body in which He is manifested.

Hinduism is the only religion in the world which has emphasised much on the motherhood of God. The Devi-Sukta appears in the tenth Mandala of the Rig-Veda. It was revealed by Bak, the daughter of Maharshi Ambrin. In this Rigvedic hymn addressed to the Divine Mother, Bak speaks of her realisation of God as Mother who pervades the whole universe. In Bengal, Mother-worship is very prevalent. 'Ma' is always on the lips of every Bengali.

Siva and Sakti are essentially one. It is said in the very first verse of Kalidasa's Raghuvamsa that Sakti and Siva stand to each other in the same relationship as the word and its meaning. Just as heat and fire are inseparable, so Sakti and Siva are inseparable. Lord Siva cannot do anything without Sakti. This is emphasised by Sri Sankaracharya in the first verse of Saundarya Lahari.

Sakti is like the snake with motion. Siva is like the motionless snake. Waveless ocean is Siva. Ocean with waves is Sakti. The transcendental Supreme Being is Siva. The manifested, immanent aspect of the Supreme is Sakti. Siva is attributeless. He is Nishkriya. Sakti is with attributes. She creates. Sakti is compared to a rope made up of tricoloured threads.

Mother Kaali dances on the breast of Siva. She has terrible form but She is not really terrible. She is all-merciful and gentle. She wears a garland made up of the skulls. What does this mean? She wears the heads of Her devotees. How loving and affectionate She is to Her devotees!

Kaali is the Divine Mother. She is the Sakti or power of Lord Siva. She is the dynamic aspect of Siva. Siva is the static aspect. Lord Siva is like a dead corpse. What does this signify? He is absolutely calm, motionless, breathless, with His eyes closed in Samadhi. He is actionless, changeless. He is untouched by the cosmic play or Lila that is eternally going on, on His breast.

He is absolutely dead to the world. He is beyond the three Gunas. There is no duality, no plurality, no relativity, no differentiation between subject and object, no distinction, no difference, no Triputi, no Dvandvas, no Raga-Dvesha, no good and evil in Him. He is ever pure, Nirlipta (unattached). And yet He is the source, substratum, support, first cause for this universe. He simply gazes. Sakti is vitalised. She works and creates. In His mere presence Sakti keeps up the play of this universe or Lila. The whole world is a mere vibration or Spandana in Him. He is superconscious and yet He has cosmic consciousness. He constitutes all the names and forms and yet He is above all names and forms. This is a great marvel and a supreme mystery which cannot be comprehended by the finite intellect.

Without Siva, Sakti has no existence and without Sakti, Siva has no expression. It is through Sakti that the Impersonal Supreme Being Siva or Nirguna Brahman becomes the Personal Being or Saguna Brahman. Siva or Nirguna Brahman becomes the Personal Being or Saguna Brahman. Siva is the Soul of Durga or Kaali. Durga or Kaali is identical with Siva. Siva is Satchidananda. Durga or Kaali is Satchidananda Mayi. Siva and Sakti are one and neither is higher than the other. Sakti is Chit, Chidrupini, Chinmatra Rupini.

SIVA AND PARVATI

O Devi! All auspicious one, giver of success and prosperity, we bow to Thee! Shower peace and amity on this earth and protect us ever more by Your kind compassion at a glance!

Parvati is the daughter of the king of Parvatas, Himavan. She is the wife or Sakti of Lord Siva. She is the matrix of the universe. She is the revealer of Brahman. She is not only Loka-Mata or World-Mother but also Brahma-Vidya. One of Her names is Sivajnana-Pradayini. She is also called Sivaduti, Sivaradhya, Sivamurti and Sivankari.

The grace of Devi is an indispensable factor for the attainment of God-realisation. Parvati or Sakti is all-in-all. You must rouse the Sakti by Yoga. Then the grace of Sakti will lead you to God-realisation and the attainment of the final emancipation and the achievement of infinite, eternal supreme bliss.

The glorious story of Parvati is related in detail in the Mahesvara Kanda of the Skanda Purana. Sati, the daughter of Daksha Prajapati, the son of Brahma, was wedded to Lord Siva. Daksha did not like his son-in-law on account of His queer form, strange manners and peculiar habits. Daksha performed a sacrifice. He did not invite his daughter and son-in-law. Sati felt the insult and went to Her father and questioned him. He gave Her a displeasing reply. Sati got enraged at this. She did not want any more to be called his daughter. She preferred to offer Her body to fire and to be born again as Parvati to marry Siva. She created fire through Her Yogic power and destroyed Herself in that Yogagni.

Lord Siva sent Virabhadra. He destroyed the sacrifice and drove away all the Devas who assembled there. The head of Daksha was cut off and thrown into the fire. Lord Siva had a goat's head stuck to the body of Daksha at the request of Brahma.

Lord Siva repaired to the Himalayas to do austerities. Asura Taraka had a boon from Brahma that he should die only at the hands of the son of Siva and Parvati. Therefore the Devas requested Himavan to have Sati as his daughter. Himavan agreed. Sati was born as Parvati, the daughter of Himavan. She served Lord Siva during His penance and worshipped Him. Lord Siva married Parvati.

Narada proceeded to Kailasa and saw Siva and Parvati with one body, half male, half female in the form of Ardhanarisvara. He wanted to see their play at dice. Lord Siva said He won the game. Parvati said that She was victorious. There was a quarrel. Siva left Parvati and went to practise austerities. Parvati assumed the form of a huntress and met Siva. Siva fell in love with the huntress. He went with her to her father to get his consent for the marriage. Narada informed Lord Siva that the huntress was Parvati. Narada told Parvati to apologise to Her Lord. They were reunited.

Siva assumed the form of Arunachala hill as a Linga. He subdued the pride of Brahma and Vishnu who were quarrelling as to their relative greatness. Arunachala is a Tejolinga. Parvati saw Siva as Arunachala-Isvara. Siva took Parvati back to His side and made Her again Ardhanari.

Asura Taraka greatly oppressed the Devas. Mahi-Sagara-Sangama-Kshetra was his capital. Lord Subrahmanya, the second son of Parvati, killed the Asura on the seventh day after his birth.

Parvati created a child with the face of an elephant for Her pleasure. He was Lord Ganesa. He was made the Lord of all creatures to remove their obstacles. One day Lord Siva offered a fruit saying that it would be given to that child who would go round the world first. Lord Subrahmanya proceeded on a tour round the world. Lord Ganesa went round His father Siva, the Maha Linga who enveloped the whole universe, and got the fruit.

Parvati had a dark skin. One day Lord Siva playfully referred to Her dark colour. She was much touched by Siva's remark. She went to the Himalayas to perform austerities. She attained a beautiful complexion and came to be called Gauri. Gauri joined Siva as Ardhanarisvara by the grace of Brahma.

One day Parvati came behind Lord Siva and closed His eyes. The whole universe lost life and light. Siva asked Parvati to practise austerities in order to make amends for Her folly. She proceeded to Kanchi (Kanjivaram) and did rigorous penance. Lord Siva created a flood. The Siva Linga which Parvati was worshipping was about to be washed away. She embraced the Linga. The Linga remained there as Ekambaresvara. She remained there as Kamakshi for the welfare of the world.

Parvati ever dwells with Siva as His Sakti. She is the Divine Mother of this universe. She sheds wisdom and grace on Her devotees and makes them attain union with Her Lord. Salutations to Parvati and Siva, the real Parents of all beings.

THE DIVINE MOTHER

Children are more familiar with the mother than with the father. Mother is an embodiment of affection, tenderness and love. She looks after the wants of the children. Whenever a child wants anything it approaches the mother rather than the father. In spiritual matters also the aspirant has more concern with Mother Kaali than Father Siva. Siva is indifferent to the external world. He is unattached. He is lost in Samadhi with His eyes closed. It is Sakti or the Divine Mother alone who really looks after the affairs of the world. She will introduce to Her Lord for the attainment of final emancipation when She is pleased with the earnestness of the devotee.

Siva and Sakti are inseparable. This is shown in Ardhanarisvara—Siva and Parvati (with one body, half male and half-female). Lord Siva has Parvati as the left half of His body.

Siva-Jnana leads us on to the realisation of Self and bestows on us eternal bliss and frees us from births and deaths. It shows us the light of life. It is the eye of intuition. It is the third eye of Siva. This third eye destroys all illusions and passions.

Sakti is thought of in various forms. Sarasvati is the Goddess of learning. Lakshmi is the Goddess of wealth. Parvati or Uma is the bliss-bestowing Goddess.

The Markandeya Purana contains seven hundred verses which are known as the Sapta-sati or the Chandi or the Devi-Mahatmya. It is one of the most famous religious texts of the Hindus. It ranks almost equal with the Gita. It describes in an allegorical form, that in the path of salvation the chief obstacles are our own desire, anger, greed and ignorance and we can overcome them through the grace of Divine Mother if we sincerely worship Her.

The book gives a beautiful description of the three aspects of the Mother as Mahakaali, Mahalakshmi and Maha Sarasvati—the Tamasic, the Rajasic and the Sattvic aspects of the Divine Mother.

The Devas were oppressed by the Asuras. The gods invoked the blessings of Divine Mother. She appeared as the above three forms and destroyed the Asuras and protected the gods. The Divine Mother has given to men as well as gods, Her definite and infallible promise that whenever they would remember Her in danger or difficulties She would save them

SAKTI ENERGISES THE TRIMURTIS

O Lord Siva! Silent adorations unto Thee! Thou art the only refuge, the only object of adoration, the one Governor of the Universe, the self-effulgent Being. Thou art the creator, preserver and destroyer of the universe. Thou art the Highest, the Immovable, the Absolute.

Sakti is the energy or the vital power that makes any activity possible. When a man does any work he does it only by virtue of his Sakti. If he is unable to do the work he says that he has no Sakti to do that work. Hence Sakti is that which enables one to work. Sakti is Devi. Sakti is the Divine Mother. Mind is Sakti. Prana is Sakti. Will is Sakti.

Devi Bhagavata deals with the forms of Prakriti. Devi took the Trimurtis to Her abode in Manidvipa, gave them their consorts Sarasvati, Lakshmi and Parvati and sent out for the life of universe in the new Kalpa.

Lord Narayana created Brahma from His navel. Brahma did not know what to do. Vishnu and Siva also did not know how to set going the life of a new universe in a new Kalpa after the dissolution. They were lifted in a Vimana or celestial car and they soon reached a strange region where they were transformed into women. They were in a land of women headed by Devi. It was Manidvipa in the Sudha Samudra, the ocean of nectar. The newly made women stayed there, for a hundred years. They did not know who they were, why they were there and what they were to do.

Then they were put in the company of men and they themselves became men. They were coupled, Brahma with Sarasvati, Vishnu with Lakshmi and Siva with Parvati. They found themselves at once in their original place and they knew what to do. They understood their functions. The Trimurtis attain Sakti through association with the Devi.

Parvati is the Sakti of Lord Siva who bestows Jnana and Mukti on men. Lakshmi is the Sakti of Vishnu who gives prosperity to the people. Sarasvati is the Sakti of Brahma who creates the world. Radha is the Sakti of Lord Krishna who leads humanity to Mukti through Bhakti.

May Sakti bless you all with Sakti!

MOTHER GANGA

The Ganga is the most sacred river of India. Lord Krishna says in the Gita: "I am the Ganga among rivers". No germ can flourish in the waters of the Ganga. It is saturated with antiseptic minerals. In the West, doctors prescribe Ganga water for rubbing in the treatment of diseases of the skin. Ganga is not merely a river. It is a sacred Tirtha. It is possessed of mysterious powers which are not found in any other rivers of the world. Even scientists have admitted the efficacy of the Ganga water.

Dr. F.C. Harrison of McGill University, Canada, writes: "A peculiar fact, which has never been satisfactorily explained, is the quick death (in three or five hours) of the cholera vibrio in the waters of Ganga. When one remembers sewage, by numerous corpses of natives (often dead of cholera) and by the bathing of thousands of natives, it seems remarkable that the belief of the Hindus, that the water of this river is pure and cannot be defiled, and that they can safely drink it and bathe in it, should be confirmed by means of modern bacteriological research." A well-known French physician Dr. D. Herelle, made similar investigations into the mystery of the Ganga. He observed some of the floating corpses of men dead of dysentery and cholera and was surprised to find that only a few feet below the bodies, where one would expect to find millions of these dysentery and cholera germs, there were no germs at all. He then grew germs from patients having the disease and to these cultures added water from the Ganga. When he incubated the mixture for a period, much to his surprise, the germs were completely destroyed.

A British physician Dr. C.E. Nelson, F.R.C.S. tells us of another striking fact. He says: "Ships leaving Calcutta for England take their water from the Hugli river which is one of the mouths of the filthy Ganga and this Ganga water will remain fresh all the way to England. On the other hand, ships leaving England for India, find that the water they take on in London will not stay fresh till they reach Bombay, the nearest Indian port, which is a week closer to England than Calcutta. They must replenish their water supply at Port Said, Suez or at Aden on the Red Sea. It is no wonder that the Indian people should hold that the Ganga is very sacred and possessed of mysterious powers."

For a Hindu the word 'Ganga' has its own sacred association. Every Hindu thirsts for a dip in the Ganga, and for a drop of water at the time of his death. Aspirants and mendicants build their huts on the banks of the Ganga for practising penance and meditation. Bhishma spoke very highly on the glory of the Ganga in his parting instructions to the Pandavas from his bed of arrows.

Whenever a pious Hindu goes to take his bath, he invokes first the Ganga, and feels Her presence in the water before he takes a plunge in the river. If he lives in a place far away from the Ganga, he intensely yearns to see Her on some day and feels blessed by bathing in the holy waters. He carries some water to his house and carefully saves it in a vessel so that he may use it for purposes of purification.

Hindus believe that all their sins are washed away if they take a dip in the sacred waters of the Ganga.

In the Satya Yuga, all places were sacred. In the Treta Yuga, Pushkara was considered as the most holy place. In the Dvapara Yuga, Kurukshetra was regarded as the most sacred place. In Kali Yuga, the Ganga has that glory. Devi Bhagavata says: "He who utters the name of Ganga even from hundreds of miles afar, is freed from sins and attains the abode of Lord Hari".

The Ganga comes out of the Supreme Being. She enters the feet of Lord Hari and reaches Vaikuntha. She issues from Goloka and passes through the regions of Vishnu, Brahma, Siva, Dhruva, Chandra, Surya, Tapah, Janah, Mahah, and reaching Indraloka flows as Mandakini.

The Ganga entered the matted locks of Lord Siva at the request of Bhagiratha who did rigorous penance for the descent of Ganga to Patala for the redemption of his ancestors, the thousand sons of Sagara, who had been burnt to ashes by sage Kapila.

Thereupon, She flowed down from the locks of Lord Siva. She was drunk up by the sage Jahnu, as the water inundated the Yajnasala of the sage. Then again She issued out of the ear of the sage and acquired the name of Jahnavi. She is also known by the name Bhagirathi, daughter of Bhagiratha. The Ganga flowed into Patala as Bhagirathi. The ancestors of the king were raised to Svarga by the touch of the sacred waters of the Ganga.

SAKTI YOGA PHILOSOPHY

Ganga had to take a human form on account of Her own fault in behaviour in the presence of Brahma. She became the wife of Santanu. Santanu also was a celestial being known as king Mahabhisha. He had to take birth in the world for his fault in conduct in the presence of Brahma by showing vanity. Ganga gave birth to Bhishma, the illustrious hero and sage.

Ganga consented to bear the seed of Lord Siva which was transferred to Her by Agni. She gave to the world Lord Subrahmanya, the great commander of the army of Devas, who killed the formidable Asura Taraka.

Ganga is the form of Vishnu. Her sight is soul-stirring and elevating. She flows in the valleys and lives by the side of Parvati, daughter of Himavan. How magnificent She is when She flows in the valley of Rishikesh! She has a blue colour like that of the ocean. The water is extremely clear and sweet. Rich people from the plains get water from Rishikesh. They take it in big copper-vessels to far off places in India.

To have a look at the Ganga in Rishikesh, is soul-elevating. To sit for a few minutes on a block of stone by the side of the Ganga, is a blessing. To stay for some months in Rishikesh on the bank of the Ganga and do Anushthana or Purascharana, is great Tapas which will take the aspirant to the abode of Lord Hari. To live for ever on the banks of the Ganga and spend the life in meditation is Sivanandam.

May Mother Ganga bless you all! May She help you to live on Her banks and practise Yoga and Tapas!

TRIPURA RAHASYA

The three cities are Anava Mala (egoism), Karma (bondage of Karma) and Maya (the illusory power of Lord Siva which veils the individual souls). Destroy the first city

Anava Mala through self-surrender to Lord Siva and consequent descent of His grace (Anugraha). Annihilate the second impurity, viz., Karma, through consecrating the fruits of your actions to the Lord and destroying the idea 'I am the doer', by developing the Nimitta Bhava, the Bhava that Lord Siva is working through your various organs and that you are a mere instrument in His hands (Chariyai and Kiriyai). You will not be bound by actions. You will attain purity of heart and through purity of heart, realisation of Sivanandam or eternal bliss of Siva. Annihilate the third impurity, viz., Maya, through the recitation of Panchakshara, worship of Guru, hearing and reflection of the attributes of the Lord and His various Lilas and meditation on His form and Satchidananda aspect.

This is the destruction of the three cities or castles. This is Tripura Rahasya.

Destroy Tamas through Rajas and convert Rajas into Sattva, by developing various virtuous qualities, by taking Sattvic food, by Satsanga, Japa of Panchakshara and meditation on Lord Siva. Transcend Sattva also. You will attain oneness with Lord Siva.

This is the destruction of the three cities or castles. This is Tripura Rahasya.

Annihilate the evil tendencies or Asubha Vasanas, viz., lust, anger, greed, hatred, jealousy, through Subha Vasanas or good tendencies, viz., Japa, meditation, study of religious books, Kirtan or singing Lord's praise. You will enjoy the eternal bliss of Siva.

This is the destruction of the three cities or castles. This is Tripura Rahasya.

Serve the Guru. Purify your heart by serving him with faith and devotion. Learn the Yogic practices which lead to the awakening of Kundalini from him and practise them.

Study the Yoga Sastras under him. Observe celibacy. Kill the Shadripus or six enemies. Look within. Take the Kundalini through the Sushumna Nadi and break the Granthis through the Chakras and unite Her with Her Lord Sadasiva at the Sahasrara Chakra at the crown of the head and enjoy the eternal bliss of Lord Siva.

This is the destruction of the three cities or castles. This is Tripura Rahasya.

Kill the three bodies, i.e., transcend the three bodies, viz., the gross or physical body (Sthula Deha), subtle body (Sukshma Deha) and causal body (Karana Sarira). Go above the five sheaths or Kosas (Annamaya, Pranamaya, Manomaya, Vijnanamaya and Anandamaya), through meditation on Lord Siva and attain Siva Sayujya.

This is the destruction of the three cities or castles. This is Tripura Rahasya.

Become a witness of the three states, viz., waking, dreaming and deep sleep states. Stand as a spectator. Withdraw yourself from the objective consciousness. Live within. Attain the Turiya state or the fourth state or Siva Pada.

This is the destruction of the three cities or castles. This is Tripura Rahasya.

Go above physical consciousness, subconsciousness and mental consciousness and attain the superconsciousness state or Nirvikalpa or Asamprajnata Samadhi.

This is the destruction of the three cities or castles. This is Tripura Rahasya.

Go above instinct, reason, understanding and open the eye of intuition, the third eye of Siva (Divya Chakshus) and merge yourself in the supreme light of Siva. Go above thinking, willing and feeling and enter the supreme silence or thoughtless state of Siva Nirvana.

This is the destruction of the three cities or castles. This is Tripura Rahasya.

Tripura Sundari is the Sakti of Lord Siva. She and Siva are one. She is extremely beautiful. She attracts the devotees to Her blissful Self and sheds wisdom, devotion and divine light on them. Hence, She is called Tripura Sundari. She helps the aspirants to destroy the three cities or castles mentioned above.

The whole world is under Her control. The entire universe is under the sway of Her three Gunas. All the ties and bonds of Karma can be broken down; the wheel of births and deaths can be rent asunder only by Her worship and benign grace. All sins can be destroyed and the eternal bliss of Siva can be realised only through singing Her praise and repetition of Her Names.

She is called Tripura, the three cities. The body of a man or a woman is one of the forms assumed by Her. The whole world is Her body. All the Devas are Her forms only. All the triplets of the sacred texts are contained in Her. The triplets, viz., the three Gunas, the three states of consciousness, the three fires, the three bodies, the three worlds, the triple power (Iccha Sakti, Kriya Sakti and Jnana Sakti), the three Svaras (Udatta, Anudatta and Svarita), the Trivarnikas, the three kinds of Karmas (Sanchita, Agami and Prarabdha), the Trimurtis, the three letters A, U, M, and the triad Pramata, Pramana and Prameya, knower, knowledge and knowable, seer, sight and seen, are all contained in Tripurasundari.

All the Devatas dwell in this body. They are the presiding deities of the various organs. The Lord Tryambaka dwells in Muladhara, Jambukesvara in Svadhishthana, Arunachalesvara in Manipura, Nataraja in

Anahata, Kalahastisvara in Visuddha, Visvesvara in Ajna and Srikanthesvara in Sahasrara.

All the sacred places are in this body—Kedar in the forehead, Amaravati in the tip of the nose, Kurukshetra in the breasts and Prayaga in the heart.

All the nine planets have their special abodes in the body. Sun is in the Nada-Chakra, moon in the Bindu-Chakra, Mars in the eyes, Mercury in the heart, Jupiter in the Manipura, Venus in the Svadhishthana, Saturn in the navel, Rahu in the face and Ketu in the thorax.

Countless rivers and hills are also allotted special places in the body. Whatever is found in the outer world is found in the body also. This body is microcosm. It is Pindanda.

This is Tripura Rahasya.

May you attain the grace of Tripurasundari and understand the Tripura Rahasya and attain Sivananda or eternal bliss of Lord Siva.

KAMAKSHI AND THE DUMB POET

The word 'Muka' means dumb. A certain devotee was performing rigorous austerities in the temple of Goddess Kamakshi at Kanchi to obtain Her Grace. Kamakshi appeared in the form of a beautiful maiden before the devotee to bless him. The devotee took Her to be an ordinary human maiden and did not show any veneration. She left him and found a person sleeping in another corner of the temple. He was dumb from his birth. She woke him up. He was extremely joyous when he saw Her. The Goddess wrote the Bijakshara on his tongue and blessed him with the power of speech. He became the celebrated Muka Kavi (dumb poet). He sang five hundred verses called the Panchasati which describe the glory of Devi, of Her lotus-feet, of Her grace, of Her gracious glance and of

Her loving maternal smile. One hundred verses are devoted to each of these five aspects. Hence the work is called 'Mukapanchasati'.

The dumb poet became the Acharya of the Kama Koti Pitha at Kumbakonam and occupied the seat for thirty-nine years.

The Mukapanchasati is read with intense devotion during the Navaratri celebrations in South India by all religious-minded persons.

Kalidasa was an unlettered shepherd. He also was turned into India's most talented poet through the benign grace of Mother Kaali. Kalidasa in his famous Syamaladandaka, has praised Devi in a charming manner.

Glory to the Devi who is the giver of the power of speech!

HYMN FOR FORGIVENESS TO MOTHER

Mother is more dear to the child than the father. Mother is gentle, soft, sweet, tender and affectionate. She is full of smiles. Father is stiff, harsh, rude, rough and hard-hearted. The child runs towards the mother for getting presents, sweets, fruits and other gifts. The child can open the heart more freely towards the mother than to the father.

Even so, poets and saints also are more familiar with the Divine Mother than with the Divine Father. They open their heart more freely towards the Divine Mother. They have found much more intimate cries of the heart when they speak of the Deity as their Mother, than when they address themselves to God as Father. Go through the following hymn to Mother by Sri Sankara. You will feel and realise the truth of the above statement.

By my ignorance of Thy commands
By my poverty and sloth
I had not the power to do that which I should have done
Hence my omission to worship Thy feet
But O Mother, auspicious deliverer of all
All this should be forgiven,
For, a bad son may sometimes be born,
                                      but a bad mother never.

O Mother! Thou hast many sons on earth
But I, Thy son, am of no worth
Yet it is not meet, that Thou shouldst abandon me
For, a bad son may sometimes be born,
                                      but a bad mother never.

O Mother of the world! O Mother!
I have not worshipped Thy feet
Nor have I given abundant wealth to Thee
Yet the affection which Thou bestowest on me
                                      is without compare
For, a bad son may sometimes be born,
                                      but a bad mother never.

Chapter VII
VIRASAIVISM AND KASHMIR SAIVISM

VIRASAIVISM

Virasaiva philosophy is only Sakti Visishtadvaita philosophy. It is a phase of Agamanta. It underwent radical changes in the hands of Sri Basavanna and his colleagues. Basava was the Prime Minister to a Jain king named Bijjala who ruled over Kalyan (1157-1167) which is sixty miles from Gulbarga in Karnataka State.

Basavanna was a magnetic personality. He exercised tremendous influence over the people. He held a spiritual conference. Three hundred Virasaiva saints assembled. There were sixty women saints also. Akka Mahadevi, the illustrious lady saint was also present on that grand occasion. Virasaivism became Lingayatism in the hands of Basava. Lingayatism is the special faith of the Karnatic Virasaivas. Sharanas are the saints of the Lingayat faith or cult.

Virasaivism or Lingayatism shows the way to attain the Lakshya or Lord Siva. Lord Siva, Lord Subrahmanya, king Rishabha, Santa Lingar, Kumara Devi, Sivaprakasa had all expounded lucidly this system of philosophy. Viragama is the chief source for this system of philosophy. Those who embrace this faith, live in great numbers in Karnataka.

Ordinary Saivites keep the Sivaling in a box and worship it during the time of Puja. The Lingayats keep a small Linga in a small silver or golden box and wear it on the body with the chain attached to the box. Wearing the Linga on the body will remind one, of the Lord and help

His constant remembrance. The Christians wear the cross in the neck. This also has the same object in view.

Sakti in Virasaiva philosophy is identical with Siva. Sakti works. Siva is the silent witness. Siva is infinite, self-luminous, eternal, all-pervading. He is an ocean of peace. He is stupendous silence. Siva illumines everything. He is all-full and self-contained. He is ever free and perfect. The whole world is an expression of the Divine Will. In Virasaiva philosophy, the world movement is not an illusion, but an integral play.

KASHMIR SAIVISM

This is known by the name Pratyabhijna system. The Agamas are the basis for Kashmir Saivism. The Agamanta called Pratyabhijna Darsana, flourished in Kashmir. The twenty-eight Agamas were written in Sanskrit in the valley of Kashmir, in order to make the meaning clear to every one. This Agamanta arose in North India long before Jainism came into prominence. Then it spread westwardly and southwards. In Western India, it was known by the name Vira Mahesvara Darsanam, and in South India, it was called Suddha Saiva Darsanam.

Siva is the only reality of the universe. Siva is infinite consciousness. He is independent, eternal, formless, secondless, omnipresent. Siva is the subject and the object, the experiencer and the experienced. The world exists within consciousness.

God creates by the mere force of His Will. Karma, material cause like Prakriti, Maya which produce illusion, forms, etc., are not admitted in this system. God makes the world appear in Himself just as objects appear in a mirror. He is not affected by the objects of His creation, just as the mirror is not affected by the reflected image in it. He appears in the form of souls by His own wonderful power inherent in Him. God is the substratum of this world. His activity (Spanda or vibration) produces all distinctions.

Siva is the changeless Reality. He is the underlying basic substratum for the whole world. His Sakti or energy has infinite aspects. Chit (intelligence), Ananda (bliss), Iccha (will), Jnana (knowledge) and Kriya (creative power) are Her chief aspects.

Sakti functions as Chit, then the Absolute becomes the pure experience known as Siva Tattva. The Ananda of Sakti functions and life comes in. Then there is the second stage of Sakti Tattva. The third stage is the will for self-expression. Then comes the fourth stage, Isvara Tattva with its power and will to create the world. It is the stage of conscious experience (Jnana) of being. In the fifth stage, there is the knower and also the object of knowledge. Action (Kriya) starts now. This is the stage of Suddha-vidya. There are thirty-six Tattvas or principles in this system.

Bondage is due to ignorance (Ajnana). The soul thinks: 'I am finite', 'I am the body.' It forgets that it is identical with Siva and that the world is wholly unreal apart from Siva.

Pratyabhijna or recognition of the reality, is all that is needed for attaining the final emancipation. When the soul recognises itself as God, it rests in the eternal bliss of oneness with God. The liberated soul is merged in Siva, as water in water, or milk in milk, when the imagination of duality has disappeared.

Vasu Gupta (eighth century A.D.) wrote the Siva Sutra and taught it to Kallata. Siva Drishti written by Somanatha may be considered equal in merit to Tirumantiram of Tirumular. Vasu Gupta's Spanda Karika, Somanatha's Siva Drishti (930 A.D.), Abhinava Gupta's Paramarthasara and

Pratyabhijna Vimarsini, Kimaraja's Siva Sutra Vimarsini are some of the important works of this school.

They accept the Siva Agamas and the Siddhanta works as authoritative. They modify them in the light of Sankara's Advaita. Somanatha's Siva Drishti, Utpala's Pratyabhijna Sutra and Abhinava Gupta's works support non-dualism.

Chapter VIII
LORD SIVA AND HIS LILAS

Siva is known by the name 'Girisa', as He is the Lord of the Mount Kailas.

Siva is called 'Tryambaka', because He has a third eye in His forehead, the eye of wisdom (Jnana Chakshus).

The word 'Hara' is derived from the root 'Hri' to take and the suffix 'Ati', for He removes (Harati) all ills. 'Hara' means He who at the time of dissolution (Pralaya) withdraws the world within Himself.

Siva is holding in His hands Parasu (axe) and deer. He is making with the other two hands the Vara and the Abhaya Mudras. The deer here is Brahma. Siva is very powerful. Even Brahma is under His control.

TRIPURARI

Siva was the destroyer of the Asuras, Tripuras. He destroyed the Tripuras or the three cities of the Asuras which were built of gold, silver and iron by Maya. The Asuras oppressed all theists, being protected by the three cities. Siva is called Tripurari because He destroyed the Asuras, Tripuras, and the cities, Tripuras.

SIVA JYOTI

Brahma and Vishnu were one day disputing which of the two was the greater. Siva appeared in the form of an Infinite Jyoti or fiery Linga, in order to destroy their pride. Brahma and Vishnu set out to measure the Jyoti. They failed in their attempts.

NILAKANTHA

When the ocean was churned, a terrible poison came out. Siva swallowed this in order to save the world. This caused a blue stain on His throat. So He is called by the name Nilakantha.

RAVANA AND SIVA

Ravana was a great devotee of Lord Siva. He used to go everyday to Mount Kailas to worship Lord Siva. He found this very troublesome. He thought within himself to bring the whole mountain to his abode in Lanka in order to save himself from the trouble of a daily journey to Mount Kailas. He began to pull up the mountain which trembled. Parvati, consort of Siva, got frightened. She embraced Lord Siva. Siva pressed Ravana with His toe and sent him down to the nether world.

HARI AND SIVA

Hari used to worship Siva daily with a thousand lotuses. One day one lotus was missing. He plucked out His own eye to make the number of a thousand. Siva gave Vishnu the Sudarsana Chakra or discus, being very much pleased with His devotion. It is this Sudarsana Chakra which Vishnu always bears. This discus is itself an embodiment of devotion.

BRAHMA'S BOON

A Rakshasa worshipped Brahma and asked Him to grant him the power to destroy the whole world. Brahma was partially unwilling to grant him this boon. He consented in a half-hearted manner and asked him to wait. The Devas, hearing this, were terribly frightened and went to Siva and told Him everything. Siva danced in order to delay the granting of this boon by Brahma, to distract him and thus save the world.

BIRTH OF SUBRAHMANYA

The Asura Taraka drove all the gods from heaven. The gods went to Brahma. Brahma said to the gods: "The Asura has acquired his power through my grace. I cannot destroy him. I shall suggest to you one plan. Go to Lord Siva. He is in Yoga Samadhi. He must be tempted to unite with Parvati. A powerful son will be born unto Him. He will destroy the Asura".

Thereupon, Indra asked Cupid (Kama) to go with his wife Rati and his companion Vasanta (the spring), to Mount Kailas, the abode of Lord Siva. The three persons at once proceeded to Kailas. Spring season appeared there. All the Rishis were surprised at this. Kama stood behind a tree and shot an arrow at Siva. At this moment Parvati was worshipping Siva and offering flowers in His hand. Her hand touched the hands of Siva. Siva felt suddenly a thrill of passion and His seed came out. Siva was wondering what was it that thus distracted Him from His Yoga. He looked around and witnessed Kama behind a tree. He opened His third eye. A fire flashed and burnt Kama to ashes.

Siva's seed was thrown into Agni (God of Fire). Agni was not able to bear it. He threw it into the Ganga. Ganga threw it into a forest of reeds where Subrahmanya, called the reed-born (Sara Janma, Saravana Bhava), was born. Subrahmanya became the commander of the Devas and destroyed the Asura as Brahma intended.

LORD SIVA AND DAKSHA

Daksha goes to attend the sacrifice of the sages who are the progenitors of the world, and not being honoured by Rudra who has come before him, Daksha reproaches Him and leaves the place. Nandisvara in his turn, curses Daksha and other Brahmins. Rudra then leaves the place of sacrifice.

Sati, daughter of Daksha, known also by the name Dakshayani, requests Siva's permission to attend her father's sacrifice, the Brihaspati-sava, and Siva shows how inadvisable it would be.

In spite of her Lord's advice, Sati goes to Daksha's sacrifice. Disregarded by her father and enraged at finding no offering made to Rudra, she praises the greatness of her Lord, censures Daksha and by the Yoga method casts off her body.

Hearing of Sati's casting off her body, Sankara creates in His anger Virabhadra out of His Jata (matted locks) and causes Daksha's death.

Informed by the gods of the destruction of Daksha, Brahma pacifies Rudra, and Daksha and others are revived.

Being pleased with Brahma's praise, Siva goes along with the gods to the scene of sacrifice; Daksha and others are revived; Vishnu issuing forth from the sacrificial fire is praised by Daksha and others. After the closing ceremony of ablutions, the gods return home. Maitreya describes the benefit of listening to this story, the birth of Sati as Parvati. and that of Skanda.

DAKSHINAMURTI

On the Mount Kailas, with Parvati Devi by His side, Lord Siva was sitting in a hall beautifully decorated by precious stones. At that time, Devi worshipped the Lord and requested Him to alter the name of Dakshayani given to her before, for being the daughter of Daksha. This Daksha was killed by Lord Siva for his disrespect and arrogance. On hearing this request Lord Siva ordained that Devi should be born as the daughter of Parvata Raj who was doing rigorous Tapas for getting a child. He also told Parvati that He would come over to her and marry her. Thus ordained, Parvati Devi was born as the child of Parvata Raj and since her fifth year, began to do rigorous Tapas for being the bride of Lord Siva.

During the absence of Devi, when Lord Siva was alone, the sons of Brahma, who are sages Sanaka, Sanandana, Sanatana and Sanatkumara, came to have Darsana of Lord Siva and prostrated before Him. They entreated the Lord to teach them the way to remove Avidya and attain salvation. They experienced that in spite of the vast study of scriptures they had no internal peace and they were in need of learning the inner secrets, by knowing which they could attain salvation.

Lord Siva, hearing this appeal made by the sages, assumed the form of Dakshinamurti and remaining as the Guru Supreme, began to teach them the inner secrets by keeping Mauna and showing the Chinmudra by His hand. The sages began to meditate on the lines shown by the Lord and attained the state of inexpressible and illimitable joy. Thus Lord Siva came to be known as Dakshinamurti. May the blessings of Lord Dakshinamurti be upon us all! May you all dive deep and enjoy the everlasting Peace and Bliss through His Grace !

TRIPURA SAMHARA

This occurs in the Karna Parva of the Mahabharata. In times of yore, there was a war between the Devas and the Asuras. The Asuras were defeated in the battle. The three sons of the Asura, Taraka, wanted to take revenge on the Devas. They performed rigorous penance and obtained a boon from Brahma, the creator. By virtue of this boon, they could not be conquered by anyone save somebody who could destroy their three castles by a single arrow.

They made three castles, one of gold in heaven, the second silver in air, and the third of iron on earth. They began to oppress the gods and the Rishis. Thereupon, all the gods made a complaint to Brahma. Brahma replied that no one save Mahadeva who knows Yoga and Sankhya, through particular penance, could vanquish these Asuras. All the gods approached Mahadeva and provided Him with a chariot out of all forms of the universe. They also supplied Him with a bow and arrow, the constituent parts of which were Vishnu, Soma and Agni. They requested Mahadeva to discharge the arrow against the three castles. Brahma became the charioteer. Mahadeva discharged the arrow against the three castles. The three castles fell down in the twinkling of an eye. Then all the gods eulogised Mahadeva and departed to heaven.

Mahadeva said to the gods that He Himself could not destroy the Asuras, as they were very strong, but that they themselves would be able to vanquish with the help of half His strength. The gods replied that they could not bear half His strength and that He should take up the task with the help of half their strength. Mahadeva agreed to this. He became stronger than all the gods. Hence He was called Mahadeva or the great God.

LORD SIVA CURSES AND PARDONS NAKIRAR

Once, a Pandya king of Madurai felt that his queen's hair had some kind of natural fragrance. A doubt arose in his mind as to whether human hair could have natural fragrance, or could be rendered fragrant only through association with flowers or scents. He went to the Sangham or the Tamil Academy the next day, suspended a bag containing one thousand gold pieces and said to the poets that anyone who would write a poem clearing the doubt he entertained in his mind would get the gold pieces as a prize. Many poets composed poems but they were not able to satisfy the king.

Darumi, a Brahmin priest in the temple, was extremely poor. He requested Lord Siva thus: "O all-merciful Lord! I am very poor. I wish to marry now. Relieve me of my poverty. Help me to get these gold pieces now. I take refuge in Thee alone". Lord Siva gave him a poem and said: "Take this poem to the Sangham. You will get the gold pieces".

The king was immensely pleased with the song as it cleared his doubt, but the Sangham poets did not accept it. Nakirar, one of them, said that there was a flaw in the poem. The poor priest was greatly afflicted at heart. He came back to the temple, stood in front of the Lord and said: "O Lord! Why did You give me the poem which contained a flaw? Nobody will take You for the Lord. I feel very much for this". The meaning of the poem is: "O fair-winged bee! You spend your time in gathering flower-dust. Do not speak out of love, but speak out of truth. Is there any among the flowers known to you that is more fragrant than the hair of this damsel who is most loving, is of the colour of the peacock and has beautiful rows of teeth!"

Thereupon, Lord Siva assumed the form of a poet, went to the Sangham and asked: "Which poet found out flaw in the poem?" Nakirar said: "It is I who said that there is a flaw." Lord Siva asked: "What is the flaw?" Nakirar said: "There is no flaw in the composition of words. There is flaw in the meaning." Lord Siva said: "May I know what defect is there in the meaning?" Nakirar said: "The hair of a damsel has no natural fragrance. It gets the fragrance from association with the flowers." Lord Siva said: "Does the hair of Padmini also possess fragrance by association with the flowers?" Nakirar said, "Yes." Lord Siva said: "Does the hair of celestial damsels also possess fragrance by association with the flowers?" Nakirar replied, "Yes. Their hairs become fragrant by association with Mandara flowers." Lord Siva said: "Does the hair of Uma Devi who is on the left side of Lord Siva whom you worship possess fragrance by association with the flowers?" Nakirar replied: "Yes. Quite so."

Lord Siva slightly opened His third eye. Nakirar said: "I am not afraid of this third eye. Even if you are Lord Siva, even if you show eyes throughout your whole body, there is flaw in this poem." The fire from the third eye of Lord Siva fell upon Nakirar. Nakirar was not able to bear the heat. At once he jumped into the neighbouring lotus-tank to cool himself.

Then all the poets approached Lord Siva and said: "O Lord! Pardon Nakirar." Lord Siva appeared before Nakirar. Through the grace of Lord Siva his body was rendered cool. He repented for his mistake and said: "I pointed defect even for the hairs of Uma Devi. No one but the Lord can pardon me." He sang a song with intense devotion. Lord Siva entered the tank and brought him to the shore.

Then Nakirar and other poets gave the purse of gold to Darumi.

KNOW YOUR GURU

Devotion to the Lord dawns in the heart of a man who has done virtuous actions in his previous births without expectation of fruits and egoism or the idea of agency. Devotion leads to knowledge of the Self (Jnana) and through Jnana, he attains Moksha or the final emancipation.

In days of yore, Virasindhu was the king of Kalinga country. He did severe Tapas, meditation and Yoga in his previous birth, but did not attain Moksha. He became a Yoga-Bhrashta as he had to enjoy the fruits of some residual Karmas in this last birth of a King. He took his birth as the son of a king. When he attained the proper age, he was crowned as the king of Kalinga. He ruled the kingdom for a period of ten years.

Owing to the force of previous spiritual Samskaras, and the grace of the Lord, discrimination and dispassion dawned in his heart. He reflected within himself: "I am doing the same acts of eating, drinking and sleeping. My several forefathers who ruled the country, had been reduced to dust. I have no peace of mind despite my wealth and dominion. I should get a Guru and obtain initiation from him to get knowledge of the Atman and reach the abode of immortality and eternal bliss."

King Virasindhu sent invitation to all Pandits, Sannyasins, Sadhus and Mahatmas. He wrote in the letter thus: "I will give half of my dominion to that supreme Guru who will give me the right initiation and make me realise the Self. If he fails to do so he will be put in the prison."

Many Pandits and Sadhus saw the king. One gave him Taraka Mantra, another gave Panchakshara, a third gave him Ashtakshara, but no one was able to satisfy the king. He put them all in the prison. He had initiation into these Mantras in his previous births.

King Virasindhu became very restless as he did not obtain his Guru. Lord Siva assumed the form of an ordinary coolie. He had a very black complexion. He wore some rags and appeared before the king. The king went in advance to receive him. Through the grace of the Lord, he came to know that this coolie was none other than the Lord. The coolie raised his hand towards the king and said "stop", and vanished immediately. The king understood that the Guru has commanded him to stop the mind and control its movements. The king closed his eyes, while he was standing, and did not allow the mind to think of the sensual objects. He controlled all the modifications of the mind. It was easy for him as he had practised Yoga and meditation in his previous birth. He entered into Nirvikalpa Samadhi and became like a statue. He did not open his eyes.

The ministers were waiting in the Durbar Hall for hours together. King Virasindhu did not open his eyes for days together. Then the ministers reflected: "The king is in Samadhi now. We do not know when he will return from the Samadhi. We will have to manage the affairs of the State." They removed the ring from his finger and used it for putting the seal in the papers of the State.

The king opened his eyes after six years, and asked the ministers: "Where is my Guru?" The ministers replied: "O venerable king! The Guru said a word to your majesty and vanished at once. You are standing here like a statue for the last six years. We are conducting the affairs of the state with the aid of your ring. Here is the seal of your ring in all the registers and papers."

The king was struck with awe and wonder. He thought within himself: "Six years have passed like a second. I enjoyed supreme bliss. I have no desire to rule the State after tasting the supreme bliss." He left the palace and entered the forest and sat in Samadhi.

The force of Yogic Samskaras of the king that was generated by the practice of Yoga in his previous birth, helped him in the attainment of the beatitude in this birth.

Those who have not much piety and religious inclination in this birth should do Japa, Kirtan, meditation, and study of religious books. They should live in the company of sages. They will develop good religious Samskaras. This will be a valuable asset for them in the next birth. They will start the practice of Yoga in the next birth in the early age.

It is difficult to say in what form the Guru or the Lord will appear before you to initiate you. He may come in the form of a leper as Sri Hanuman did, or in the form of an untouchable as Lord Krishna did, or in the form of a groom as Lord Siva did. The aspirants must be very careful and vigilant to detect the Lord in the various forms which He assumes.

LORD SIVA DRINKS POISON

Once, the Devas and the Asuras had a formidable fight for a very long period. Many Devas and Asuras died in the fight. The Devas thought that they should prolong their lives by drinking nectar and then continue the war. They approached Brahma with this desire in view. Brahma said: "This work cannot be done by me. It can be done only by Lord Vishnu." Thereupon, Brahma and the Devas approached Lord Hari in Kshirasagara.

Lord Hari asked the Devas and Asuras to churn the ocean with the help of Mandaragiri as churning-rod and Vasuki, the serpent, as the rope. As they went on churning, poison (Halahala) came out first from the ocean. The terrible poison began to burn the people into ashes. The Devas, the Asuras and the Rishis began to fly away. Lord Vishnu was not able to destroy the poison. His body also became very black. He ran to Kailas along with the Devas and Brahma to see Lord Siva. He reported to Lord Siva all that had happened. Thereupon, Lord Siva collected the poison and kept it as a drop in the palm of His hand and swallowed it. Then Lord Vishnu and Brahma requested Lord Siva to keep it in His neck as a mark of their protection. Lord Siva did it accordingly. Due to the effect of the poison His throat became blue. From that day onwards Lord Siva is called by the name 'Nilakantha' (blue-necked one) or 'Kalakantha Murti'. Then Lord Siva said to them: "If you churn again, you will get nectar and several other things." They all started again the churning of the ocean and obtained nectar and many other things. All the Devas drank the nectar and rejoiced heartily.

LORD SIVA RIDES ON THE BULL

Turning of Chatur-Yuga two thousand times, is a day of Brahma. Such thirty days make a month for him. Such twelve months make an year for him. Such hundred years make the full life of Brahma. The whole life-period of Brahma is a day for Lord Vishnu. After one hundred years, Lord Vishnu also will pass away or merge himself in Parabrahman. All the Andas will perish. On account of the heavy blowing of Prachanda Vayu, the seven oceans will ebb high and cover the whole world. Lord Siva alone will exist. He will burn everything into ashes through His fiery third eye and then dance.

The Dharmadevata or the Lord of Virtue reflected within himself: "How can I attain immortality? If I approach Lord Siva only, I can attain this." He assumed the form of a bull, went to Lord Siva and said: "My venerable Lord! Kindly accept me as Thy vehicle and thus protect me."

Lord Siva agreed to the humble request of the God of Dharma and said: "Conduct the Dharma with four feet in the Krita Yuga, with the three feet in the Treta Yuga, with two feet in the Dvapara Yuga, and with one foot in the Kali Yuga. On account of My grace, you will be endowed with all splendour and powers. You will be always My vehicle. You will be one with Me."

When Lord Siva destroyed Tripuras or the three cities, Lord Vishnu assumed the form of a bull and supported Lord Siva.

LORD SIVA WEARS THE GANGA ON HIS HEAD

Once upon a time in Mount Kailas, Parvati closed the eyes of Lord Siva with her hands. Thereupon the sun, moon and fire did not shine forth. This caused terrible havoc in the world. All were enveloped by darkness for a long period. Lord Siva opened His third eye a bit. The sun, moon and fire began to shine again and all darkness vanished.

Parvati was frightened. She removed her hands and dropped down the perspiration from her fingers. This perspiration was turned into ten Gangas with countless branches. These rivers did much havoc to the world. Thereupon Lord Brahma, Vishnu and Indra ran to Lord Siva and requested Him to avert this catastrophe.

Lord Siva felt compassionate and brought the whole waters in one hair of His matted locks. Lord Brahma, Vishnu and Indra requested Lord Siva to give a little of the water of the Ganga for their worlds. Lord Siva gave them a little. They became Virajanadi in Vaikuntha, Manasa Tirtha in Satyaloka and Devaganga in Indraloka. King Bhagiratha brought down the Ganga from Brahmaloka to save the sixty thousand sons of Sagara.

LORD SIVA'S LILA OF BEGGING

The Rishis of Darukavana thought that there was no use in loving and adoring Lord Siva and they could attain

Moksha through the performance of sacrifices. They left off worship of the Lord and did sacrifices vigorously.

Then Lord Siva said to Lord Hari: "Assume the form of Mohini and enter the abode of all Rishis in Daruka forest. They have no regard for Me now. They are treading the wrong path now. We should teach them a severe lesson. Excite their passion and delude them. Destroy their Vratas." He also put on the form of a mendicant-beggar.

Thereupon, Lord Hari assumed the form of Mohini and entered the dwelling places of the Rishis in Darukavana. All the Rishis lost their power of understanding and discrimination and followed Mohini under strong excitement of passion.

Lord Siva entered the Parnakutirs of the wives of the Rishis, sang the Srutis and hymns beautifully and roamed about as a mendicant-beggar. The wives of Rishis became excited and followed Lord Siva. They entreated Him in a variety of ways to satisfy them. Lord Siva multiplied Himself and appeared in the mind of each woman. All the wives of the Rishis enjoyed heartily. They all brought forth in the morning eighteen thousand Rishis with matted locks, Danda and Kamandalu. They all prayed to Lord Siva. Lord Siva blessed them to do Tapas in the forest. The Rishis acted accordingly.

The Rishis witnessed the condition of their wives and said: "We were deluded by the enchanting Mohini. The mendicant-beggar spoiled the chastity of our wives. Lo! How powerful is lust! Mysterious is Maya!"

LORD SIVA WEARS TRIDENT, DEER, ETC.

The Rishis of Darukavana performed a Yajna to destroy Lord Siva. A cruel tiger came out of the fire. They commanded the tiger to kill Lord Siva. Lord Siva killed the tiger and wore the skin around His waist. Then they created a trident to kill the Lord. Lord Siva wore it in His hand as His instrument. Then they created a deer with sharp horns, to kill the Lord. Lord Siva wore it in His left hand.

Later on they created countless black cobras to kill the Lord. Lord Siva wore them as His ornaments. Then they created countless Bhuta Ganas to kill the Lord. Lord Siva made them as His army. Then they created a Damaru to kill the Lord. Lord Siva wore it in His hand. Then they created an Asura, Muyalaka, to kill the Lord. Muyalaka marched with the Yajna fire to destroy Lord Siva. Lord Siva held the fire as Malu in His hand and kept the Asura under His feet.

LORD SIVA HAS UMA ON HIS LEFT

After the Samhara was over, Lord Brahma born of the grace of Lord Siva thought of creating all beings. He created Sanaka, Sanandana, Sanatkumara and Sanatsujata. They did not enter the life of householders. They developed wisdom and became great Yogis.

Lord Brahma went to Vaikuntha and saw Lord Hari and said to Him: "O venerable Lord! I am not able to continue the creation. Sanaka, Sanandana, etc., have become Yogis. They do not wish to become householders. Kindly suggest to me a way to continue my work of creation." Lord Vishnu said: "This is not in my power. Let us go to Lord Siva who abides in Kailas."

Brahma and Vishnu saw the Lord of Kailas and said to Him: "O God of gods! The creative work of Brahma has been stopped as the four Kumaras have become Yogis. Kindly bless him to continue his creative work."

Lord Siva looked at the left side of His chest. Uma took Her birth from Lord Siva's left side. Lord Siva said to them: "Now there is no difficulty in creation. It will continue without any hitch." Thereupon Brahma and Vishnu repaired to their respective abodes. Then Lord Brahma created the worlds through the grace of Lord Siva. Men and women lived together happily and brought forth offsprings. The whole appearance is Saktimaya. Lord Siva witnesses Prakriti's activities.

LORD SIVA WEARS ELEPHANT'S SKIN

In days of yore, Gajasura did severe penance. Brahma appeared before him and asked him: "O Gajasura! I am pleased with your penance. What boon do you want?" Gajasura said: "O venerable Lord! Give me prowess and inexhaustible wealth." "I have given you what you desired. But if you fight against Lord Siva, you will lose your boon." Then Lord Brahma vanished.

Thereupon, Gajasura did Digvijaya, and defeated Devas and Indra. He troubled the Munis and the Rishis also. They repaired to Banares and fell at the feet of Lord Visvanatha and said: "Gajasura is trying to kill us. Protect us. O Lord! There is no other refuge for us."

Gajasura attacked Lord Visvanatha also. The Lord killed the Asura, tore the skin and wore it as His garment. Then the Devas and the Rishis praised the Lord and became happy.

LORD SIVA THE FUEL-SELLER

Varaguna Pandian was the king of Pandya kingdom. His capital was at Madurai. He was like Indra. Yemanathan, skilled in Vina, came to his Durbar from Northern India. He played thrilling songs on Vina. The king appreciated Yemanathan's music, gave him rich presents and kept him in a separate bungalow. Yemanathan was very much puffed up owing to his skill in music.

Varaguna Pandian understood that Yemanathan was proud of his knowledge of music. He called his Durbar-musician Bhanabhadra and said to him: "O Bhadra! Will you be able to attain victory over the new musician Yemanathan?" Bhanabhadra replied: "I can certainly defeat him through your grace and the blessings of Lord Somasundara of Madurai." The king said: "Well then, come tomorrow and exhibit your skill in music."

The disciples of Yemanathan roamed about in all the streets and lanes of Madurai, played on Vina and vigorously advertised about their skill in music. Bhanabhadra heard this and reflected within himself: "These disciples are very efficient in music and Vina. If the disciples possess such knowledge, what must be the splendour and glory of their Guru! How can I attain victory over this master-musician?" Then he prayed to Lord Siva: "Kindly help me now to defeat Yemanathan. I am in need of Thy grace."

Then the Lord assumed the form of a wood-cutter, wore a rag around his body and torn shoes on his feet. He had a Vina in his hand and a bundle of fuel on his head. He went to the house where Yemanathan was living and sat on the verandah. He took his Vina and played in a marvellous manner. He sang beautifully along with Vina.

Yemanathan was struck with wonder when he heard the wonderful music. He came out and asked the fuel-seller: "O fuel-seller! Who are you?" The fuel-seller replied: "I am one of the disciples and a servant of Bhanabhadra, the Durbar-singer of Varaguna Pandian. He has many disciples. As I became old, my master abandoned me and told me that I am unfit for singing."

Yemanathan requested the fuel-seller to sing again. He sang again Satari Raga which melted the heart of

Yemanathan. Lord Siva, who acted the part of fuel-seller, vanished with his bundle of fire-wood.

Yemanathan thought within himself: "I have not heard this Satari Raga till now. It is Devaraga. If this old man can sing this Raga in such a beautiful manner, what must be the knowledge and glory of his master! Surely God only ought to have taught him this Raga. I cannot stand before Bhanabhadra. Let me leave this place at once." Yemanathan's heart was filled with fear and shame. He left all the things and left the house at midnight along with his disciples.

Lord Somasundara appeared in the dream of Bhanabhadra and said: "Do not be afraid. I put on the form of fuel-seller, sat on the verandah of the house in which Yemanathan lived and played on the Vina. He was struck with wonder and ran away at midnight. Be at ease now."

Bhanabhadra got up in the morning, went to the temple at Madurai and worshipped Lord Somasundara. Then he went to the Durbar of Varaguna Pandian. The king sent a servant to call Yemanathan. The servant searched him in several places. He was not able to find out the new musician. The neighbours of the house in which Yemanathan lived said: "One fuel-seller came and sang. The new singer left the place at midnight. This only we know."

The servant reported the matter to the king. The king said to Bhanabhadra: "Could you tell me what you did after leaving me?" Bhanabhadra told the king: "My venerable Lord! I went to my house and prayed to Lord Somasundara to bless me. He appeared in my dream and said: 'I put on the form of a fuel-seller, sang Satari Raga in the house of Yemanathan. I drove him away.' I at once woke up. This is what happened."

Varaguna Pandian came to know that this was the Lila of Lord Siva. He admired the devotion of Bhadra and gave him rich presents. He said to Bhadra: "The Lord who made Brahma and the other Devas His servants, became your servant and blessed you. We are all your servants only. I am your servant. In future sing the praise of Lord Somasundara always."

Bhanabhadra rejoiced heartily. He was ever devoted to Lord Somasundara.

THE TWENTY-FIVE LILAS OF LORD SIVA

The following are the 25 Lilas (sportive plays) or manifestations of Lord Siva:

1. Wearing of moon on the head, 2. Living with Uma Devi, 3. Riding on ox, 4. Tandava dance with Kaali, 5. Marriage with Parvati, 6. Begging, 7. Burning of Manmatha or the God of Love, 8. Victory over Yama or the God of Death, 9. Burning of Tripuras, 10. Killing of Jalandarasura, 11. Killing of Gajasura, 12. Incarnation of Virabhadra, 13. Harihara, 14. Ardhanarisvara, 15. Transforming into Kirata, (hunter), 16. Assuming the form of Kankala, 17. Blessing Chandisvara, 18. Drinking poison, 19. Giving of Chakra to Lord Vishnu, 20. Destroying of obstacles, 21. Having sons of Uma Devi with Him, 22. Becoming Ekapada Rudra, 23. Being in easy pose (Sukhasana), 24. Assuming the form of Dakshinamurti, and 25. Assuming Linga form.

Chapter IX

SIVA YOGA SADHANA

SECRET OF PANCHAKSHARA

Panchakshara is a Mahamantra which is composed of five letters, Namassivaya. A Mantra is that which removes all obstacles and miseries of one who reflects on it and bestows eternal bliss and immortality. Panchakshara is the best among seven crores of Mantras. There are seven Skandhas in Yajurveda. There is Rudradhyayi in the centre of the middle Skandha. In this Rudradhyayi there are one thousand Rudra Mantras. Namassivaya or the Siva Panchakshara Mantra shines in the centre of these one thousand Rudra Mantras.

Yajurveda is the head of Paramesvara, who is the Veda Purusha. Rudram which is in the middle is the face, Panchakshara is His eye, Siva which is in the centre of the 'Namassivaya' is the apple of the eye. He who does Japa of this Panchakshara is freed from births and deaths and attains eternal bliss. This is the emphatic declaration of the Vedas. This Panchakshara is the body of Lord Nataraja. This is the abode of Lord Siva. If you add 'Om' to the 'Namassivaya' in the beginning, then it becomes Shadakshara or six-lettered Mantra. 'Om Namo Mahadevaya' is the eight-lettered Mantra or Ashtakshara.

Panchakshara is of six kinds, viz., Sthula Panchakshara (Namassivaya), Sukshma Panchakshara (Sivaya Namah), Karana Panchakshara (Sivaya Siva), Mahakarana Panchakshara (Sivaya), Mahamanu or Mukti Panchakshara (Si).

'Namah' means 'Prostration'. 'Sivaya Namah' means 'Prostration unto Lord Siva'. The Jiva is the servant of Lord Siva from the Deha-Drishti. 'Namah' represents Jivatman. 'Siva' represents Paramatman. 'Aya' denotes 'Aikyam' or identity of Jivatman and Paramatman. Hence 'Sivaya Namah' is a Mahavakya, like 'Tat Tvam Asi' which signifies the identity between the individual and the supreme soul.

Pranava denotes the external form (husk) of the Lord (paddy) and Panchakshara, the internal Svarupa (rice). Pranava and Panchakshara are one. The five letters denote the five actions or Pancha Krityas of the Lord, viz., Srishti (creation), Sthiti (preservation), Samhara (destruction), Tirodhana (veiling) and Anugraha (blessing). They also denote the five elements and all creations through the combination of the five elements.

'Na' represents Tirodhana; 'Ma', the Mala or impurity; 'Siva' Lord Siva; 'Va', the Arul Sakti; and 'Ya', the individual soul.

Take bath or wash your face, hands and feet. Wear Bhasma and Rudraksha Maala. Sit on Padmasana or Sukhasana. facing East or North, in a quiet place or room. Repeat silently the Panchakshara and meditate on the form of Lord Siva. Keep the image in the heart or space between the eyebrows.

If you practise meditation regularly, your heart will be purified. All Samskaras and sins will be burnt in toto. You will attain Siva-Yoga-Nishtha or Nirvikalpa Samadhi. You will attain the glorious Siva-Pada or Siva-Gati and become one with Lord Siva. You will enjoy the eternal bliss of Sivanandam and become immortal.

May Lord Siva bless you all!

MEDITATION ON LORD SIVA

Saguna Meditation: Saguna meditation is meditation on a form. An archer first aims at a gross, big object. Then he takes up a medium object. Finally, he shoots at very small and minute objects. Even so, one should take to Saguna meditation to start with, and when the mind is trained and disciplined well, he can have Nirakara, Nirguna meditation. Saguna meditation is meditation on a concrete object. Saguna meditation is peculiarly pleasing the Bhakta, who loves to gaze on the peculiar form of his Ishta. Saguna Upasana removes Vikshepa. For three or six months, practise Trataka on Siva's picture.

Meditate on the mental picture of the Murti from half an hour to two hours only in the Trikuti (space between the eyebrows). See and feel that the Lord is present in every object of the universe. When you meditate, mentally repeat the Mantra of the Devata, 'Om Namah Sivaya'; think of the attributes of the Deity such as omnipresence, omnipotence and omniscience. Feel that Sattvic qualities from the Ishtam flow towards you. Feel that you possess these Sattvic qualities. This is Sattvic or Suddha Bhavana. You will have Darsana of your Ishtam in one or two years, if you are sincere in your Sadhana. Follow this plan. This will help concentration. Move the mind on the various parts of the Murti, the picture or idol of Lord Siva, and meditate. Sit upon your usual Asana. Repeat His Name and think of His attributes like bliss, radiance, love, etc., gazing at His picture all the while. Then enthrone Him in the lotus of your heart or between your eyebrows amidst a blazing light. Now mentally think of His lotus-feet, offering your devout salutations. Take the mind to the elephant-skin worn round the waist, then to the necklace of Rudraksha beads, adorning His chest, and the beautiful blue hue of His throat (Nilakantha), serene countenance, radiating the majestic aura of profound meditations, the indrawn half-closed meditative eyes, the mysterious third eye in the centre of the forehead. Next take the mind up to the matted locks, the cool crescent moon, and the sacred Ganga sprouting from the Jata. Rotate your mind on the trident (Trisula) in one hand, and then, the Damaru, in the other. Run your mind over the whole form till you complete all the details. Then fix your mind either on the face or upon the starting point (feet). Repeat the entire process again and again, as many times as you can. By constant practice, you will ultimately be established in meditation and have communion with Siva.

Nirguna Meditation: This is meditation on Lord Siva, in His all-pervasive, unmanifested aspect, as the Supreme Para Brahman. In this form of meditation, you meditate on Lord Siva as the Supreme Brahman without form, attributeless, eternal, infinite. Meditate on Him as the Suddha, Satchidananda, Vyapaka Atman; Nitya, Suddha, Siddha, Buddha, Mukta, eternally free Brahman; an unlimited Ocean of Pure Consciousness. Now, identify yourself with this transcendental Svarupa of Siva. Feel that you are Chaitanya, Akhanda, Paripurna, Ekarasa, Santa, Unchanging Existence.

Every atom, every molecule, every nerve, vein, artery, should powerfully vibrate with these ideas. Lip-repetition of 'Sivoham' will not produce much benefit. It should be through heart, head and soul. This feeling should be kept up continuously. Negate the body-idea while repeating Sivoham mentally. When you chant Sivoham feel:

Infinity I am	Sivoham Sivoham
All light I am	Sivoham Sivoham
All joy I am	Sivoham Sivoham
All glory I am	Sivoham Sivoham

>   All power I am   Sivoham Sivoham
>   All knowledge I am   Sivoham Sivoham
>   All Ananda I am   Sivoham Sivoham

Meditate on the above ideas constantly. Constant effort with zeal and enthusiasm, is an indispensable requisite. Repeat mentally the above ideas incessantly. You will realise.

WORSHIP OF SIVA

Lord Siva is worshipped in His Saguna aspect in the form of Sivalingam. Generally Sivabhaktas do Panchayatana Puja. In this Puja, Lord Siva, Ganesa, Parvati, Suryanarayana and Saligram are duly worshipped.

Get the Panchayatana Murtis on an auspicious day. Install them with great faith in your own house. Conduct special prayers, Archana, Puja, Abhisheka, and feeding of Brahmins, Mahatmas and the poor on a grand scale. Install the deity in a separate room. Worship the Lord daily with all sincerity and faith. You will have all wealth, peace of mind, attainment of Dharma, Artha, Kama and Moksha also. You will lead a prosperous life and enter the Immortal abode of Siva-Sayujya, on death.

Collect plenty of Bael or Bilva leaves for Lord Siva's worship. Get ready Dhupa, Dipa, camphor, sandal-sticks, fresh water, plenty of flowers, food offerings to the Lord, a seat to sit upon, a bell, conch and other things required for the Puja before you begin the worship. Get up in the early morning before sunrise. Wash your face. Take bath. Wear silk dress separately kept for Puja purposes. Decorate the Puja room nicely. Enter the room chanting Lord's names, glorifying Him, repeating Hymns in His praise and prostrating before the Lord. Wash your feet before entering the room. Sit in a comfortable posture and commence your worship. You have to first of all do

Sankalpa for beginning the Puja in the prescribed method. You should then do Kalasa (water vessel), Sankha (conch), Atma (self) and Pitha (Lord's seat) Puja in their order. You should then offer Shodasopachara Puja to the Lord and then repeat Mahamrityunjaya Mantra, Rudrapatha, Purushasukta, Gayatri, and do Abhisheka with pure water, milk, sugarcane juice, ghee and other articles according to your capacity or with pure water alone. Rudrabhisheka is highly beneficial. If you do Rudra Japa and Abhisheka, all your worries and agonies will disappear and you will attain the highest beatitude of human existence by the grace of Lord Visvanath. Rudra is a great purifier. There is invisible hidden power in Rudra and Purushasukta. There is a wonderful inspiration in the recitation of Rudra. Start the worship and realise its glory and splendour for yourself.

After Abhisheka, decorate the Lord nicely with sandal paste and flowers. Then do Archana repeating His names, 'Om Sivaya Namah', 'Om Mahesvaraya Namah', etc. Do daily 108 or 1008 Archanas if possible. After Archana, do Arati with different kinds of lights—single Arati, Triple Arati, Pancha Arati and Karpura Arati. Ring bells, cymbals, conch, etc., during Arati. Offer sacred Prasad or Naivedya to the Lord.

After Arati is over, sing the praises of the Lord like Mahimna Stotra, Panchakshara Stotra, etc., waving the Chamara. In the end repeat the prayers *'Kayena vachah'* *'Atma tvam Girija matih',* and *'Kara-charana-kritam'.* Offer everything to the Lord. Feel that you are a mere instrument in His hands. Do everything for obtaining the divine grace only. Develop Nimitta Bhava. Serve the Bhaktas. The Lord is much pleased with the service of His devotees. Distribute the Prasad among the Bhaktas in the end. Take the Prasad with great faith. The glory of

Bhagavan's Prasad is indescribable. Vibhuti is taken as Prasad and applied to the forehead.

When you advance in Saguna worship with external objects of worship, you can begin Manasa Puja. You will have Darsana of the Lord and final emancipation.

Have special Pujas on Mondays and Pradosha (thirteenth day of every fortnight—Trayodasi) days. These days and Sivaratri (in the month of February-March) are very sacred for Lord Siva. Celebrate the Sivaratri on a grand scale. Fast the whole day. Have Trikala Puja, special Abhisheka, Ekadasa-rudra-japa, Sahasrarchana, vigil in the night, study of hymns of Lord Siva, Sivapurana, hearing discourses on the Lilas of Lord Siva. After Puja on the next day, break your fast with Abhisheka water. Offer sacred food offerings and partake of the Divine Prasad. You will have great mental peace, and spiritual advancement. Never miss this opportunity. Daily worship is a sure remedy for all ills. You will never suffer from poverty. Take my word and begin the Puja right from this day onwards.

SIVA MANASA PUJA

Manasa Puja is mental worship. Manasa Puja is more powerful and effective than the external worship with flowers, sandals, etc. You will have more concentration when you do Manasa Puja.

Mentally enthrone the Lord on a Simhasana, set with diamonds, pearls, emeralds, etc. Offer Him a seat. Offer Arghya, Madhuparka and various sorts of flowers, clothes, etc. Apply sandal paste to His forehead and body. Burn incense and Agarbatti (scented sticks). Wave lights. Burn camphor and do Arati. Offer various kinds of fruits, sweetmeats, Payasa, coconut and Mahanaivedyam. Do Shodasa-upachara or the sixteen kinds of offerings in worship.

PANCHAKSHARA MANTRA WRITING

Write down in a fine note book 'Om Namah Sivaya' for half an hour or more. You will have more concentration by taking recourse to this Sadhana. Write the Mantra in ink clearly. When you write the Mantra observe Mauna. You may write the Mantra in any language. Give up looking hither and thither. Repeat the Mantra mentally also when you write the Mantra. Write the whole Mantra at once. When the Mantra notebook is completed, keep it in a box in your meditation room. Be regular in your practice.

Keep a small notebook in your pocket and write Mantra when you get leisure in the office. Have three things in your pocket, viz., the Gita, Mantra notebook and a Japa Maala or rosary. You will be immensely benefited.

SIVA JNANAM

Japa and meditation of the sacred Names of Lord Siva will free you from all sins and lead you to the attainment of Siva Jnanam or eternal bliss and immortality. Siva-nama is the very soul of all Mantras.

Lord Siva has manifested in the world in sixty different aspects. Vrishabharudha, Hari-hara, Nataraja, Bhairava, Dakshinamurti, Ardhanarisvara, Bhikshatana, Somasekaramurti, Urdhvanatana, Kalasamhara, Jalandhara, Surasamhara, Lingodbhava are His forms.

Siva means that which is eternally happy or auspicious, Parama-mangala. Om and Siva are one. Mandukya Upanishad says: *'Santam Sivam Advitam'*. Even an outcaste can meditate on the name of Lord Siva.

Siva manifests in the Gayatri Mantra, Agni and in the Sun. When you repeat Gayatri and when you worship the Agni and the Sun, you should meditate on Lord Siva.

Japa of Panchakshara and meditation of Lord Siva should be particularly done in the Pradosha Kaala or just before the sunset. The Pradosha on the thirteenth Tithi after a full moon or a new moon day, is known as the Mahapradosha. The Devas visit Siva temples for the worship of the Lord at this period. You can worship the Devas also if you visit temples during Mahapradosha. Devotees of Lord Siva observe full fast on Mahapradosha days.

A devotee of Lord Siva should apply Vibhuti to his forehead and body. He should wear a Rudrakshamaala. He should worship the Sivalinga with leaves of the Bilva tree. He should do Japa and meditation of the Panchakshara 'Om Namah Sivaya'. Lord Siva is propitiated by everyone of these actions. Vibhuti or Bhasma is very sacred. It is worn by Lord Siva Himself. The bead of a Rudrakshamaala represents the third eye on the forehead of Lord Siva. Bilva leaves are regarded to be one of the five abodes of Lakshmi or the Goddess of wealth.

It is Siva only who causes bondage and Mukti for the Jivas. It is Siva who makes the Jivas realise their essential Divine Nature. Siva made Maya as the body, senses and the Universe and thrust the Jivas into the Maya. He created the idea of egoism, 'I'-ness in them. He bound them in Karma and made them experience pleasure and pain according to the nature of their Karmas, virtuous actions or vicious deeds. This is the stage of bondage of the Jivas.

Gradually it is Siva only who releases them from the fetters of egoism, Karma and Maya and makes them shine as Siva. This is the state of Moksha or freedom. It is only through the grace of Lord Siva, they attain the state of final emancipation.

The Jivas have no independence, when they are under the influence of the three impurities, i.e., Anava, Karma and Maya. They are endowed with a little knowledge (Alpajnana).

The Jiva must first know his nature and his relationship with Lord Siva in order to attain His grace. Life or Prana is in the body. Lord Siva is within the Prana. He is the Prana of Pranas, and yet He is distinct from the Pranas and body. If there is no Prana in the body, the body becomes a corpse. It cannot perform any action. Siva is the support for this body, Prana and Jiva. The Jiva cannot do any action without Siva. It is Siva who illumines the intellect. Just as the eye cannot see without the light of the sun, although it is endowed with the power to see, so also the intellect cannot function without the light of Lord Siva.

The four Sadhanas, viz., Charya, Kriya, Yoga and Jnana are the four steps to attain Salvation. They are like the bud, flower, unripe fruit and ripe fruit.

Lord Siva gradually frees the individual souls from egoism, Karma and Maya. The Jivas gradually become disgusted with the sensual pleasures. They become balanced in pleasure and pain. Through the grace of the Lord they understand that Karma is the cause for births and deaths. They begin to do actions for the Lord, serve the devotees of the Lord and attain purity of mind. They understand that the soul or Siva is distinct from the body, senses and mind and is beyond the reach of mind and speech. They get initiation into the significance of 'Om Namah Sivaya', the Panchakshara Mantra and meditate on Siva.

They practise Siva Yoga. Their hearts melt. Seer, sight and seen vanish. All the activities of senses, mind and intellect cease. They bathe Lord Siva with the stream of

Divine Love that is generated in their heart and offer their heart as flower unto the Lord.

They hear the sound 'Chilambosai' and march forward through the path of the sound and behold the vision of Nataraja in the Chidakasa and are immersed in the ocean of Sivananda. They become one with the Lord, just as camphor melts in the fire.

WORSHIP OF SIVA LINGA

The popular belief is that the Siva Lingam represents the phallus or the virile organ, the emblem of the generative power or principle in nature. This is not only a serious mistake, but also a grave blunder. In the post-Vedic period, the Linga became symbolical of the generative power of the Lord Siva. Linga is the differentiating mark. It is certainly not the sex-mark. You will find in the Linga Purana: *Pradhanam prakritir yadahurlingamuttamam; Gandhavarnarasairhinam sabda-sparsadi-varjitam* — The foremost Linga which is primary and is devoid of smell, colour, taste, hearing, touch, etc., is spoken of as Prakriti (Nature).

Linga means 'mark', in Sanskrit. It is a symbol which points to an inference. When you see a big flood in a river, you infer that there had been heavy rains the previous day. When you see smoke, you infer that there is fire. This vast world of countless forms is a Linga of the Omnipotent Lord. The Siva Linga is a symbol of Lord Siva. When you look at the Linga your mind is at once elevated and you begin to think of the Lord.

Lord Siva is really formless. He has no form of his own and yet all forms are His forms. All forms are pervaded by Lord Siva. Every form is the form or Linga of Lord Siva.

There is a mysterious power or indescribable Sakti in the Linga, to induce concentration of the mind. Just as the mind is focussed easily in crystal-gazing, so also the mind attains one-pointedness, when it looks at the Linga. That is the reason why the ancient Rishis and the seers of India have prescribed Linga for being installed in the temples of Lord Siva.

Siva Linga speaks to you in the unmistakable language of silence: "I am one without a second, I am formless". Pure, pious souls only can understand this language. A curious passionate, impure foreigner of little understanding or intelligence says sarcastically: "Oh, the Hindus worship the phallus or sex organ. They are ignorant people. They have no philosophy". When a foreigner tries to learn Tamil or Hindusthani language, he first tries to pick up some vulgar words. This is his curiosity nature. Even so, the curious foreigner tries to find out some defects in the worship of symbol. Linga is only the outward symbol of the formless being, Lord Siva, who is the indivisible, all-pervading, eternal, auspicious, ever-pure, immortal essence of this vast universe, who is the undying Soul seated in the chambers of your heart, who is your Indweller, innermost Self or Atman, and who is identical with the Supreme Brahman.

A Siva Linga consists of three parts, the lowest of which is the Brahma-Pitha, the middle one, the Vishnu-Pitha and the uppermost one, the Siva-Pitha.

Some are Svayambhu-lingas, some are Narmadesvaras. There are twelve Jyotirlingas and five Pancha Bhuta Lingas in India. The twelve Jyotir-lingas are: Kedarnath, Kasi Visvanath, Somanath, Baijnath, Ramesvar, Ghrusnesvar, Bhimasankar, Mahakaala, Mallikarjuna, Amalesvar, Nagesvar and Tryambakesvar. The five Pancha Bhuta Lingas are: Kalahastisvar, Jambukesvar, Arunachalesvar, Ekambaresvar of Kanjivaram and Nataraja of

Chidambaram. The temple of Lord Mahalinga at Tiruvidaimarudur known also as Madhyarjuna is regarded as the great Siva temple of South India.

Sphatikalinga is also a symbol of Lord Siva. This is prescribed for Aradhana or worship of Lord Siva. It is made up of quartz. It has no colour of its own, but takes on the colour of the substances which come in contact with it. It represents the Nirguna Brahman or the attributeless Supreme Self or formless and attributeless Siva.

For a sincere devotee, the Linga is not a block of stone. It is all radiant Tejas or Chaitanya. The Linga talks to him, makes him shed profuse tears, produces horripulation and melting of heart, raises him above body-consciousness and helps to commune with the Lord and attain Nirvikalpa Samadhi. Lord Rama worshipped the Siva Linga at Ramesvar. Ravana, the learned scholar, worshipped the golden Linga. What a lot of mystic Sakti there should be in the Linga!

May you all attain the formless Siva through the worship of the Linga, the symbol of Lord Siva which helps concentration of mind and which serves as a prop for the mind to lean upon in the beginning for the neophytes!

SIVA LINGA IS CHINMAYA

The light of consciousness manifesting out of Sadasiva is, in reality, the Sivalinga. From Him all the moving and unmoving creations take their origin. He is the Linga or cause of everything. In Him, the whole world merges itself finally. The Siva Purana says: *"Pitham Ambamayam Sarvam Sivalingascha Chinmayam."* The support or Pitham of all is Prakriti or Parvati, and Linga is Chinmaya Purusha, the effulgent light which is self-luminous. Union of Prakriti or Parvati, and Purusha or Sivalinga is the cause of the world. In Sanatkumara-samhita of the Siva Purana, Lord

Siva Says: "O Parvati, daughter of mountain, there is none dearer to Me than the man who worships Me in the Linga, knowing that Linga is the root-cause of everything and knowing the world to be Linga-maya or Chaitanya-maya."

The Linga is like an egg. It represents the Brahmanda (cosmic egg). Whatever that is contained in the Brahmanda is in the Linga. The whole world is the form of Lord Siva. The world is a Linga. Linga also is the form of Lord Siva.

Linga signifies that the creation is effected by the union of Prakriti and Purusha. It means Laya, Jnana, Vyapya, Prakasa, Arathaprakasa, Samarthya and the symbol which denotes the above meaning. Linga means the place of dissolution for the world and all beings. It signifies also Satya, Jnana and Ananta—Truth, Knowledge and Infinity. It indicates that Lord Siva is endowed with all-pervading and self-luminous nature. Linga is a symbol which makes us understand the various kinds of Artha which are indicated above.

There are six Lingas, viz., Anda Linga, Pinda Linga, Sadasiva Linga, Atma Linga, Jnana Linga and Siva Linga. These Lingas are taken to mean the characteristics by which the Anda (the Universe), Pinda (the body), Sadasiva, etc., are to be recognised and understood.

The union of Linga with Yoni is a representation of the Eternal Union between the static and the dynamic aspects of the Absolute Reality. This represents the Eternal Spiritual Communion of the paternal and the maternal principles from which all the phenomenal diversities have originated. This is an eternal communion of the Changeless Being and the Dynamic Power or Sakti from which all changes flow.

Further, the lower sexual propensities in the aspirants are eradicated by this sublime conception. The spiritualisation and divinisation of Linga and Yoni, helps the aspirants to free themselves from sexual thoughts. All base thoughts gradually vanish by entertaining this lofty idea. All sexual relations in this world are spiritualised as the manifestations of the ultimate Creative Principle, of the eternal Self-enjoyment and Self-multiplication of Lord Siva in and through His Power or Sakti.

The union of Linga with Yoni symbolises the creation of this universe by Lord Siva in conjunction with His Sakti or Power.

The so-called educated men of the modern age have no spiritual insight and philosophical penetration. Hence, they criticise the union of Linga with Yoni as immoral and obscene, owing to their extreme ignorance and lack of enquiry, deep thinking and Satsanga or association with sages. This is highly deplorable and lamentable indeed! May Lord grant wisdom to these poor ignorant souls!

WAY TO ATTAIN LORD SIVA

Tirumular's Tirumantram is a poetical work, said to be composed in the course of three thousand years. It deals with the practical and theoretical aspects of Saiva religion and philosophy. The treatment of Pati (Lord Siva), Pasu (the individual soul) and Pasa (attachment) in the old method, is found in this book. The following is Tirumular's exposition in his Tirumantram.

God alone is the Guru or the spiritual teacher. He shows Siva or Sat. Sat-Guru is Ambalam or Chidakasa Siva. You will have to search the Guru in your own heart. Knowledge, devotion, purity and Siddhis are obtained through the grace of the Guru. The grace descends in virtuous aspirants who have purity, dispassion, etc.

The thirsting aspirant should get help from Guru Param. Guru Param imparts spiritual instructions to the aspirant. Then Suddha Guru confers upon him Divine Grace. When the aspirant obtains the Divine Grace, he gets several powers, purity, the power to know the Mantras, higher Siddhis, etc. Then the Sat-Guru reveals himself in the Chidakasa, breaks the three bonds, viz., Anava (egoism), Karma (action) and Maya (illusion) and helps him to enter the illimitable domain of Moksha or supreme abode of eternal bliss. Siva Guru presents himself later on and manifests Sat, Asat and Sadasat. When the Jiva attains this final knowledge, he becomes Siva himself. The Guru who presents himself in the earlier and later stages, is Siva himself.

The devotee attains the grace of the Lord when he meditates on Him in the chambers of his heart, in the space between the two eyebrows and in the head. The holy feet of the Lord are highly eulogised. Tirumular says: "The holy feet of my Lord are Mantra, beauty and truth."

Jneya or that which is to be known, is Siva Ananda which is a product of Siva and His grace, Sakti. The Jnata (knower) is the individual soul or Jiva. He knows Siva by abiding in Siva Ananda and obtains Jnana or knowledge.

Moksha is the attainment of Siva Ananda. He who attains Moksha will attain supreme knowledge of Siva. He who gets established in Siva Ananda will attain knowledge and Moksha (the final emancipation). The Jiva who knows Siva Ananda dwells for ever in it. He attains Siva and Sakti in Siva Ananda. He is endowed with true knowledge which is really union of Siva and Sakti. Lord Siva shows the path which leads on to Moksha, to the aspirant who is endowed with dispassion, non-attachment, renunciation, who praises Him always and performs regular worship.

The devotee of Lord Siva gets strength to resist the temptations of the world and of Indra, through his Tapas or austerity. He does not care at all for the celestial pleasures offered by Indra. He is quite contented with the supreme bliss attained through union with Lord Siva.

When the Sadhaka does rigorous austerities and practises concentration, he attains several powers. Indra and other Devas get terribly afraid that they will lose their position. Hence, they put several obstacles on his path and tempt him in a variety of ways by offering celestial car, damsels and various sorts of celestial pleasures. But the firm Sadhaka stands adamant. He never yields and marches direct to the goal, viz., Siva-Pada or the Immortal seat of eternal Bliss. He who yields gets a downfall. Visvamitra had a downfall.

Sage Tirumular says: "Abandon pride of learning. Introspect. Look within. You will be firmly established in Siva. Nothing will shake you. You will be freed from the trammels of births and deaths."

Saiva Siddhanta teaches Advaita only. It is Siva Advaita.

GREATNESS OF THE PRASAD

Prasad is that which gives peace. During Kirtan, worship, Puja, Havan and Arati, Badam, Kismis, milk, sweets, fruits are offered to the Lord. Puja is done by Bael leaves, flowers, Tulasi, Vibhuti, and these are given as Prasad, from the Lord. They are charged with mysterious powers by the chanting of Mantras during Puja and Havan.

Prasad is a great purifier. Prasad is a panacea. Prasad is a spiritual elixir. Prasad is the Grace of the Lord. Prasad is an embodiment of Sakti. Prasad is divinity in manifestation. Many sincere aspirants get wonderful experiences from Prasad alone. Many incurable diseases are cured. Prasad energises, vivifies, invigorates and infuses devotion. It should be taken with great faith.

Live for a week in Brindavan, Pandharpur or Banares. You will realise the glory and miraculous effects of Prasad. Prasad bestows good health, long life, peace and prosperity on all. Glory to Prasad, the bestower of peace and bliss. Glory to the Lord of the Prasad. Giver of immortality and undying happiness.

Vibhuti is the Prasad of Lord Siva, to be applied on the forehead. A small portion can be taken in.

Kumkum is the Prasad of Sri Devi or Sakti, to be applied at the space between the eyebrows (Ajna or Bhrumadhya).

Tulasi is the Prasad of Lord Vishnu, Rama or Krishna, not to be taken in. Badam, Kismis, sweets, fruits, etc., are to be taken in.

All these Prasads are given on all important religious functions.

BENEFIT OF PILGRIMAGE

You will find a description of Oertel's treatment in books on medicine, for certain cardiac afflictions (heart-troubles). The patient is asked to climb up hills slowly. So, the Kailas trip, besides the spiritual benefit, removes many kinds of minor heart-troubles. The heart is invigorated and strengthened. The whole cardiac-vascular, nervous, pulmonary, alimentary, integumentary systems are thoroughly overhauled and purified. There is no necessity for Kuhne's steam bath. You perspire profusely during the march. The whole body is filled with fresh, oxygenated blood. The gentle breeze blowing from the tall pine trees all over, surcharged with natural oil of pine, disinfects the lungs and a consumptive is cured of phthisis when he returns. The excessive fat is reduced. A Kailas trip is the best treatment for reduction of obesity in corpulent persons. Many kinds of stomach troubles, uric acid troubles and various sorts of skin diseases are cured. You will not get any disease for a period of 12 years, as you are charged with new electrons, new atoms, new cells, new molecules and new nuclei with renovated protoplasm. This is no Arthavada (glorification). You get two birds by throwing one stone. The Kailas trip brings spiritual blessings and good health. Hail! Hail to Sambhu, the Lord Siva who dwells in Kailas with His Sakti, Parvati, who gives Mukti to His devotees and who is known by the different names, Hara, Sadasiva, Mahadeva, Nataraja, Sankara, etc.

The goal of life is God-realisation which only can free us from the miseries of Samsara, the wheel of birth and death. The performance of the daily obligatory rites, Nitya-Naimittika Karmas, Yatras, etc., unselfishly, leads to the acquisition of virtue. This leads to the destruction of sin, which in turn results in the purification of the mind. This purification of the mind leads to the comprehension of the true nature of Samsara or relative existence, its false and worthless nature. From this results Vairagya (renunciation), which arouses a desire for liberation. From this desire results a vigilant search for its means. From it comes the renunciation of all actions. Thence, the practice of Yoga, which leads to a habitual tendency of the mind to settle in the Atman or Brahman. This results in the knowledge of the meaning of such Sruti passages as 'Tat Tvam Asi', which destroys the Avidya (ignorance), thus leading to the establishment in one's own self. Thus you see that Yatra like Kailas trip is a Parampara Sadhana for God-realisation, as it causes Chitta Suddhi and Nididhyasana. Dhyana is a direct Sadhana. Householders who are shut up in the world amidst various sorts of cares and anxieties, find a great relief in a Yatra. Their minds get quite refreshed by a Yatra. Further, during the travel they come across Sadhus and Sannyasins. They can have good Satsanga. They can clear their doubts. They can get various sorts of help from them in spiritual Sadhana. That is the main object of Yatra.

Let me bring to your memory, once more, the last word of the Vedas, Upanishads—'Tat Tvam Asi', my dear readers. Om Tat Sat, Om Santi, Peace be unto all beings.

BENEFITS OF PARIKRAMA

Parikrama is the devout perambulation or Pradakshina around a sacred and holy spot. This is either a mountain peak, a sacred Tirtha, a place of pilgrimage or an entire area regarded as holy and sanctified by tradition. This practice of making a circuit is ordinarily done at any time, and especially undertaken by devotees en masse at particular periods during the year.

When done on a smaller scale within a small ambit as round a Murti installed in a shrine, round the sacred Tulasi plant or Pipal tree, the perambulation is in common parlance termed 'Pradakshina.' A Parikrama also doubtless constitutes Pradakshina, but by convention, it is being referred mainly to big circuit.

More difficult forms of Parikrama are in vogue. Additional measures involving greater physical exertion and strain are combined with Parikrama. Some lay themselves fully stretched upon the ground and roll along over the entire route. Some others proceed slowly prostrating full length at every three or ten steps; still others walk step by step, placing one foot in close proximity to the other and cover the whole distance of Parikrama; and others do the circuit themselves gyrating in a continuous Atma-Pradakshina. All these difficult features are adopted by devotees at times as special penance, or in accordance with some vow previously made, or as spontaneous expression of their zeal or fervour. Your mental attitude and motive will bestow on you the highest, maximum spiritual good.

Undaunted Yatris in the icy Himalayas do the difficult Parikrama of Mount Kailas and even longer circuit of Lake Manasasarovar. Other Yatris complete a round of entire Uttarakhand, in doing the Kedar-Badri-Yatra by going via one route and returning via another, after circling the Chardham.

Far off in the South, pious devotees make Pradakshina of the holy Arunachala at Tiruvannamalai. Rama Bhaktas and Krishna Premis go round Chitrakuta Parvata, Ayodhya, Brij, Brindavan, Govardhana and Badrinath.

The deep significance of Parikrama lies in the fact that the devotee considers not the physical aspect of the place, hill or Tirtha, but the spiritual power it symbolises and the Divine Presence that is manifested and felt through it. Through the Lord's revelation in the tenth chapter of the Bhagavad-Gita, you will understand how much special places are saturated with the Divine Presence. By the fervent attitude of faith and veneration, you make yourself fully receptive to the inflow of the spiritual vibrations of the holy place. These powerful spiritual currents enter and purify all the sheaths, gross and subtle, destroying bad Vasanas and Samskaras. Tamas and Rajas are reduced. The concentrated influence of Sattva awakens the dormant spiritual tendencies. By Parikrama, the devotee drinks deep the Divine atmosphere pervading the place and comes out of this spiritual path steeped in Sattvic vibrations. This is the inner working and significance of doing Parikrama.

Being a great purifier, it is enjoined on all devotees as a method of penance or Tapascharya by wise tradition and convention. It is an act of great spiritual benefit and religious merit too. The devotee takes bath, wears clean clothes, smears Tilak or sacred ash and wears Tulasi or Rudraksha Maala and starts with God's Name on his lips. On the Parikrama route, you gain valuable Satsanga by meeting Sadhus and Sannyasins living there. Your sins are destroyed by taking bath in sacred rivers (on big Parikramas) or ponds and Kunds. You are elevated and blessed by Darsana of many holy shrines situated on the way. You develop patience and endurance putting up with various discomforts in the sun or rain or cold. Difficult Parikramas mean giving up many dear articles to which the mind is attached. You have your mind freed from all thoughts and you are absorbed in the one idea of the Divine presence. A devoutedly conducted Parikrama constitutes in one single act a triple Sadhana elevating your body, mind and spirit. The spiritual vibrations of the holy places of pilgrimage and shrines purify your base Asuric Vrittis and fill you with Sattva and purity. You need not go in for Satsanga. Mahapurushas come to you of their own accord. They are always in search of real and sincere Sadhakas. Therefore, they also remain in holy places like Badri, Kedar, Kailas, Haridwar, Brindavan, Mathura, etc.

Blessed indeed are those who take part in Parikrama, because they will soon attain peace, bliss and immortality! Glory to Lord Rama, the Lord of Ayodhya! Glory to Krishna the Indweller of all hearts, whose special seat is Brindavan! Glory to Bhaktas! May their blessings be upon you all!

REAL FLOWER AND ARATI

The tower of a temple represents Brahmarandhra. Balipitha represents the navel or Manipura Chakra. Nandi represents Ajna Chakra. Dhvajastambha represents Sushumna Nadi which runs from Muladhara to Brahmarandhra.

Dig-devata dwells in the ears, Vayu in the skin, Sun in the eyes, Varuna in the tongue, Asvins in the nose, Vishnu in the feet, Indra in the hands, Agni in the speech, Prajapati in the generative organ, Yama in the anus, Sutratman in the Prana, Hiranyagarbha in Antahkarana, Chandra in mind, Brahma in the intellect, Rudra in egoism, Siva in Chitta, Sarasvati in the end of the tongue, Parvati in Anahata Chakra, Lakshmi in Manipura Chakra, Ganesa in Muladhara and Satchidananda Brahman in Brahmarandhra at the crown of the head.

Satya, Ahimsa, Tapas, mercy, love, self-restraint, contentment, forgiveness, Jnana, equal vision, peace are the real flowers of Puja. All the Nadas are the waters for Abhisheka. The virtuous actions are the offering of incense. Vedanta is Pitambar. Jnana and Yoga are the Kundalas. Tapas and meditation are the lights. Japa is Chamara. Anahata is the music. Kirtan is umbrella. Pranayama is the fan.

Tattvas are the attendants of the Lord. Jnana-Sakti is the Devi. Agama is the commander. The eight Siddhis are the door-keepers of the Lord. Turiya is the Bhasma. Veda is the bull or Nandi. Kalyana Gunas represent the Trident in the hand. Panchakshara is the holy thread. Suddha Jiva is the ornament. The Vrittis are the Pujopakaranas. The Panchabhutas and the five Tanmatras are the Rudrakshamaalas of Lord Siva. Tiger skin represents Ahankara.

Kriya-Sakti and virtuous actions are Dhupa or incense for the Lord. Chit-Sakti which produces knowledge is also Dhupa. Offering of the ego and the mind at the lotus-feet of the Lord is real Naivedya. Just as camphor melts and becomes one with the fire, so also the mind of a sage melts and the individual soul gets merged in the Supreme Soul. This is real Karpura Arati.

Chapter X
THE SAIVA UPANISHADS

RUDRA OF THE UPANISHADS

Some ignorant persons think that Rudra is a malevolent, terrific deity who causes destruction. They believe that Rudra is a God of punishment. It is not so. Rudra is the God who bestows prosperity and destroys suffering. He is a benevolent Deity who confers auspiciousness, offspring and cattle. He is the bringer or source of prosperity.

Siva or Rudra means He who removes sin or suffering. The names Bhava, Sarva, Pasupati, Ugra, Mahadeva, Isana and Asani are applied to Rudra. Pasupati means the Lord or Protector of cattle.

In the Vedas you will find prayers such as: "O Rudra! May we increase in offspring". "Thou, O Rudra, art the most eminent of beings, the strongest of the strong, wielder of the thunderbolt; protect us, carry us happily across our calamity, drive away all evils". "Remove from us whatever sins we have done." Therefore, Rudra is not a terror-inspiring God, but a bestower of welfare or prosperity. He is the one great Lord of the Universe.

Rudra is the ideal of mendicants, because Rudra alone, of all the deities, is spoken of in the scriptures as the mendicant-God. He is mentioned as having the ascetic water-pot in the Rigveda hymns.

You will find in the Svetasvatara Upanishad, chapter III: "There is one Rudra only who rules all the worlds by His powers. There is no one besides Him who can make Him the second. He is present inside the hearts of all beings. He creates all the worlds and maintains and finally withdraws them into Himself".

Rudra represents here Para Brahman or the Supreme Self, the Infinite or the Absolute.

Rudra, after having created all objects, draws together or takes them all back into Himself at the end of time, i.e., during cosmic Pralaya or dissolution.

Rudra is the destructive aspect of Siva. There are eleven Rudras in the cosmic hierarchy. Esoterically, the Pranas (or the ten senses) and the mind represent the eleven Rudras. Sri Hanuman is a manifestation or aspect of Rudra only.

In Siva-Purana, Rudra is another name for Siva. Rudra is one who destroys the sins and removes the miseries of His devotees and confers on them wisdom and bliss. Rudra is the Antaryamin or indweller of all beings. He witnesses silently the actions and thoughts of men and dispenses the fruits of their actions.

"That one God, having His eyes, His face, His arms and feet in every place, when producing heaven and earth, forges them together with His arms and His wings".

May Rudra, the creator and supporter of the gods, the great seer, the Lord of all, who created at first Hiranyagarbha, endow us with good thought (pure intellect).

"Rudra, with Thy form which is auspicious, which is not dreadful, and which manifests what is holy, with that all-blessed form, appear to us, O Dweller among the mountains".

RUDRAKSHA JABALA UPANISHAD

Hari Om! I praise the Effulgent State of Absolute Peace, belonging to Sri Maharudra, which is to be known through the Rudraksha Jabala Upanishad.

Bhusunda questioned Lord Kalagnirudra: What is the beginning of Rudraksha beads? What is the benefit of wearing them on the body?

Lord Kalagnirudra answered him thus: I closed my eyes for the sake of destroying the Tripura Asuras. From my eyes thus closed, drops of water fell on the earth. These drops of tears turned into Rudrakshas.

By the mere utterance of the name of 'Rudraksha', one acquires the benefit of giving ten cows in charity. By seeing and touching it, one attains double that benefit. I am unable to praise it any more.

I closed my eyes one thousand celestial years. Then from my eyelids, drops of water dropped down and attained the state of immobility for blessing the devoted persons.

This Rudraksha destroys the devotees' sins that are committed both night and day, by wearing it.

By mere vision of the Rudraksha, the benefit will be say, a lakh. But by wearing them, it will be a crore. Why, it will be equal to hundred crores.

But it will be a thousand lakhs of crores and hundred lakhs of crores times powerful when one does Japa with Rudraksha and wears it at all times.

Among Rudrakshas, one as big as Amalaka (myrobalan), is considered to be the best. One as big as the Badari fruit (Indian berry) is considered to be of the middle sort. But that as big as Chana (Bengal gram) is considered to be the worst of all. This is my idea about the size of Rudraksha beads.

The four kinds of people, Brahmins, Kshatriyas, Vaisyas and Sudras are born as merely a worthless burden on the earth. The real Brahmin is the white Rudraksha. The red is a Kshatriya. The yellow is a Vaisya. And the black is a Sudra.

Therefore, a Brahmin should wear white Rudrakshas, a Kshatriya the red, a Vaisya the yellow and a Sudra the black.

One should use those Rudraksha-beads which are nice, handsome, strong, big, auspicious and thorny. One should avoid those eaten by worms, broken, without thorns, and having sores.

The self-holed Rudraksha is of the best variety. But that which is holed by man's attempt, is considered to be worse. Those best Rudrakshas should be strung in white thread. A worshipper of Siva should wear Rudraksha all over the body. He should wear one bead on the crest, three hundred round the head, thirty-six round the neck, sixteen round each arm, twelve round the chest and five hundred round the waist. He should wear a Yajnopavita consisting of one hundred and eight beads of Rudrakshas. He should wear two, three, five or seven Maalas of Rudraksha round the neck.

A Siva-Bhakta should wear Rudrakshas round his crown, ear-ring, chain, round the ear, armlet, at all times, and specially round the stomach, irrespective of the fact whether he is sleeping, drinking, etc.

If the devotee wears three hundred beads, it is the worst, if he wears five hundred it will be medium, but one thousand will be the best of all.

The devotee, when wearing Rudrakshas on the head, should repeat his Ishta Mantra, and when wearing them round the neck, should repeat the Tat-Purusha Mantra and when wearing round the throat, should repeat the Aghora Mantra. The same Mantra (Aghora) should be recited when wearing round the chest also.

He should wear them round the arms with the Aghora Bija Mantra.

Then again Bhusunda asked Lord Kalagnirudra: What are the different forms and effects of Rudraksha beads? Please tell me about the secret of these blessed ones including their various faces, which is the means of getting rid of all evil.

Lord Kalagnirudra said: The bead with one face is of the form of the Supreme Truth. A disciplined one (controlling his senses) mingles himself with the one Eternal Truth, after wearing these Rudrakshas. (The following is a list of different faces of Rudrakshas and their effects).

Faces Form	Effect of wearing
1. Supreme Truth	Attainment of Eternity
2. Ardhanarisvara	Grace of Ardhanarisvara
3. Tretagni	Grace of Agni
4. Brahma	Grace of Brahma
5. Pancha-Brahmas	Destruction of homicide sin
6. Karttikeya or Ganesa	Attainment of Chitta-Suddhi and Jnana
7. Saptamala	Attainment of good health and wealth
8. Ashtamatras (Ashta Vasus) or Ganga	Grace of these Devatas and becoming truthful
9. Nava-Saktis	Grace of Nava-Saktis or nine Powers
10. Yama	Attainment of Peace
11. Ekadasa Rudras	Increase of all kinds of wealth
12. Mahavishnu or 12 Adityas	Attainment of Moksha

13. Cupid	Attainment of fulfilling desires and grace of Cupid
14. Rudra	Destruction of all diseases

One who wears Rudrakshas, should not use intoxicants, meat, garlic, onions, carrots and all such prohibited things. By wearing Rudrakshas during eclipses, Vishusankranti (the end of Mina and beginning of Mesha Masa), new moon, full moon and other such auspicious days, one is freed of all sins.

The base of the Rudraksha bead is Brahma, its navel is Vishnu, its face is Rudra and its hole consists of all gods.

One day Sanatkumara asked Kalagnirudra: "O Lord! Tell me the rules for wearing Rudrakshas". At that time Nidagha, Jadabharata, Dattatreya, Katyayana, Bharadvaja, Kapila, Vasishtha, Pippalada, etc., came to Kalagnirudra. Then Lord Kalagnirudra asked them why they all had come in a group. They all answered that they came to hear the method of wearing Rudrakshas.

Kalagnirudra said: Those that are born out of Rudra's Akshis (eyes) are called Rudrakshas. When these beads are even once touched by hand, one attains the glory of giving in charity two thousand cows at a time. When they are worn in ears, he gets the effect of giving out eleven thousand cows in charity. He also attains the state of the eleven Rudras. When the beads are worn on the head, one has the benefit of giving a crore of cows in charity. Of all these places, I am unable to tell you the benefit when worn in the ears.

Whoever studies this Rudraksha Jabala Upanishad, be he a boy or a youth, becomes great. He becomes the Guru of all and the teacher of all Mantras. Havan and Archana should be done with these Mantras (of the Upanishad).

That Brahmin who recites this Upanishad in the evening, destroys the sins committed during day time; who recites at noon, destroys the sins of six births; who recites in the morning and evening, destroys the sins of many births. He attains the same benefit of doing six thousand lakhs of Gayatri Japa.

He becomes purified from all sins of killing a Brahmin, drinking toddy, stealing gold, approaching Guru's wife, having intercourse with her, speaking with corrupted person, etc.

He gets the benefits of all pilgrimages and river-baths. He attains Siva-sayujya. He does not come back (to rebirth).

BHASMA JABALA UPANISHAD

I am that Absolute Brahman only which, after being understood in its true aspect (as one with this Atman), entirely burns into ashes (Bhasma) the ignorance (illusion or Maya) of considering this universe to be existing (real) and separate from one's own Self, through the destructive fire of (Supreme) Knowledge!

Once Bhusunda, a descendant of Jabali went to the Kailas Peak and prostrated before Lord Mahadeva Siva, who is the form of Omkara and who is beyond the trinity of Brahma, Vishnu and Rudra.

Bhusunda worshipped Siva with great devotion again and again through fruits, flowers and leaves. Then he questioned Lord Siva: "Lord! Kindly impart to me the essential knowledge of all the Vedas, embodying the process and technique of using the Bhasma (sacred ash), because it is the only means for attaining Liberation. What is the Bhasma made of? Where should it be applied? What are the Mantras to be recited? Who are the persons fitted for this? What are the rules regarding it? Kindly instruct me, born from depressed class."

The kind Lord Paramesvara said: At first the devotee after understanding the influence of the celestials at the prescribed time, should fetch some sacred and pure cow-dung early in the morning, keep it in the leaf of a Palasa-tree and then dry it with the Vedic Mantra 'Tryambakam' etc. (in the sun).

Then he should burn that dry cow-dung, placed in a convenient place, with any fire that is available, according to the rules laid down in the Grihya Sutras of his sect, and then pour Ahutis of seasamum and paddy together with ghee, with the Mantra 'Somaya Svaha'. The number of Ahutis should be 1008, or if possible, 1½ times this. The instruments for pouring ghee should be made of leaf; in that case man does not commit any sin.

Then, at the end, the devotee should offer the oblation of Sveshtakruta at the time of Purna-Ahuti, with the Mantra 'Tryambakam' etc. With the same Mantra Bali (an offering) should be placed in the eight directions (of the fire).

That Bhasma should be sprinkled with water by the Gayatri Mantra. Then that sacred ash should be placed in a gold, silver, copper or earthen vessel and sprinkled again with the Rudra Mantras. It should then be kept in a clean and decent place.

Then the devotee should honour the Brahmins with a grand feast.

Then only he will become purified. Then he should take the Bhasma from the vessel with the Pancha-Brahma-Mantras, 'Manastoka', 'Sadyo Jatam', etc., and with the idea that 'fire is Bhasma, air is Bhasma, water is Bhasma, earth is Bhasma, ether is Bhasma, gods are Bhasma, Rishis are Bhasma, all this universe and existence are Bhasma; I prostrate to this sacred and purifying Bhasma which destroys all my sins.'

Thus, the devotee should keep a little Bhasma with the decent left hand saying, 'Vamadevaya' (this is to Vamadeva) sprinkling with the Mantra 'Tryambakam' etc., and cleaning it with the Mantra 'Suddham suddhena' etc. Then he should filter it nicely. Then he should apply it from head to foot, with the five Brahma-Mantras. With the first finger, middle finger and ring finger, he should apply the same to the middle of the head saying 'to the head' and 'O Bhasma! Thou hast come from Agni!'

Places where Bhasma is to be applied	Mantra to be used
1. Forehead	Tryambakam etc.
2. Neck	Nilagrivaya etc.
3. Right side of neck	Tryayusham etc.
4. Cheeks	Vama etc.
5. Eyes	Kalaya etc.
6. Ears	Trilochanaya etc.
7. Face	Srinavama etc.
8. Chest	Prabravama etc.
9. Navel	Atmane etc.
10. Below right shoulder	Nabhih etc.
11. Middle of right shoulder	Bhavaya etc.
12. Right side of chest	Rudraya etc.
13. Back of right arm	Sarvaya etc.
14. Below left shoulder	Pasupataye etc.
15. Middle of left shoulder	Ugraya etc.
16. Middle of left arm	Agrevadhaya etc.
17. Back of left arm	Durevadhaya etc.
18. Armpits	Namo Hantre etc.
19. All parts	Sankaraya etc.

The devotee should then prostrate to Siva with the Mantra 'Somaya' etc. He should wash the hands and drink that ash-water with the Mantra 'Apah Punantu' etc. The water should never be spilt down from any cause.

Thus, this practice of Bhasmadharana should be done in the morning, noon and evening. If he does not do this, he will become fallen. This very thing is the prescribed Dharma of all Brahmins. Without having Bhasmadharana in this fashion, he should never take any food, water or anything else. Accidentally if this practice is forgotten, that day, Gayatri should not be repeated. No Yajna should be done on that day; no Tarpana should be offered to gods, Rishis or Pitrus. This is the eternal Dharma that destroys all sins and gives the final state of Moksha.

This is the daily rite of Brahmins, Brahmacharins Grihasthas, Vanaprasthas and Sannyasins. If this is overlooked even once, he should stand in water upto the neck, repeating Gayatri 108 times, and fast the whole day. If a Sannyasin does not wear Bhasma, even a single day, he should fast during the whole day and do 1000 Pranava Japa, for being purified once again. Otherwise, the Lord will throw these Sannyasins to dogs and wolves.

In case this kind of Bhasma is not available, any other Bhasma that may be at hand should be used with the prescribed Mantras. This kind of practice shall destroy any kind of sin that may be committed by man.

Then again Bhusunda asked Siva: What are the daily rites to be performed by a Brahmin, by neglecting which he will commit a sin? Who is to be then meditated upon? Who is to be remembered? How to meditate? Where to practice this? Please tell me in detail.

The Lord answered all in a nutshell: First of all the devotee should get up early in the morning before sunrise, and after finishing the purificatory actions, should take his bath. He should clean the body with the Rudra Suktas. Then he should wear a clean cloth. After this, he should meditate on the sun-god and apply Bhasma to all the prescribed parts of the body. He should then wear white Rudraksha, as prescribed. Some prescribe the following way of applying Bhasma:

Places	*No. of times (lines)*
1. Head	40
2. Chest	1 or 3
3. Ears	11
4. Neck	32
5. Arms	16 each
6. Throat	12 each side
7. Thumbs	6 each

Then the devotee should observe Sandhya with the Kusa grass in his hand. He should do Japa of either Siva-Shadakshara or Siva-Ashtakshara. 'Om Namah Sivaya' and 'Om Namo Mahadevaya' are the two Mantras. This is the highest truth and the greatest instruction. I myself am that Great Lord Siva, God of all gods, the Supreme Controller of all the universes. I am that Impersonal Brahman, I am Omkara, I am the Creator, Preserver and Destroyer of all. Through My terror only, all are working properly. I am this world and the five elements. I am the Highest Truth that exists, the Brahman of the Upanishads. This is the greatest Vidya.

I am the only giver of Moksha. Hence all people come to Me for final help. That is why I absorb into My Being those creatures who leave their Pranas at Banares which is standing at the top of My Trisula (trident). Therefore, everyone should perform penance at Banares only. Banares should not be neglected under any circumstance.

Everybody should try to live at Banares as far as possible. No place is better than Banares.

Even at Banares, the most celebrated is the temple of Siva, where in the East, there is the place of Wealth, in the South, the place of Vichara, in the West, the place of Vairagya and in the North, the place of Jnana. There in the middle, I, the Eternal Spirit should be worshipped. That Linga at Banares, is not illumined by the sun, moon or the stars. That self-luminous Linga called 'Visvesvara' has its root in Patala. That is Myself. I should be worshipped by one who wears the sacred Bhasma and Rudrakshas in the prescribed manner. I shall deliver him from all sins and sorrows.

By performing My Abhisheka, he attains My Sayujya state. Nothing exists other than Myself. I initiate all with the Taraka Mantra. Those who want Mukti should live in Banares. I will take care of them. I am the Lord of Brahma, Vishnu and Rudra. The most corrupt man or woman will attain Moksha, if he or she dies at Banares. Other sinners will be fried in burning pits of live coals after death. Therefore, everybody should try to live at Banares which is My Pranalinga Itself.

TRIPURA-TAPINI-UPANISHAD

I praise that Supreme Truth which is Knowledge Absolute, which is to be known through the Vidya of the Tripura-Tapini-Upanishad.

The Lord assumed the form of destructive ferociousness and then He covered Himself all over the three worlds, Bhuh, Bhuvah and Svah. Then He had that power of the Adi-Sakti, i.e., the Adi-Sakti burst out from His heart. This is the Sakti called the Maya of Siva and She is understood by the fundamental syllable 'Hrim'. The whole universe was then covered by this Sakti. Since She covered the three worlds or Tripuras, She has been styled as 'Tripura'.

This Tripura Sakti has the following Vidya called Sri Vidya which can be derived from the following Vedic Mantras:

तत्सवितुर्वरेण्यं भर्गो देवस्य धीमहि। धियो यो नः
प्रचोदयात्। परो रजसे सावदोम्॥

जातवेदसे सुनवाम सोममरातीयतो निदहाति वेदः।
सनः पर्षदति दुर्गाणि विश्वा नावेव सिन्धुं दुरितात्यग्निः॥

त्र्यंबकं यजामहे सुगन्धि पुष्टिवर्धनम्।
उर्वारुकमिव बन्धनान्मृत्योर्मुक्षीय माऽमृतात्॥

This Vidya consisting of one hundred letters is the Supreme Vidya in its entirety. This is Paramesvari, Tripura Herself.

Out of the above Mantras, the first four stanzas deal with the exposition of the glory of the Para-Brahman. The second set of stanzas deals with the Mahima of Sakti. The third set deals with the glory of Siva Himself.

In this Vidya, all the worlds, all the Vedas, all the Sastras, all the Puranas and all the Dharmas have been dealt with and this is the Effulgence that has come out of the combination of Siva and Sakti.

Now, we shall comment on the most important and the hidden meanings of these verses. Here the great word 'Tat' means Para-Brahman Itself, the Eternity. This is the symbol used for that Lord who is beyond all definitions and arguments. This Lord is the embodiment of Supreme Knowledge itself That is, He wishes to be in the form of Knowledge Absolute. He alone is the great Lord Siva who is always desired by sages, Yogins, etc., in Yajnas. Therefore there is the creation of desire.

Thus, this Lord who is beyond the reach of all desires, still desires and is being desired. He creates the alphabetical list of language. Therefore, the Lord is called 'Kama' or desire. The letter representing Kama is called 'Ka'. Therefore the word 'Tat' represents the letter 'Ka'. This is the meaning of the word 'Tat'.

'Savituh' comes from the Sanskrit root-word 'Sunj Praniprasave', which means the Generator or producer of all beings. He is the great Power. Power means Sakti. This great Sakti or Devi called Tripura, is embodied in the Mahakundali (Yantra). Thus, the fire-globe (of the sun) should be known by the intelligent. This Sakti or power of Trikona (triangular figure) bears out the letter called 'E'. Therefore we should learn the word 'E' from the word 'Savituh'.

'Varenyam' means that which is fit to be adored and worshipped, which is the imperishable and the praiseworthy. Therefore, it should be understood that the letter 'E' should be taken from the word 'Varenyam'. 'Bhargo' and 'Dhimahi' will be now commented upon. The letter 'Dha' means Dharana or concentration. The Lord is always concentrated upon by the 'Dhi' or the intellect or Buddhi. 'Bharga' is the Lord Himself who can be understood only by reaching the fourth stage or Avastha and this is the Being that pervades all and all. The letter representing this fourth stage is called 'I' and this is the real meaning of the above-mentioned words of the Mantra. We shall now talk of the word 'Mahi'. 'Mahi' means greatness, idleness, strength, stubbornness, and this applies to that element which possesses all these qualities. That is the earth which is represented by the letter 'La'. This is the

Supreme state. Thus, this Lakara shows the quality of the earth in its being the embodiment of all oceans, forests, mountains and the seven islands. Therefore the form of Devi called the earth, is termed 'Mahi'.

Now about, 'Dhiyo Yo Nah Prachodayat'. Para or the Supreme is the Imperishable Siva Himself, the Eternal Soul. The underlying meaning here is this: We should meditate on the immobile form of Lakara or Jyotirlinga or Lord Siva which is the most supreme thing that ever exists anywhere. Here, there is no desire for any Dhyana whatsoever. It is beyond all Dhyanas. Therefore, we are requesting the Lord to direct our minds to be established in that Nirvikalpa State where there is no thinking at all. This request should not be made through the mouth. It should be simply thought of in the mind.

Then 'Paro Rajase Savadom'. After meditating on the form of the Supreme Truth, there will come out a big effulgence, pure and blissful, full of knowledge which is residing inside the heart. This is the essence of all speech and Knowledge. This is the true Sakti. And this is called the Panchakshara, since it is the creator of the Pancha Bhutas or the five elements. This should be understood correctly by the intelligent.

This is the Vidya giving all desires to the devotee. Thus, after understanding in its true aspect, this Vidya of thirty-two letters, the devotee should think of the letter called 'Ha' which is the form of Siva, who is the Imperishable, pure State. The letter derived out of the combination of the sun and the moon, that is, the combination of Siva and Sakti is 'Ha' and it is also named as 'Hamsa'. This is the seed of Kama. Through this Vidya, we can know the Supreme Lord Siva.

This combination is also understood as being the merging of the Jivatma in the Supreme Paramatman. Thus 'Ha' means the Eternal Stage or the Final Emancipation.

This is the derivation of the Sri Vidya. One who knows this, attains the form of Rudra. He bursts open the residence of Vishnu and reaches the Para-Brahman.

Then about the second Mantra. This Mantra glorifies the Mahima of Tripura Devi.

By the word 'Jata' Lord Siva is meant. He who gave birth to the first letters of the 'Varna-Matrika' of the form of the 'Bindurupa' of Omkara in the very beginning is called 'Jata'. Or else, it may also be said that because He desired at the very beginning the fulfilment of His Kama, when He was just born, He is called 'Jata'. The Knowledge of Devi Tripura should be thus carefully analysed in the same manner by dissecting the Mantra into its different words (according to Mantra-Sastra). Then all kinds of 'Raksha' or defence can be had from this Mantra. The first thing that is to be understood here is that 'Jata' is the One Lord, the Effulgent Being. This should be taken as the foundation of all Vidyas pertaining to Tripura. Here, it should also be understood that the letter 'Sa' refers to the power of Sakti and the letter 'Somam' refers to the State of Siva. Whosoever knows this becomes famous and important.

Thus, this Vidya where Devi Tripura resides at all times should be taken to be the basis of all Vidyas and the devotee should always be studying this Vidya and reciting it. This Vidya is the embodiment of the Powers of Siva and Sakti. This Vidya is called the limb of Sri Tripuramba Herself. The same Vidya, when used for meditating purposes, is called 'Sarvatodhira'.

The Sri Vidya Chakra of Tripura is the King of all Chakras. This gives one, anything that he wants and this can be worshipped by anybody, without restriction. This Chakra is the gateway to Moksha, and Yogins after bursting the Brahman through this Vidya, attain that permanent Bliss. This Chakra is the house of Tripuradevi.

Then about the Mrityunjaya Anushtup Mantra. 'Tryambakam' (Trayanam Ambakam) means the 'Lord of the three' worlds. 'Trayanam' means 'of the three' worlds. 'Ambakam' is the Lord of it. 'Yajamahe' means 'Sevamahe' or do service. Besides this, the word 'Mahe' means 'Mrityunjaya' or the destroyer of death. Therefore, the word 'Yajamahe' is very important here.

The word 'Sugandhim' means 'to derive fame from all quarters'. And the word 'Pushtivardhanam' means 'one who creates all the worlds, preserves all the worlds, pervades all the worlds and gives salvation to all the worlds'.

'Urvarukam' means 'cucumber'. 'Urvarukamiva Bandhanan Mrityormukshiya Mamritat'. A cucumber is tied with a creeper. Similarly the human being and other creatures are tied by the bonds of Samsara. Here, it means to deliver the earthly beings from the Mayaic bond to the Eternal Bliss, just as a cucumber is delivered free from the creeper.

A person who wants to conquer death should repeat the Mantra 'Mrityunjaya', etc. One who wishes to become Rudra, should make use of the Mantra 'Om Namah'. Then he will certainly derive the best benefit out of it.

Then there is another Mantra. 'Tad Vishnoh Paramam Padam', etc. Vishnu is one who pervades all the universe. His supreme state which is just like the sky is called 'Paramam Padam'. 'Surayah' means scholars or those intelligent who have understood the Reality, i.e., Brahma, etc. That Supreme State of Vishnu is lying or residing in each and every being. By 'residing', we mean 'Vasati.' Therefore, He is called 'Vaasudeva'. The powerful twelve letters of Sri Vaasudeva 'Om Namo Bhagavate Vaasudevaya', are everything. They are sufficient to absolve one from all sins. The knower of this Mantra reaches that Brahma-Purusha who is in the form of the embodiment of the three letters A, U and M.

Then, we have got another powerful Mantra 'Hamsa Suchishat', etc. This is the great Mantra of the Sun-God. And the other Mantra which is to be known is 'Gananam Tva', etc. This is the Mantra of Ganapati. One who knows and repeats these Mantras that belong to Siva, Vishnu, Surya and Ganapati, will get the direct revelation of Devi Tripura.

In the Gayatri, there are four forms. In the morning, She is called Gayatri. In the noon, She is called Savitri. In the evening, She is called Sarasvati. She is always called Ajapa when She is having the fourth Pada with Her. This Devi is having the form of fifty alphabets from the letter 'A' to the letter 'Ksha'. All the Sastras and the world are covered by the Devi in this form. Prostrations to Her again and again.

So, any devotee who worships Devi Tripura with these Mantras, becomes the true seer of the Reality. He then attains Moksha. This should be known correctly by everybody.

Now, we shall expound the Karmakanda of the Tripura-worship. This Sakti or the Adimaya directs the Supreme Brahman. That Brahman is Knowledge Absolute, and is termed Paramatman. This Supreme Being is the Hearer, Knower, Seer, Commander, Perceiver and the Supreme Purusha who resides in the Atman of all beings. This is to be known. There is no world, no non-world, no God, no non-God, no being, no non-being, no Brahmin and no non-Brahmin, at all. Thus shines the Nirvana called Para-Brahman.

The mind that is thinking of something, is called Baddha. That which does not think of anything is called Mukta. Then only this Brahman can be understood. Therefore, everybody should keep his mind free from thoughts of objects.

Until the mind is devoid of all thoughts, one should try to control the Pranas. This is the eternal knowledge. All other things are merely unnecessary scriptural descriptions. There is no difference between thinking and non-thinking in the Para-Brahman. All are same there. There is nothing to be thought of and there is nobody to think.

Thus finally, the devotee should understand gradually that Brahman is his own Self and then he will attain the Blissful Emancipation.

Now the Supreme Truth is revealed. There is no one who longs for liberation, there is no one who is liberated, there is no Vairagya, there is no Sadhana, there is no destruction.

There are two Brahmans, namely Sabda Brahman and Para Brahman. One who has mastered the Sabda Brahman, attain to the Para Brahman. After acquiring all the knowledge through books, the intelligent man should throw away those books, just like the husk thrown away by one who wants only the internal kernel of the grain.

Thus the Supreme Brahman-State is described. One who knows this Great Vidya should be worshipped by others. There is no doubt about it. This is the great Upanishad.

RUDRA UPANISHAD

Now, at this moment, I take refuge in that Pure State of the Supreme Absolute which can be known by the Vidya, called the Rudra Hridaya Upanishad.

After prostrating before the celebrated form of Sri Mahadeva-Rudra in his heart, adoring the sacred Bhasma and Rudraksha and mentally reciting the great Mahavakya-Mantra, Tarasara, Sri Suka asked his father Sri Vyasa Maharshi, thus:

Who is the real God of gods? In whom are all these existences established? By worshipping whom, can I please the Devas in whole?

Hearing these words, Sri Veda Vyasa replied thus:

Rudra is the embodiment of all Devas. All devas are merely different manifestations of Sri Rudra Himself. On the right side of Rudra, there is the sun, then the four-headed Brahma, and then three Agnis (fires). On the left side, there exist Sri Umadevi, and also Vishnu and Soma (moon).

Uma Herself is the form of Vishnu. Vishnu Himself is the form of the moon. Therefore, those who worship Lord Vishnu, worship Siva Himself. And those who worship Siva, worship Lord Vishnu in reality. Those who envy and hate Sri Rudra, are actually hating Sri Vishnu. Those who decry Lord Siva, decry Vishnu Himself.

Rudra is the generator of the seed. Vishnu is the embryo of the seed. Siva Himself is Brahma and Brahma Himself is Agni. Rudra is full of Brahma and Vishnu. The whole world is full of Agni and Soma. The masculine gender is Lord Siva. The feminine gender is Sri Bhavani Devi. All the mobile and immobile creation of this universe, is filled up with Uma and Rudra. The Vyakta is Sri Uma, and the

Avyakta is Lord Siva. The combination of Uma and Sankara is Vishnu.

Hence everybody should prostrate to Sri Maha Vishnu with great devotion. He is the Atman. He is the Paramatman. He is the Antaratman. Brahma is the Antaratman. Siva is the Paramatman. Vishnu is the Eternal Atman of all this universe. This whole creation of Svarga, Martya and Patala Lokas is a big tree. Vishnu is the top portion (branches) of this tree. Brahma is the stem. The root is Lord Siva.

The effect is Vishnu. The action is Brahma. The cause is Siva. For the benefit of the worlds. Rudra has taken these three forms.

Rudra is Dharma. Vishnu is the world. Brahma is Knowledge. Therefore, do Kirtan of His name, 'Rudra' Rudra. By singing like this, the hallowed name of this great Lord, all your sins will be destroyed.

Rudra is man. Uma is woman. Prostrations to Him and Her.

Rudra is Brahma. Uma is Sarasvati. Prostrations to Him and Her.

Rudra is Vishnu. Uma is Lakshmi. Prostrations to Him and Her.

Rudra is Sun. Uma is shadow. Prostrations to Him and Her.

Rudra is moon. Uma is star. Prostrations to Him and Her.

Rudra is day. Uma is night. Prostrations to Him and Her.

Rudra is Yajna. Uma is Vedi. Prostrations to Him and Her.

Rudra is Agni. Uma is Svaha. Prostrations to Him and Her.

Rudra is Veda. Uma is Sastra. Prostrations to Him and Her.

Rudra is tree. Uma is creeper. Prostrations to Him and Her.

Rudra is scent. Uma is flower. Prostrations to Him and Her.

Rudra is meaning. Uma is word. Prostrations to Him and Her.

Rudra is Linga. Uma is Pitha. Prostrations to Him and Her.

The devotee should worship Sri Rudra and Uma with these Mantras referred to above. O my son, Suka! With these hymns, you should meditate on the Eternal Para-Brahman, which is beyond the reach of the senses, which is pure Existence, knowledge and Bliss and which cannot be understood either by the speech or by the mind. After knowing this, there is nothing more to be known, because everything is the form of That, and there is nothing separate from That.

There are two Vidyas to be known. They are Para and Apara. Apara Vidya is the embodiment of the four Vedas and their six Angas. They do not deal with the Nature of the Atman. But the Para Vidya is called the Moksha-Sastra. It deals with that supreme philosophy of the Absolute Truth, unununderstandable, impersonal, Nirguna, Nirakara, without ears, without eyes, without hands, without feet, eternal, omnipresent, imperishable, and knowable by the intelligent daring sages.

From that Lord Siva who performs a terrible penance in the form of Supreme Jnana-Marga, this whole world is created which is the food of the mortals. This world is

Maya. It seems to appear just like a dream. It is superimposed on the Lord just like a rope on a serpent. This is the eternal Truth. There is no creation in reality. All is absolute. All is Truth. Knowing this, one is liberated at once.

Only through Jnana, you can get rid of this Samsara. Only through Jnana, you can understand this existence and never through Karma. Understand this through the guidance of a Brahmanishtha-Srotriya Guru. The Guru will give the disciple all the necessary knowledge of Brahman, the Absolute. By cutting off the bondage of Ajnana or Avidya, one should take refuge in Lord Sadasiva. This is the real wisdom to be understood by an aspirant seeking after Truth.

The Pranava is the bow. The Atman is the arrow. The Para-Brahman is the target. Just like the arrow, the Atman will become one with Brahman.

But all these three, the bow, the arrow and the target are not different from that Sadasiva. There do not shine the bodies of the sun, moon or the stars. There does not blow the wind, there do not exist many Devatas. He, the One Lord only exists. He only, the Purity of purities, shines for ever and ever.

There are two birds in this body, the Jiva and the Paramatman. The Jiva eats the fruit of his Karmas, but the Paramatman is untouched by anything. The Paramatman is only the Sakshi. He does not do anything. He only assumes the form of the Jiva through His Maya, just as the Akasa inside a pot seems to be different from the Akasa outside and assumes the form of the pot. In reality all is Siva, Advaita, the One Absolute. There is no difference of whatever kind.

When all is understood to be One, Omkara, the Absolute, there is no sorrow, there is no Maya. Then the attainment of the Advaita-Paramananda is very easy. Think that you are the basis of all this universe, you are the One, Kevala, Sat-Chit-Ghana. All people cannot understand this Truth. Those devoid of Maya can know this secret. After knowing this, the Atman does not move towards any place at any time. It becomes one with the Absolute, just like Ghatakasa with Paramakasa. Just as Akasa does not move anywhere, similarly this Atman does not have any movement. It becomes one with OM.

One who knows this great secret Truth is the real Muni. He becomes the Para-Brahman Itself. He becomes Satchidananda. He attains permanent peace.

Chapter XI
THE SAIVA ACHARYAS

APPAR OR TIRUNAVUKARASAR

Appar is one of the four Tamil Samaya Acharyas. He was a contemporary of Sambandhar. He was a Vellala of Tiru Amur in the district of Cuddalore, Tamilnadu. He was born of Pugalenar and Mathiniar. The parents gave the name Marulneekiar (dispeller of darkness or ignorance) to Appar. Appar means father. Sambandhar gave Marulneekiar this name. The name Appar was first used by Sambandhar in addressing him in one of the several meetings between them. Appar's soul-stirring and sublime odes earned the title Tirunavukkarasar or the Lord of speech. He was a God-inspired soul. He sang devotional odes or Padigams during his pilgrimage to various shrines. He flourished in the middle of the seventh century A.D. He was a mystic and poet.

Tilakavadhiar was the elder sister of Appar. She was betrothed to Kalippahaiyar, a military commander under the Pallava king. Kalippahaiyar had to fight against some invader from the North. He died in the battle-field. Tilakavadhiar's parents also died. The news of the death of Kalippahaiyar reached the ears of Tilakavadhiar. She made up her mind to enter the funeral pyre. Marulneekiar came to know of the intention of his sister. He ran to his sister, prostrated before her and said: "I am keeping my life on account of your support only, after the death of our parents. If you want to give up your life, I will give up my life before you do so". The heart of Tilakavadhiar melted.

She changed her determination and resolved to lead the ascetic life and bring up her helpless younger brother.

Appar became a convert to Jainism. He studied all the Jain scriptures. He went to Pataliputra itself and became one of the spiritual heads there, as he was an erudite scholar in the Jain scriptures.

Appar's sister was very much afflicted at heart when she came to know that her brother became a convert to Jainism. She left her native village and went to Tiru Atikai, a neighbouring town. She spent her time in meditation and prayer at the Siva's temple. She prayed to the Lord for his return.

Appar fell a victim to a severe colic which could not be cured. He threw off the garb of a Jain, his bowl and went to his sister. She smeared the holy ashes on the forehead of Appar and took him to the temple of Siva and asked him to prostrate before the Lord and worship Him. Appar acted accordingly. The severe colic vanished at once. He praised Lord Siva.

The spiritual head of the Jains at Pataliputra reported to Kadava, the Jain king, about the absconding of Appar. The district of Cuddalore was under the sway of the Pallava king Kadava. The spiritual head induced the king to persecute Appar.

Appar proceeded to the Pallava capital and appeared before the king. Appar was persecuted in various ways. He was thrown into a burning lime-kiln. He was compelled to drink poisoned milk. An elephant was sent to kill him. A heavy stone was tied to him and he was thrown into the sea. Lord saved him. He floated alive and reached the shore at Tiruppatirupuliyur.

The Pallava king recognised the greatness of Appar and prostrated at his feet. He gave up Jainism and embraced

Saivism. He built a magnificent temple of Siva called Gunathara Vicharam at Tirunadhikai.

Thereupon, Appar proceeded on a pilgrimage to various sacred places. He visited Chidambaram, Sirkali and other places and sang Tevaram or odes in praise of Lord Siva.

Appar met the saint Appudi Adigal at Tingalur. Appar brought to life Appudi's son, who was bitten by a cobra.

Thereupon, Appar visited holy places such as Tiruvanainallur, Tiruvamathur, Tirukoilur and Tirupennakatam and worshipped Lord Siva. He finally reached Tirutunganaimadam and prayed to Lord Siva: "O Siva Sankara! O Ardhanarisvara! O source and end of all beings! I do not wish to keep the body which was in touch with the Jains. Let me have the stamp of Your trident and Nandi on my body". He sang a Padigam. At once a Sivagana approached Appar through the grace of Lord Siva, and put the stamp of trident and Nandi on the shoulder of Appar.

Then Appar proceeded to Sirkali to meet Sambandhar. He fell at the feet of Sambandhar. Sambandhar addressed the Vellala saint: "O my beloved Appar".

Once, Sambandhar went in a palanquin to Tiruppuntiruti in the district of Tanjore to meet Appar. Appar went in advance and carried the palanquin. Sambandhar asked: "Where is Appar?" Appar replied: "Here am I carrying the palanquin". Sambandhar at once got down from the palanquin, embraced Appar and shed tears of love.

Appar went to Tiruchattimutram. He sang a Padigam and said: "O Lord, place Thy lotus-feet on my head before I leave this physical body". He heard an Akasavani or voice in the sky: "Come to Tirunallure". Appar acted accordingly and went to Tirunallure. Lord Siva placed His feet on the head of Appar. Appar prostrated on the ground. His heart was filled with indescribable delight.

Then Appar went to Tiruvambhar, Tirukadavur and Milalai. There was great famine in Milalai. Appar and Sambandhar were very much grieved at heart as the devotees of Lord Siva were starving. Lord Siva appeared in the dream of both and said: "Do not be afflicted, I shall give you gold-pieces". They found gold-pieces daily in the temple and fed the people sumptuously.

Appar and Sambandhar visited the temple at Vedaranyam in the district of Tanjore. Here, an old temple of Lord Siva had long remained with doors shut. The Vedas themselves had come and worshipped Siva in the temple and they now did not offer their worship, because people neglected the study of Vedas on account of the influence of Jainism. Sambandhar said to Appar: "Come, and sing that these doors may be opened". Appar sang and the doors opened. Sambandhar sang and the doors shut.

On one occasion, Appar was very hungry during his pilgrimage tour. Lord Siva created a tank and garden on the way and gave him food also.

Appar started on a journey to visit Mount Kailas. He had a tiresome journey. He had severe bruises on his feet. He heard a voice in the sky. It was the voice of Lord Siva. The voice said: "O Appar, wake up. Take a dip in this tank. You will see Me and Mt. Kailas in Tiruvayur". Appar took a dip in the tank and appeared in a temple in Tiruvayar on the banks of Kaveri. He came outside the tank and saw Siva and Sakti everywhere. He entered the temple and saw Mt. Kailas and the Lord Siva of Mt. Kailas. Appar rejoiced heartily at the marvellous sight and sang Padigams.

Finally Appar stayed at Pumpukalar near Tiruvalur and spent here the last years of his life. He was tested here by the Lord, in order to show his greatness to the people. When he was serving in the temple, gold and diamond appeared under his feet. Appar regarded them as stones and threw them away. On another occasion celestial damsels appeared before him and tempted him in a variety of ways; but Appar remained undisturbed in his meditation. He merged himself in the Light of lights, Lord Siva, when he was much advanced in age.

II

Appar laid the foundation of Saiva Siddhanta school of philosophy, by means of his poems. Appar's poems are full of imagination, spiritual insight, religious emotion and high spiritual realisation.

Appar was more learned than Sambandhar. He had a very powerful personality. He led an exemplary life as a Siva Bhakta. He put an end to the influence of Jainism. He always praised the five letters, the Panchakshara. He says: "The rare jewel of the Brahmins is the Veda with six Angas; the rare jewel for the Saivites is the Panchakshara". His exemplary life, mellifluous poetry, vast erudition and profound religious fervour attracted countless people. He had countless admirers and disciples. He had great influence. Appar's works consist of three hundred poems which form three books out of twelve in the Tamil collection of Saivite poetry known as Tirumurai.

Appar says: "Everything is the manifestation of Lord Siva. Siva is Narayana, Brahma, the four Vedas, the holiest, the oldest, the perfect. Though Siva is all these, He is none of these. He is without name, without birth, death or disease. He is at once the transcendent and immanent.

"Love of Lord Siva must be felt and manifested. Sing. Pray. Worship. Weep. Dance. Lord Siva is the music or melody in the song, the sweetness in the fruit, the thought in the mind, the lustre in the eyes. He is neither male nor female. He is without dimensions.

"Subdue the senses. Practise regular meditation. Practise Chariyai, Kriyai, Yoga and Jnana. Practise regular meditation. Develop dispassion (Vairagya). Transcend the three bodies. Unite the individual soul with the Supreme Soul or Lord Siva. You will attain eternal bliss and immortality. You can behold Lord Siva if you look for Him with the light of wisdom issuing forth from the wick of life, fed with the ghee of meditation, in the lamp of the mind, within the house of your body.

"Plough with truth. Plant the seed of desire for knowledge. Weed out falsehood. Irrigate the mind with the water of patience. Supervise your work by looking within or introspection and self-analysis. Build the fence of Yama and Niyama or right conduct and right rules. You will soon attain Sivanandam or eternal bliss of Siva.

"Regard your body as the temple of Lord Siva, your mind as the worshipper, truth as purity which is necessary for worship, the jewel of the mind as the Linga, love as the ghee, milk, etc. Perform Puja to Lord Siva thus. Lord Siva cannot be obtained without making the mind one-pointed and meditation on the Panchakshara."

May you all follow the precepts and teachings of Appar and attain the Siva-Pada, the immortal abode of eternal bliss!

TIRUJNANA SAMBANDHAR

Sambandhar took his birth in a Brahmin family in Sirkali in the district of Tanjore which is also known by the name Brahmapuri. He was born of Bhagavati and Sivapadahridayar.

Bhagavati and Sivapadahridayar went to the tank to take their bath. The child also accompanied his parents. They left the child on the bank and proceeded to take bath. The child cried aloud: "O father!" as he did not see his parents. The parents did not hear the cry of the child, but Lord Siva and Parvati heard his cry. They both appeared before the child. Parvati gave milk to the child. The child drank the milk of divine knowledge along with the milk. From that moment he began to sing the praises of Lord Siva in various temples. He sang soul-stirring, sublime Tevarams or odes. This incident occurred when the child was three years old.

The parents finished their bath and came near the child. Milk was flowing from his mouth and there were tears in his eyes. The parents asked: "My beloved child, who gave you milk?" The child sang a hymn and narrated everything to his parents. The parents rejoiced heartily and gave to the child the name Tiru-Jnana Sambandhar as he attained divine wisdom through the grace of Lord Siva and Parvati. He was also known by the name Pillayar.

Thereupon Sambandhar proceeded to Tirukkolakka. He sang a hymn or ode in the temple. Lord Siva presented him with a gold cymbal.

There was a devotee of Lord Siva in Tiruyerukkattampuliyur. He could play well on the musical instrument Yal. His name was Tirunilakantha Yalpanar. He went to Sirkali to pay his respects to Sambandhar. Sambandhar took him to the temple of Lord Siva and heard his music. Yalpanar prayed to Sambandhar and said: "Let me always live with you playing thy hymns on Yal. Grant me my prayer". Sambandhar agreed. Thereupon, Sambandhar and his parents and Yalpanar proceeded to Chidambaram and worshipped Nataraja. One day, Sambandhar saw the three thousand Brahmins of Chidambaram as the three thousand Siva Ganas.

Sambandhar wanted to worship the Lord at Aratturai. He walked on foot. He got tired and so he rested on the way in Maranpadi during the night. As he was a small boy, his tender feet were much affected by the long walk. The Lord of Aratturai appeared in the dream of the priests and told them: "Sambandhar is coming to Me. Take the pearl umbrella and the pearl palanquin which are now in the temple and hand them over to him". The priests woke up and went to the temple. They saw the articles which they saw in their dream there. They took them, went to Maranpadi and gave them to Sambandhar. They informed Sambandhar about the command of the Lord. Sambandhar knew this already as the Lord informed him also about this, in his dream.

Thereupon, the thread ceremony of Sambandhar was performed by the priests. Sambandhar did not study the Vedas and the Vedangas, but he repeated them and explained them to the priests. The priests were struck with wonder.

Appar heard all about the glory of Sambandhar. He came from Chidambaram to Sirkali to pay his respects to Sambandhar. Sambandhar came forward to receive Appar. They both spoke words of affection and love. Appar remained in the house of Sambandhar for some days.

The daughter of the king of Malaya country was suffering from an incurable disease. The king tried all sorts of medicines. Finally, he took her to the temple at Tiruppaccil Acciramam and left her there before the Lord Sambandhar visited the temple and saw the princess in an unconscious state. His heart melted. He sang a Padigam and worshipped Lord Siva. The last line in every stanza ends: "Is it right for the Lord to cause suffering to this girl?" At once, the princess became all right. She got up and prostrated at the lotus-feet of Sambandhar.

Then Sambandhar proceeded to Tiruppattisvaram temple. It was a very hot day. Lord Siva of Tiruppattisvaram temple sent a pearl palanquin through His Ganas to ward off the heat of the sun.

Sambandhar sang a Padigam and received one thousand gold coins from the Lord of Avadutturai. In the Padigam, he asks in every stanza: "Is this the way of Your looking after my interests? If You do not give me anything, is that Your grace?" He gave the gold coins to his father.

Sambandhar proceeded to Tirumarugal. There a traveller was bitten by a snake. His wife was bemoaning the death of her husband. Sambandhar sang a Padigam. The traveller was brought back to life.

There was severe famine at Tiruvilimilalai. Sambandhar received one measure of gold every day from the Lord at Tiruvilimilalai. He purchased provisions for this money and fed all Siva Bhaktas.

Kulaccirai, minister of the Pandyan king invited Sambandhar to his place. He was a devotee of Lord Siva. Mangayarkkarasi, the queen was also a devotee of Lord Siva. Sambandhar visited Madurai and worshipped the Lord there.

The Jains set fire to the camp of Sambandhar. Sambandhar sang a Padigam. The fire was extinguished, but the Pandyan king got severe fever. The doctors and the Jains were not able to cure him. The king requested Sambandhar to cure him. Sambandhar sang a Padigam in praise of the holy ashes and applied them to the king's body. At once, the king became all right.

Thereupon it was decided that both Sambandhar and the Jains were to put their writings into the fire and that if

Sambandhar's religion was the better one, the palm leaves which he put into the fire should not be burnt. Sambandhar came out successful in the test.

Afterwards, there was another test. The Jains said that the palm leaf which contained the writings of a true religion should go against the current of the Vaigai river. The minister said: "What is the punishment for those who are defeated in the test?" The Jains replied: "Those who are defeated will be hanged". The Jains put a palm leaf in the river. It went along the current of the river. Sambandhar wrote one of his poems and threw it into the Vaigai. It went against the current and reached the place known as Tiruvedangam. Sambandhar sang a Padigam to stop the palm leaf. It stopped. The minister ran, took the leaf and showed it to the king.

Then some of the Jains were hanged. The rest embraced Saivism. Sambandhar went with the king and queen to the temple at Madurai and praised the Lord there.

Sambandhar wanted to go to Tirukkollampudur to have Darsana of the Lord there, but there was flood in the river. The boatmen gave up the idea of crossing it. They tied the boat somewhere and left the bank. Sambandhar took the boat, sang a Padigam and went over to the other side along with his party.

The devotees of Sambandhar were blowing the trumpet of victory when they were travelling. The Buddhists became very jealous of this. They informed their spiritual head, Buddhanandi. Buddhanandi called Sambandhar for discussion.

Sambandhararanalayar, a disciple of Sambandhar who was recording all the songs of his master, sang a Padigam sung by Sambandhar and said: "A thunder will fall on the head of this Buddhanandi". At once, a thunder fell on the head of Buddhanandi. He died immediately. Some Buddhists ran away. Some others embraced Saivism and applied the holy ashes on their forehead.

Thereupon Sambandhar visited Tiruvottur. One man came to Sambandhar and said: "O Swami, all the palmyra seeds have become male palmyras. People are mocking at me. Kindly bless me". Sambandhar sang a Padigam. The male palmyras were converted into female palmyras.

In Mylapore, there lived a devotee of Siva named Sivanesa Chettiar. A daughter was born to him after doing penance. He gave her the name Poompavai. Sivanesar heard about the glory of Sambandhar and surrendered all his wealth and daughter to the saint. One day, Poompavai was bitten by a cobra, while she was gathering flowers in the garden. She died immediately. Sivanesar kept her bones in a pot and kept the pot in the Kannikaimatam. He decorated the pot with silk cloth. Sivanesar invited Sambandhar to the place. Sambandhar came to Mylapore and had Darsana of Kapalisvarar. The devotees informed Sambandhar about the death of Sivanesar's daughter. Sambandhar asked Sivanesar to bring the pot which contained the bones of his daughter. Sivanesar brought the pot at once. Sambandhar sang a Padigam. Poompavai came out of the pot just as Lakshmi emerged from the lotus. Sivanesar's heart was filled with intense delight. There was a rain of flowers from the celestial regions. Then Sambandhar went to Sirkali.

The Brahmins approached Sambandhar and said: "O Swami, you will have to marry a girl now in order to perform the sacrifices mentioned in the Vedas". Sambandhar agreed. The Brahmins and the father of Sambandhar selected the daughter of Nambiandar Nambi as the bride. The marriage ceremony was arranged at

Nallur Perumanam. Sambandhar went along with his chosen bride into the temple. When he-approached the Lord, he, his bride and his followers got merged in the Jyotis or the effulgence of the Lord.

Sambandhar says in one of his Padigams: "O foolish man, do not allow days to pass. Serve Lord Siva who has a blue neck. Hear His praise. Meditate on His form. Repeat always the Panchakshara. Live in the company of devotees of Siva. Serve them. His name will remove all evils and dangers likely to fall on you and your children. Worship Lord Siva. He will confer on you eternal bliss and immortality".

SUNDARAMURTI

There was a Brahmin by name Sadayanar in Navalur in Tamilnadu. He was very pious and devoted to Lord Siva. He had a pious son named Nambiyarurar or Alala Sundarar. He attained manhood. He was known by the name Sundaramurti Nayanar also.

Sundaramurti Nayanar was a great devotee of Lord Siva. He is one of the four Saiva Acharyas. Lord Siva of Tiruvennainallur appeared before Sundaramurti in the form of an aged Brahmin on the eve of his marriage. The Lord said that Sundarar was His bond slave and so ought to work for Him in His house. The name of the Lord is Taduttatkonda Isvar or the Lord who obstructed and saved Sundarar from Samsara.

Sundaramurti visited several temples. He went to Adigai Virattanam. Lord Siva appeared before him and placed His sacred feet on his head. Sundarar then went to Tiruvarur. Lord Siva made Sundarar His friend.

Kamalini was the maid servant of Umadevi at Kailas. She entertained a desire to marry Alala Sundarar. So she was forced to take birth in the world at Tiruvarur. She was named as Paravai. She came of age. Lord Siva of Tiruvarur appeared in the dream of the devotees and told them: "Arrange for the marriage of Paravai and Sundaramurti". Lord Siva informed Paravai and Sundarar also. Sundarar married Paravai and both lived happily.

There was a famine in Tiruvarur. Lord Siva appeared before Sundaramurti and gave him heaps of grain. It was impossible to remove this large quantity of grain. Sundaramurti asked Lord Siva to help him. The grain was removed to the house of Paravai by the Ganas, the agents of Lord Siva.

When Sundarar was at Tiruppugalur he asked for gold for his wife. He kept his head on bricks and slept. He woke up and found the bricks converted into gold. He got again gold on his way to Vriddhachalam. He threw the gold in the river Manimukta according to the Lord's command. He took it again in the tank at Tiruvarur. Lord Siva showed him the way to Tirukkudalaiyarrur.

Lord Siva gave Sundarar food when he was going to Tirukkarukavur. On another occasion Lord Siva begged food for Sundarar.

Sundaramurti went to Tiruvottiyur. He married Sangili, a great devotee of Lord Siva through the grace of Lord Siva. Aninditai, maid servant of Umadevi who lived in Kailas, took her birth as Sangili.

Sundaramurti requested Lord Siva to stay under the Magila tree when he was to swear to Sangili that he would not leave her. Sundarar wanted Sangili to go inside the temple, but Lord Siva already informed Sangili that He was under the tree and not inside the temple. Thereupon, Sangili asked Sundaramurti to come to the tree and not inside the temple, to take the oath. Sundaramurti had to give consent to Sangili's request. Later on, he broke the oath by going to Tiruvarur to see the Utsava leaving Sangili, and became blind.

Sundaramurti said to the Lord: "If it is just that You should make me blind, kindly give me a stick". Lord Siva gave a stick at Tiruvenpakkam. Sundarar's left eye became all right when he came to Kanjivaram. When he praised Lord Siva at Tiruvarur his right eye also became all right.

When Sundaramurti was passing through a street in Tiruppukoliyur he saw that some people were crying in a house and some people were rejoicing at the opposite house. He asked the people: "What was the matter in both the houses?" They said: "Two boys aged five took bath in a tank. One boy was devoured by a crocodile and the other boy escaped. The parents of the boy who was killed by the crocodile are bitterly weeping. The parents of the boy who escaped, are celebrating his thread-ceremony and so they are rejoicing."

Sundarar was greatly moved. He sang a Padigam in praise of Lord Siva-Avinasi. The crocodile brought the child to the shore through the order of Lord Yama. The parents of the boy greatly rejoiced and prostrated before Sundarar.

During the pilgrimage tour, Sundarar came to the bank of Kaveri. There was flood in the river. He wanted to have Darsana of Lord Siva at Tiruvayur. He sang a Padigam. The river gave way to Sundarar. He reached Tiruvayur and worshipped the Lord.

There was a great devotee of Lord Siva in Tiruperumangalam named Kalikamar. He was a Pillai by birth. He heard the news that Sundarar sent Lord Siva as a messenger to Paravai, and said: "A devotee has ordered the Lord to do some work. He has made the Lord his servant. That too for the sake of a woman. Is this man who has behaved like this, a devotee? I am a great sinner. My life has not yet departed from me as I have heard such news. I have not destroyed my ears, with an iron rod, which heard such news of a so-called devotee."

Sundarar came to know of the condition of Kalikamar Nayanar. He knew already that what he did was a grave error. He prayed to the Lord to pardon him. Lord Siva wanted to unite these two devotees. He caused the disease gastritis in Kalikamar, appeared in his dream and said: "This disease can be cured only by Sundarar". Kalikamar reflected: "It is better to bear the pains of this disease, than to be cured by Sundarar". The Lord commanded Sundarar: "Go and cure the disease of Kalikamar".

Sundarar sent a message to Kalikamar about his coming to him. Kalikamar thought: "Let me give up my life before Sundarar comes to cure me." He cut open his bowels and gave up his life. The wife of Kalikamar received Sundarar with great honour.

Sundarar said to the wife of Kalikamar: "I wish to cure the disease of your husband and live with him for some time". She kept quiet and asked those who were around her to tell Sundarar that her husband was not suffering from any disease and he was sleeping. Sundarar informed the people that he had a strong desire to see Kalikamar. Then they showed Kalikamar. Sundarar saw the dead body of Kalikamar. He also drew the sword and wanted to kill himself. Kalikamar came back to life through the grace of Lord Siva. He at once caught hold of the hands of Sundarar. Sundarar fell at the feet of Kalikamar. Kalikamar also prostrated at the lotus-feet of Sundarar. They both embraced each other. They both went to the temple of Lord Siva and worshipped Him. Thereupon, they proceeded to Tiruvarur.

Paravai was very much annoyed towards Sundarar for having left her and married Sangili. Sundarar requested Lord Siva to pacify Paravai. Lord Siva went twice to the house of Paravai, pacified her and united them both. The Lord acted the part of a messenger for His devotee. The Lord becomes a perfect slave of His sincere devotees.

Sundaramurti became quite disgusted with this worldly existence. He requested Lord Siva to take him back to Kailas. Then Lord Siva sent him a white elephant.

Sundaramurti sang the glories of Siva in different sacred places. These hymns are called Tevaram. They are collected in a book-form. All devotees sing Tevaram even today. The hymns sung by Sundaramurti, Appar or Tirunavukarasar and Tirujnana Sambandhar are called Tevaram. The hymns sung by Manickavasagar are called Tiruvasagam.

Sundaramurti had the Sakhya Bhava with Lord Siva. Therefore, he was quite friendly with the Lord, took any kind of liberty with Him and asked for gold, pearl garland, musk, a garland of precious stones, spectacles, clothes, fragrance, jewels, horses which can go with the swiftness of the wind, golden flowers, palanquins, one-third of the riches of Tiruvarur. He did not ask for these things on account of desire for enjoyment. He had no selfish desires. He did not keep them. He utilised them for those who depended on him.

Sundaramurti showed to the world the path of Sakhya Marga or Sakhya Bhava in Bhakti.

MANICKAVASAGAR

Manickavasagar was a Brahmin by birth. He took his birth in Tiruvadavur seven miles from Madurai on the banks of Vaigai river. He must have lived between 650 and 692 A.D. Some say that he flourished in the tenth or eleventh century. He secured the friendship of the king of Madurai, Arimardana Pandyan, and became his chief minister. He was also known by the name Vadavurar.

The Pandya king sent Manickavasagar with a lot of money to purchase horses for the State. Manickavasagar started on his journey. On his way, he heard the Kirtan of Siva in a garden in Tiruperundurai. Lord Siva assumed the form of a Siva Yogi and seated Himself, underneath a tree with His Siva Ganas as disciples. He came here to initiate Manickavasagar in Siva Jnana.

Manickavasagar fell at the feet of the Lord and surrendered himself. Lord Siva initiated Manickavasagar into the mysteries of Siva Jnana. Manickavasagar spent away all the money he had brought, in the construction of temples and feeding Siva Bhaktas. He renounced everything, wore a Kowpin and became a Sannyasin. The matter was reported to the king.

The Raja sent a letter to Manickavasagar and ordered him to see him at once. Manickavasagar did not pay any attention. Lord Siva said to Manickavasagar: "I will bring the horses on Avani Mulam. You go in advance. Give this diamond to the Raja". Manickavasagar proceeded to Madurai, gave the diamond to the Raja and said: "The horses will come here on Avani Mulam". The Raja became impatient. He did not get any information about the horses two days before Avani Mulam. He thought that Manickavasagar had cheated him. Therefore, he put Manickavasagar in jail and tormented him severely.

The horses came in the morning of Avani Mulam. Lord Siva assumed the form of a groom. How merciful is the Lord towards His devotees! The Raja was highly pleased. He released Manickavasagar from jail and made an apology to him. Through the Lila of the Lord, jackals came in the form of horses. All the horses were turned into jackals. The Raja became terribly angry. He again tortured Manickavasagar. He made him stand in the hot sand-bed of Vaigai river at 12 noon. At once the Lord caused flood in the river to cool His devotee. The whole town was inundated.

The ministers told the Raja that this calamity had happened on account of his ill-treatment of the great Mahatma. The Raja at once released Manickavasagar. He prostrated before him and requested him to stop the flood. As soon as Manickavasagar marched on the bank, the flood subsided. The Raja ordered all the subjects to put one basketful of mud on the bank of the river. All the breaches were made all right except that portion of the breach given to an old woman Vandi. She was in distress. Lord Siva Himself out of compassion appeared as a coolie before that old woman and offered His services to her in return for a handful of rice-flour. He was simply playing. He kept the mud in His hands. The Raja came to know that the coolie of Vandi did not do any work. He became very angry and beat the coolie with a stick. The blow was felt by the Raja and everyone in the town. The coolie vanished. The Raja came to know that this was the Lila of the Lord Siva. He recognised the glory of Manickavasagar also.

Thereupon Manickavasagar met Lord Siva. The Lord ordered him to visit all places of pilgrimage and then go to Chidambaram. Manickavasagar visited Tiruvannamalai, Kanjivaram and other places, sang his Tiruvasagam and lastly went to Chidambaram. Tirukoovai was written by him here.

Then Manickavasagar entered into discussion with a Buddhist teacher and defeated him. Goddess Sarasvati made the Buddhist teacher and his disciples dumb. Then the Buddhistic king approached Manickavasagar and said: "You made my teacher and all his disciples dumb. If you can make my dumb daughter speak, I and my subjects will embrace Saivism". Manickavasagar then put some questions to the dumb daughter of the king. She began to speak. Then the Buddhistic king and all his subjects became Saivites. Manickavasagar then made the Buddhistic teacher and his disciples speak.

Then Lord Siva approached Manickavasagar in the form of a Brahmin. Manickavasagar repeated the whole Tiruvasagam to the Brahmin. The Brahmin wrote down everything on the palmyra leaves and wrote in the end: "Manickavasagar repeated this, Tiruchittambala Udayar wrote this". The Brahmin kept this in the step of Panchakshara of the Chitsabhai. Then the Brahmins of Chidambaram showed this to Manickavasagar and requested him to tell the meaning of the verses. Manickavasagar said: "This Tillai Nataraja is the purport of these stanzas". He at once merged himself in the feet of Nataraja at the age of thirty-two.

The poems of Manickavasagar are fifty-two in number. They are all collected together under the title of Tiruvasagam. They are most beautiful, sublime and inspiring. They contain ornamental poetry. South Indians sing Tiruvasagam daily. The hearts of those who hear these hymns melt at once.

Dear readers! You can understand from the life of Manickavasagar, that Lord Siva becomes the slave of His devotees.

TIRUMULAR

Tirumula Nayanar was the author of Tirumandiram, one of the most authoritative works embodying the Siva doctrine.

He was a great Siva Yogi who had obtained the grace of Nandi, the door-keeper of Lord Siva. He came to South India from Kailas. He had a desire to see Agastya Rishi on Pothigai hills, Tirunelveli, Tamil Nadu. He went to Kedarnath, Nepal, Avimuktam, the Vindhyas, Kasi, Kalahasti, Tiruvalangadu, Kanjivaram, Tiruvadigai, Chidambaram and Perumbarrappuliyur. Then he came to Avaduturai and worshipped the Lord there.

He left this place and was moving on the banks of Kaveri. Here, some cows were crying on account of the death of cowherd Mula who lived in Sattanur. The Siva Yogi became very compassionate when he saw the condition of the cows. He entered into the body of the cowherd and drove the cows homeward. When he reached the cowherd's house, the wife of Mula approached him, but he would not permit her to touch him. He did not even talk to her. She was much afflicted at heart and spent a sleepless night. Then those who saw him said that he was a great Yogi. The Siva Yogi who entered the body of Mula sat in meditation and entered into Samadhi. He came down from his Samadhi and proceeded to enter into his old body. He did not find the body in the place. Through his Yogic vision, he found out that Lord Siva wanted that he should write a book on Saiva philosophy which would be useful to the people of South India and He hid his body for this purpose.

Then he went to Avaduturai, meditated upon the Lord and wrote out the doctrine of Saiva philosophy in three thousand stanzas at the rate of one stanza in one year. He rendered into Tamil the Saiva doctrine of the Sanskrit Saiva Agamas. His work became the foundation upon which the later structure of Saiva Siddhanta philosophy was built. After finishing this great work, he went back to Kailas or the world of Lord Siva.

Tirumular gives a description of the fruits that can be obtained by the practice of the eight limbs of Raja Yoga. The Yogi obtains the blessing of Uma and attains Amarapati by the practice of Yama (self-restraint). He attains Sivapadam by the practice of Niyama (religious canons). He hears Nadam by the practice of Asana (pose). He attains a stage by the practice of Pranayama (restraint of breath) in which all the gods eulogise him. He attains the form of Siva by the practice of Pratyahara (abstraction of senses) and the gods become confused as they cannot differentiate him from Siva. He can go anywhere including the worlds of Brahma and Vishnu by the practice of Dharana (concentration). He can walk into any place just as one can walk on earth. He attains the abode of Brahma, Vishnu, Rudra and Indra by the practice of Dhyana (meditation). He frees himself from all the Upadhis or fetters and unites with Lord Siva (Tat Padam) by the practice of Samadhi (superconscious state).

BASAVANNA

Basavanna was the great Vira Saiva socio-religious teacher. He was also known by the names Basavaraja, Basavesvara. He was a deep thinker. He brought about vital changes in social adjustment and thought.

He was the Saivite reformer of the Karnataka state. He gave the present form to the cult known as Sivachara.

He flourished in the twelfth century. He was born in a Brahmin family. He left the practices of his own community as they were too ritualistic and formal. He joined the Vira Saiva cult which was very prevalent at that time.

He was the Chief Minister in the court of king Bijjala in Kalyan. He was a very popular minister. He was very kind, noble, modest, very lovable and courageous. He had intense reliance on God. People deified him and worshipped him. He would freely mix with common people. He redressed their grievances. He was in close intimacy with them. He worked very hard for the dissemination of his faith. He created many enemies on account of this active propaganda. There was civil disturbance in the country. Bijjala met his end in this disturbance, Basavanna's life too ended in this period of agitation, although it is difficult to find out how he exactly met his end.

He was a reformer. He became the leader of the Vira Saiva movement. He established a cult that is accepted today by many people. It developed a school of poor priests. It abolished the old priestly class. It adopted the vernacular as the medium for inculcating the supreme truth into the people. It gave to women an important place in religious and social life. It prescribed one ideal of realisation for every individual, high or low.

Basavanna made great sacrifice for Truth. People accepted him as a teacher. His sayings have come straight from his heart. They go straight to the heart. They are simple, direct and powerful. His rules of conduct are lofty and admirable. He was a sincere seeker after Truth and could make great sacrifices for attaining the Truth. He was all love and kindness. Love for all life or universal love was the central teaching of Basavanna.

Chapter XII
SIVA BHAKTAS

SAINTS AND SAGES

Who is a saint? He who lives in God or the Eternal, who is free from egoism, likes and dislikes, selfishness, vanity, mine-ness, lust, greed and anger, who is endowed with equal vision, balanced mind, mercy, tolerance, righteousness, cosmic love and who has divine knowledge is a saint.

Saints and sages are blessings to the world at large. They are the custodians of superior divine wisdom, spiritual powers and inexhaustible spiritual wealth. Even kings bow their heads at their lotus-feet. King Janaka said to Yajnavalkya: "O venerable sage, I am grateful to your exalted Holiness for obtaining the ancient wisdom of the Upanishads through your lofty and sublime instructions. I offer my whole kingdom at thy feet. Further I am thy servant. I will wait on thee like a servant".

Such is the magnanimous nature of saints and sages. Their very existence inspires others and goads them to become like them and attain the same state of bliss as achieved by them. Had it not been for their existence, there would not have been spiritual uplift and salvation for you all. Their glory is indescribable. Their wisdom is unfathomable. They are deep like the ocean, steady like the Himalayas, pure like the Himalayan snow, effulgent like the sun. One crosses this terrible ocean of Samsara or births and deaths, through their grace and Satsanga or association with them. To be in their company is highest education. To love them is highest happiness. To be near them is real education.

They wander from village to village and disseminate divine knowledge. They move from door to door and impart wisdom. They take a little for their bare maintenance and give the highest education, culture and enlightenment to the people. Their very life is exemplary. Whether they deliver lectures or not, whether they hold discourses or not, it matters little.

Saints and sages only can become real advisers of kings because they are selfless and possess highest wisdom. They only can improve the morality of the masses. They only can show the way to attain eternal bliss and immortality. Sivaji had Swami Ramadas as his adviser. King Dasaratha had Maharshi Vasishtha as his adviser.

Study the 'Lives of Saints', you are inspired at once. Remember their sayings, you are elevated immediately. Walk in their footsteps, you are freed from pain and sorrow. Therefore, the book 'Lives of Saints' must be your constant companion. It must be in your pocket. It must be underneath your pillow.

Do not superimpose defects on them on account of your Dosha-drishti or evil-eye. You cannot judge their merits. Be humble and sit at their feet. Serve them with your heart and soul, and clear your doubts. Get instructions and practise them in right earnest. You will certainly be blessed.

Every school, every college, every boarding house, every jail, every institution, every house, should have a saint for their guidance. Saints are in abundance. You do not want them. You do not wish to approach them. You do not wish to serve them. You do not aspire for higher things. You are perfectly satisfied with some broken shells and glass-pieces. There is no thirst or spiritual hunger in you for achieving higher, divine knowledge and inner Peace.

There is no caste among saints and sages. Do not look to their caste. You will not be benefited. You cannot imbibe their virtues. In higher religion, there is neither caste nor creed. Cobblers, weavers and untouchables had become the best saints. Wisdom and Self-realisation are not the monopoly of Brahmins alone. South Indian Brahmins pay respects and give food only to the Brahmin Dandi Sannyasins. This is a serious mistake and grave blunder. What a sad state! That is the reason why saints do not visit South India. Punjab, Sindh and Gujarat have devotion to all saints. Hence, they move in these parts and people derive much spiritual benefit from them.

May this world be filled with good saints and sages! May you all attain the supreme goal through their Satsanga and advice! May the blessings of saints and sages be upon you all!

MARKANDEYA

Markandeya was a great devotee of Lord Siva. His father Mrikandu performed rigorous austerities to get a son. Lord Siva appeared before him and said: "O Rishi, do you want a good son who will die in his sixteenth year or a bad and foolish son who will live for a long time?" Mrikandu replied: "O my venerable Lord, let me have a good son".

The boy came to know about his fate and began to worship Lord Siva whole-heartedly with intense faith and devotion. The boy entered into deep meditation and Samadhi on the day decreed as the day of his death. The messengers of Lord Yama were not able to approach him. Hence, Yama himself went to take away his life. The boy prayed to Lord Siva for protection and embraced the

Linga. The Yama threw his noose round the Linga and the boy. Lord Siva came out of the Linga immediately and killed Yama to protect the boy. Lord Siva was called Mrityunjaya and Kala-kala from that day.

Then the Devas approached Lord Siva and said: "O adorable Lord, salutations unto Thee. Pardon Yama for his mistake. O ocean of mercy, bring him back to life". Then Lord Siva brought Yama back to life at the request of the gods. He also conferred a boon to the boy Markandeya that he should live for ever as a boy of sixteen years of age. He is a Chiranjivi. In South India, even now men and women bless a boy when he does prostration to them: "Live as a Chiranjivi like Markandeya".

Through Tapas and meditation you can achieve anything in the three worlds.

THE STORY OF RISHABHA YOGI

This story is related in seven chapters in the Brahmottara Kanda of Skanda Purana.

Mandara, a Brahmin of Avanti was a man of great erudition. But he lived with a prostitute named Pingala. Rishabha, a great Siva Yogi, was the guest of Mandara one day. Both Mandara and Pingala served the Yogi with intense faith and devotion and obtained his grace.

After some time both of them died. Mandara was born as the son of Vajrabahu, the king of Dasarna. When he was in the womb of his mother Sumati, the other wives of the king gave poison to Sumati on account of jealousy. Both the child and Sumati became very sick. They could not be cured of their illness. They were abandoned in the forest by the order of the king.

They were taken by a rich merchant through the grace of the Lord and were protected by him nicely. The child grew worse day by day and died. The mother was wailing bitterly over the death of her son. Now Rishabha appeared on the scene, consoled the mother and imparted her philosophical instructions. But she could not be consoled. Then the Yogi touched the dead child with the Bhasma of Siva. The child came back to life. He made the mother and son quite healthy and beautiful through his Yogic powers. He gave the name Bhadrayu to the boy and taught him the Siva Kavacha. He gave him a sword, a conch and the strength of ten thousand elephants. He gave him also the Bhasma of Siva. Then the Yogi left the place.

Bhadrayu and Sunaya, the son of the merchant, lived together happily. Bhadrayu heard that his father had been deposed and imprisoned by Hemaratha, the king of Magadha. He went with Sunaya, defeated the enemies and freed his father, all the ministers and the queens who had been imprisoned by the king of Magadha. He left the king of Magadha and his retinue as prisoners in the possession of his father and returned home. He did not reveal his identity to his father. The father admired the valour of the boy and expressed his keen sense of indebtedness to the boy. Thus Rishabha, the great Siva Yogi showed his grace to Bhadrayu who as Mandara, had once served him with faith and devotion despite his loose living.

Chitravarma, the king of Aryavarta had a daughter by name Simantini. Chandrangada, the son of Indrasena, the son of Nala and Damayanti of Nishadha, married Simantini. Chandrangada was drowned in Yamuna soon after marriage, while he was sporting in a boat. The Naga girls took Chandrangada to Takshaka, their chief in Nagaloka.

Simantini learnt from an astrologer of the court that she would become a widow in her fourteenth year. Therefore, she got initiation into the worship of Lord Siva on

Mondays and at Pradosha, from Maitreyi, wife of the sage Yajnavalkya. She continued the worship even after she became a widow.

Takshaka sent Chandrangada back to the banks of Yamuna as he wished that he should live with his wife. One evening on Monday, when Simantini went to the river for taking a bath, she met her husband.

Chandrangada defeated the enemy king who had deposed his father in his absence and replaced his father on the throne. Simantini and Chandrangada were reunited by the grace of Lord Siva.

Simantini used to adore and give presents to Brahmins and their wives every Monday in honour of Lord Siva and Parvati. Two Brahmin boys approached the king of Vidarbha for getting money for their marriage. The king asked the boys to be dressed as man and wife and go to Simantini. He did this in order to test the devotion of Simantini. The boys acted accordingly. Simantini laughed and adored them as Lord Siva and Parvati. One of the boys become a woman. The father of the boy who had become a woman by the power of Simantini requested the king to help him out of the trouble. The king prayed to Parvati. Parvati refused to interfere with the act of Her devotee, but promised a son to the father of the boy. The two boys had to marry and live as husband and wife.

Simantini had a daughter by name Kirtimalini. This Kirtimalini was really the prostitute Pingala who had obtained the grace of Rishabha, the Siva Yogi, by serving him with great devotion. Rishabha went to Chandrangada and asked him to marry Kirtimalini to Bhadrayu. The Siva Yogi related the whole story of Bhadrayu to Chandrangada. Chandrangada gave his daughter Kirtimalini to Bhadrayu in marriage. He invited the father of Bhadrayu to the marriage. When Vajrabahu saw the son-in-law of Chandrangada, he found him to be the very boy who had defeated the king of Magadha and given him his kingdom. The story of the mother and son, Sumati and Bhadrayu, was related to Vajrabahu. Vajrabahu took his queen and son with the daughter-in-law to his kingdom.

The great Siva Yogi Rishabha, reunited his devoted worshippers Mandara and Pingala. Though they led a loose life they were saved and made happy through the grace of the Siva Yogi, Rishabha. One day Bhadrayu went to the forest. He heard the cry of a Brahmin's wife, who was being carried away by a tiger. The king tried his level best to save the woman but could not kill the tiger. The Brahmin abused the king and said: "O timid king, you have no valour to kill the tiger. What sort of king you are!" Bhadrayu promised to give anything including his wife to the Brahmin. The Brahmin demanded the queen. Bhadrayu gave his queen to the Brahmin and prepared himself to enter the fire and lose his life which was not worth living thereafter.

Then, Lord Siva and Parvati appeared before the king who was a great Siva-Bhakta and said: "We have done this to test your strength and Dharma". Thereupon, Lord Siva gave Siva Sayujya to Bhadrayu, Kirtimalini, their parents, the Vaisya and his son, according to the request of Bhadrayu and his wife. The Brahmin's wife was once again brought to life and they both received the blessing of Lord Siva.

The story clearly reveals the glory of Siva Bhakti, the greatness of Siva Bhaktas, the importance of Siva Puja on all days, particularly on Mondays and in Pradosha, the hour just at sunset.

PUSHPADANTA

Pushpadanta was a great devotee of Lord Siva. He was the chief of the Gandharvas. His teeth were like the petals of the jasmine flower. Hence he was called by the name Pushpadanta, 'flowery toothed'.

Pushpadanta had the power of moving in the air. He used to collect flowers from the garden of king Vahu at Banares, in order to worship Lord Siva. As he had the power of moving in the air, the gardeners were not able to detect him. The gardeners suspected that some mysterious being with some supernatural powers, was stealthily plucking the flowers of the garden. They made a device to catch him.

They scattered some flowers which had been offered to Lord Siva in different places in the garden. They thought that the mysterious being would tread on the flowers.

As usual Pushpadanta visited the garden to pluck flowers. He walked on the flowers which were scattered on the ground. He unconsciously insulted Lord Siva and lost his power of moving in the air. He was caught by the gardeners and brought before the king.

Pushpadanta recited a hymn to Lord Siva to propitiate Him and free himself from the fear of the king whom he had offended by the theft of the flowers. He again obtained the power to move in the air through the grace of Lord Siva.

This celebrated hymn is known by the name 'Mahimnastava'. It is full of sublime, soul-elevating thoughts. It is sung daily in the Siva temples of Northern India, during evening prayers and Arati. This hymn touches the heart of all. It is sonorous, rhythmical and musical and full of profound devotion. You should get this by heart and repeat it daily. You will attain supreme, immortal, blissful abode of Lord Siva.

KANNAPPA NAYANAR

Tinnanar, known as Kannappar, was born of Nagan, the king of the Vyadhas (hunters), in Uduppur, in South India. King Nagan was a great Bhakta of Lord Subrahmanya. From his boyhood, Tinnanar was well trained in the skill of a hunter and archery and in his prime age, he had to assume the reins of government which his old father bestowed on him. One day, Tinnanar went out for a hunt with some of his followers. While wandering in the forest they came across a hog, escaping from a net. They at once chased the hog for a long time, up and down the hills. After a long time, Tinnanar killed the hog and as they were much tired due to the long chasing, they at once arranged to cook the flesh of the animal and it was removed to another place in the Kalahasti Hill which was nearby. While walking towards the hill one of the followers of Tinnanar suggested to him to pay a visit to Kudumi Thevar, the presiding deity of the hills, and they proceeded to have Darsana of the Lord on the hill.

While climbing up the hill Tinnanar felt as if some great burden which was on him uptill now, was gradually diminishing and he decided now to go to the temple nearby, have Darsana of the Lord there and then to take their meals. As soon as he came near the temple, to his great joy he saw a Siva Linga. At the very sight of Isvara, he was transformed to an embodiment of love and devotion and extreme joy. Like a mother who met her child that was missing for long, Tinnanar was merged in deep feeling of divine ecstasy and Prem. Ha! What a boundless and inexpressible and illimitable joy and exhilaration he had at the very sight of Lord Siva! He began to cry, weep and shed tears of joy and love towards the Lord. He forgot everything about his meals and his followers and even his own body.

He felt very much for the loneliness of the Lord on the hills without being protected against the animals and others that might do harm to Him, and he decided to keep watch over the temple throughout the night against any danger from animals or evil-doers. On seeing that the Lord was hungry, he at once ran out to prepare meals for the Lord out of the meat he had got by killing the hog. He carefully took the flesh, tasted it and thus selected the pieces which were palatable and roasted them. The remaining portion he threw away as bad. Then he proceeded towards the river to fetch water for the Abhisheka and he got the water in his mouth. On the way, he plucked some flowers and kept them in the locks of his hair. With these preparations he entered the temple, removed the old flowers that were lying on the Lord by shoe, did Abhisheka with the water in his mouth and decorated Him with the flowers he had on his locks of hair. Then he offered the Prasad of meat to the Lord. Finishing all these, with bow and arrow in his hand he kept a keen watch over the temple by standing in front of the temple throughout the night. Early in the morning, he went out for hunt to bring Prasad for the Lord.

When Tinnanar left for hunting, the temple priest, Sivakasariar, an earnest and sincere devotee of Lord Sankara, came to the temple and to his great surprise and disappointment, saw bones and flesh all round the Lord and the decorations have been spoiled. But he could not identify the man who has done such an act, and meddled with the sanctity of the place. So uttering the necessary Mantras, he cleaned the place and performed his usual

Puja for the Lord and recited the prayers. After the Puja he closed the temple and went out.

Tinnanar now returned with the Prasad of meat and flesh and as before, he removed the old decorations done by the priest, decorated in his own way as usual, and offered Prasad. At night, he kept vigil and keen watch over the temple. Early in the morning, he went out to bring Prasad. Thus he was with the Lord serving Him for five days and in spite of the entreaties of his parents to come home, he persisted in remaining with the Lord and Lord alone.

Sivakasariar, who was vexed with the incident being repeated day by day, complained to the Lord and requested Him to put an end to these mishappenings. Lord Siva appeared in the priest's dream and narrated to him what was happening in the temple during the absence of the priest and told him also that what all actions Tinnanar was doing was only out of pure, unsophisticated love that he bore towards the Lord. Further, the Lord said: "I welcome, and rather I am immensely pleased with the mouthful of water by which he is doing my Abhisheka. This has greater value to Me than by the Tirthas of the Ganga. Whatever action that is performed out of pure and deep love and faith, I merit it with greater value than those rituals and austerities done by the Vedic injunctions". Then Lord Gangadhar asked the priest to come to the temple next day and hide himself behind the Murti and witness what Tinnanar does.

Tinnanar, after bringing the Prasad, arranged in his own usual way for the Abhisheka and decoration of the Lord. Now Lord Siva willed that the priest, Sivakasariar should see and feel the degree of devotion and faith that Tinnanar was having for Him. So, while Tinnanar was doing the Puja and offering the Prasad of meat, to his great astonishment, he saw the Lord shedding tears of blood, in the right eye. He got perplexed and was at a loss to know what to do. He ran hither and thither to bring some leaves for stopping the bleeding but found they were of no use. He wept bitterly, cursed himself for being unable to stop the bleeding from the eye. At last, a plan came to him. He at once plucked out his right eye with his arrow and fixed it on the right eye of the Lord. To his great joy and ecstasy, he saw the bleeding stopped. While he was dancing in divine ecstasy for having cured the bleeding, all on a sudden, he perceived that the left eye also was bleeding. Though he was overtaken by surprise and sorrow, the previous plan came to him and he decided to pierce his left eye with his arrow with the intention of plucking it out and fixing it on the left eye of the Lord. But when his both eyes were gone, how could he see the bleeding on the left eye of the Lord so as to stop it by fixing his own eye? Hence, in order to identify the left eye of the Lord, he first fixed it up with the shoe on his right foot, and began to pierce his own left eye with the arrow in his hand. But Isvara will not be so cruel as to see His Bhaktas suffer so much. On the spot, the Lord appeared and addressed Tinnanar as *'Kannappa'* and stopped him from plucking out the left eye. He was much pleased with the filial devotion and staunch faith that Kannappar had for Him and kept him by His right side.

The above story of Kannappar is illustrative of the highest degree of devotion and faith that was evinced by the Bhakta towards Lord Siva, even though he was a hunter by caste and never cared for the rituals and austerities by which the Lord should be worshipped. It was only mere love and intense devotion to the Lord that bestowed on him the greatest boon from the Lord, i.e., Self-realisation. It is only a matter of six days that he performed the Puja ceremonies to the Lord in his own way, but the amount of devotion and love he had to the Lord, was boundless.

May the blessings of Kannappar be upon you all! May you all attain the highest goal of human life by following the example of Kannappa Nayanar, the great South Indian Bhakta of Lord Siva!

SIRUTONDA NAYANAR

Paranjotiar of Tiruchettangudi was general under the Chola king. He was skilful in all the methods of warfare and had won many a war for the Chola king. In spite of the fact of his being a general, his devotion to Lord Siva and Siva Bhaktas was increasing. As a Bhakta of Lord Siva, he was noted for his humility and he was aptly named Sirutonda Nayanar. He left his post of general and spent his lifetime in worshipping Lord Siva and serving and feeding Siva Bhaktas. Never a day was known when he took food without feeding Siva Bhaktas. Such was the intensity of his devotion. In this way, he was happily living with his wife and a son, Seeralan by name.

Once, it happened that Lord Siva in the guise of Vairavar came to his doors for Bhiksha. Just at that moment, Sirutondar had gone out to get some Siva Bhaktas for feeding. Vairavar waited for a while and there came Sirutondar returning from his quest of Sadhus, quite disappointed as he found none to feed with. To his great joy Vairavar was waiting at his doors. Now Vairavar, expressing his wish to dine in his house, informed him that he would do so provided Sirutondar complied with his wishes. On getting his consent, Vairavar told him that he required the cooked flesh of a boy of 5 years old with robust health and without any deformities of mind and body. Though at first the Bhakta was bewildered in getting the thing required, at last happily decided to offer their own son, Seeralan, for the feast of Vairavar.

Both the wife and husband hurried up in preparing the required meals, the mother keeping her son on the lap and the father cutting the throat, and every limb was cooked except the head. Even this part was nicely prepared after getting the consent of Vairavar. When everything was prepared, Sirutondar and Vairavar began to take their meals. But at the moment Vairavar stopped and refused to take food unless Sirutondar got his son by his side for eating. Though Sirutondar told Vairavar that his son would not serve the purpose at that hour, still Vairavar insisted. Sirutondar got up and with increased devotion and staunch faith in Him, went outside his house and called out the name of his son, Seeralan, as if his son was coming from school. But to his astonishment, his son responded to his call and was coming down the other end of the street as if from school. With his son, he entered the house. But now, neither the cooked flesh not Vairavar were to be seen. What a dismay? Instead, Lord Mahadev appeared on the scene with His consort Parvati and Lord Subrahmanya by His side, blessed both the husband and wife for their intense love towards Him, and took Sirutondar and his family along with Him. Such was the reward for the Bhakta who offered his son's flesh for the feeding of the Sadhu.

May you all develop intense love and faith to the Lord! May the blessings of Sirutondar be upon us all!

LORD SIVA'S MOTHER

In ancient days, there lived a rich merchant named Dhanadatta in Karikal in South India. He had no child. He worshipped Lord Siva. He had a daughter through the grace of the Lord. The child was called by the name Punitavati. Punitavati came to be later on called by the name Karikal Ammaiar also. She is counted as one amongst Nayanars (the famous Siva Bhaktas of South India).

Punitavati was very intelligent, beautiful, pious. She chanted the names and praise of Lord Siva. She applied holy ash to her forehead.

She married Paramadatta, the son of a rich merchant at Nagapattam. Paramadatta also was beautiful and intelligent. He possessed good character. He lived in his father-in-law's place with the permission of his father.

Punitavati used to feed with intense devotion and joy, the Bhaktas day and night and hear them singing the names of Lord Siva. She always remembered the utterance of the Vedas: "Let the guest be a God unto you—*Atithi devo bhava*". She and her husband took the food that remained after serving the devotees, as if it were nectar.

One day, a wandering mendicant came and gave two ripe mangoes to Paramadatta. Paramadatta gave them to his wife and attended to his business. A devotee came and asked Punitavati to give him something to eat as he was very hungry. The food was not ready. So she gave him one of the mangoes and some milk.

Paramadatta returned home and took his food. Punitavati served him with mango fruit that remained. Paramadatta found it very delicious. He asked her to bring the other fruit also. She prayed to Lord Siva. Immediately, a mango fell into her hands. It looked exactly like the one served before. She gave it to her husband. He found it a thousand times more palatable than the first one. He asked Punitavati: "My beloved Punitavati, where did you get it from?" She narrated everything. Paramadatta said: "Get me another". Punitavati got another mango in the twinkling of an eye.

Paramadatta was struck with awe and wonder. He understood that his wife was a beloved devotee of Lord Siva. He reflected within himself: "I am a great sinner. I have treated a great devotee of Lord Siva as my servant. I cannot consider her as my wife any longer. It will be a great sin to leave her alone. But what to do now?"

He was in a dilemma. Finally, he resolved to part from her. He told his wife that he was going out on professional business. He obtained her permission and proceeded to Madurai. He settled there and married another wife. The second wife gave birth to a daughter. Paramadatta named her Punitavati.

Punitavati was anxiously awaiting the return of her husband at the promised time. She had no news of him. She became very miserable and unhappy. After some time, she came to know about the whereabouts of her husband. She proceeded to Madurai and met her husband.

Paramadatta welcomed her with intense joy and prostrated at her feet. He said to his wife: "I am a worldly man. I am passionate and greedy. You are a goddess. I cannot take you now as my wife. Pray, pardon me".

Punitavati replied: "My lord, I have preserved my youth and beauty for your sake only. As you do not want me, I shall seek my Lord Siva now."

She distributed all the jewels to those assembled around. She worshipped the pious Brahmins and shook off all the flesh by the power of Yoga and looked as a mere skeleton. She marched northward.

She came to Mount Kailas. She thought it a sin to walk with one's feet in the holy Himalayas. She moved on her head through the power of her austerities.

Parvati asked Lord Siva: "Who is that person, O Lord, who is coming towards us?" Lord Siva replied: "That pious woman is My Mother, who nourished My devotees".

Lord Siva got up, moved a few steps forward, welcomed Punitavati and said: "My dear Mother, are you keeping fit?"

Punitavati fed the devotees like a mother. The Lord makes no distinction between Himself and His devotees. He has said: "The devotees form My heart and I, theirs. They do not think of anyone other than Me and I other than them".

The supreme Lord abides in the hearts of all beings. Therefore, the guests deserve worship. The Srutis declare: "*Atithi devo bhava* — Let the guest be your God."

THE SIXTY-THREE NAYANAR SAINTS

The Nayanars were the sincere and ardent devotees of Lord Siva. Some were the contemporaries of Appar and Sambandhar. Only a few had made a study of the Agamas. The rest were pure and simple Bhaktas only. They served the devotees of Lord Siva and made absolute self-surrender to the Lord. They were quite ignorant of philosophy. They practised Chariyai. They cleaned the temple premises, made garlands of flowers for the Lord, lighted the temple lamps, planted flower gardens and fed the devotees of Lord Siva and served them. Worship of Siva Bhaktas was regarded even superior to the worship of Lord Siva Himself.

What is wanted is true devotion. Kannappa, the hunter, was totally ignorant of Saiva doctrine, philosophy or worship, but attained within six days, the highest place possible for devotees of Siva through the intensity of his devotion. The nature of Kannappa's devotion was quite different from that of the ordinary worshippers of Siva.

The names of some of the Nayanars are: Nedumara Nayanar, Kannappa Nayanar, Sirutondar, Appudi Adigal, Muruga Nayanar, Tirunilanakka Nayanar, Kunguliakkalaya Nayanar, Gananata Nayanar, Seraman Perumal Nayanar, Somasi Mara Nayanar, etc.

Tirunilakantha Nayanar was a potter of Chidambaram. Enadi Nayanar was a Sanar (toddy-drawer). Tirukkurippu-tondar was a washerman. Adipatta Nayanar was a fisherman by caste. Nesa Nayanar was a weaver by caste. Siva Bhaktas of the higher castes ate with the Bhaktas of other castes. They had no caste-distinctions. They regarded that a life of devotion to Lord Siva was much more important than the little distinctions of caste, etc.

Tirunilanakka Nayanar was one day performing the Puja. A spider fell upon the image of Siva. His wife at once blew it away and spat on the place where it fell. The saint was very much annoyed. He thought that the image had become impure. He wanted to abandon his wife. But Lord Siva appeared before him in his dream and showed the saint how his whole body except where it had been spat upon, was blistered owing to the fall of the spider. This opened the eyes of the saint. He now realised that Bhakti is more important than the knowledge of the Sastras.

Sirutondar killed his child with his own hands and prepared meat to please the devotee of Siva. He was prepared even to go against the rules of the scriptures, in order to practise what he considered as Siva virtue. He was not a man of great erudition. He was not a philosopher and a Yogi, but he had intense devotion to the devotees of Siva. What a great sacrifice he did in order to serve the devotee! The Lord appeared before him with Parvati and Lord Subrahmanya and blessed Sirutondar. The devotee and the dish of meat disappeared. Sirutondar went out and called his son. The son came running towards him. The Lord does anything and everything for His Bhakta.

Kungilik-Kalaiya Nayanar was supplying incense to the Lord in the temple of Tirukkadevur. He lost all his wealth. There was nothing left in the house. Then his wife gave him a plate and asked him to buy some rice in exchange for it. The Nayanar bought incense and took it to the temple. The Lord blessed his wife that night with abundant wealth and asked the Nayanar to go to his house and take his meal. The Nayanar came to know that the king was not able to make erect the Siva Lingam in the temple of Tiruppanandal. He tied the rope which was attached to the Lingam round his own neck and pulled the Lingam to make it erect. The Lingam stood upright. Everybody had now proof of the intensity of the Nayanar's devotion. Nayanar had no knowledge of the Vedas or the Agamas, but he was a true devotee of the Lord. What is wanted is sincere Bhakti. Study of scriptures makes one proud of his learning and keeps him away from God.

Kannappa Nayanar plucked his own eye and replaced Siva's bleeding eye with his own. He resolved to give his second eye also. But Lord Siva stopped him from doing it. Kannappa regained his eye-sight and became, from that moment, a God himself and took his seat by the side of Lord Siva. He did not chant Rudra and Chamakam. He was not a Brahmin. He was a hunter. He did his worship in his own way by bathing the image with the water carried in his own mouth, threw the flowers down from his own tuft and offered the best part of the cooked pig after examining with his teeth. Pandits and Sastris do thousand and one Rudras, and yet they are far from God, because there is not an iota of real devotion. They have a stony, barren, sin-hardened heart.

Iyarpagai Nayanar was observing the vow of giving everything that the devotees of Siva wanted. Lord Siva wanted to test him. He came in the garb of a Brahmin Siva devotee, in the garb of a libertine. The devotee asked the Nayanar: "Give me your wife". Nayanar willingly gave his wife. His relatives objected and fought with him. The Nayanar escorted the pseudo-Yogi into the forest. The pseudo-Yogi vanished to reappear in his real form of Siva on the sacred bull.

Eripatta Nayanar killed the elephant and five men as the elephant destroyed the flowers which were in the possession of Sivakam Andar for the worship of the Lord. Lord Siva appeared and saved the king and the Nayanar and the elephant with the five people who were lying dead.

Arivattaya Nayanar began to cut his throat as he was not able to give the usual food of red rice to Lord Siva. Lord Siva stopped him from cutting his throat and took him to His abode.

Murti Nayanar used to offer sandalwood paste to Lord Siva at Madurai. When sandalwood was not available he began to rub his elbow very hard upon the sandstone. Lord Siva was moved. The Nayanar was máde the king. He reached the abode of Siva.

Nanda, the untouchable saint, entered the fire and came out of it in the form of a holy ascetic with sacred thread on his shoulders through the grace of Lord Siva.

Tirukkuripputondar was a washerman by caste. He washed the clothes of the devotees of Siva. Lord Siva wanted to test him. He appeared as a poor man with a very dirty rag. The saint washed the rag. As there was a very heavy rain, he could not dry the rag. He was very much afflicted at heart. He began to dash his head against the stone on which he washed the clothes. Lord Siva appeared before him and gave him salvation.

Nami Nandi Adigal lighted the lamp with water through the grace of Lord Siva. A devotee can do anything through the grace of the Lord.

Kali Kamba Nayanar used to welcome the devotees of Siva to his house and feed them after washing their feet. His wife helped him to do that. On one occasion, one who had been some time back their servant, came into the house as a Siva devotee. The Nayanar as usual began to wash his feet but his wife refused to help him. Nayanar cut off her hands and did the service himself. He also attained the abode of Lord Siva.

Kalianayanar used to light the temple lamps with oil supplied by himself. He lost all his property. He thought of selling his wife but no one would purchase her. Then he resolved to offer his own blood in the place of oil. When he was trying to do this Lord Siva blessed him.

Kanampulla Nayanar was lighting the lamp in Siva temples. He lost all his property. He began to cut grass and purchase oil out of the money realised by selling grass. He could not sell the grass one day and so he burnt the grass itself. He could not get even the grass one day. He resolved to burn his hair. Lord Siva showered His grace upon the Nayanar and took him to His abode.

Saint Seruttunai Nayanar cut off the nose of the queen for smelling a flower which had been gathered for the sake of Siva and which had accidentally fallen on the floor. The king came to know of this and gave an additional punishment to the queen by cutting of her head also. There was a rain of flowers. Kalarunga Nayanar, the king, attained the grace of the Lord.

The Nayanars were not much concerned with Siva doctrines or Saiva Philosophy. They attached the greatest importance to Siva worship, even though it was against the ordinary rules of right and wrong. They had the utmost regard for the externals of Siva worship. They were prepared to do anything to preserve these outward forms, even at the cost of their lives. Even bigotry was not considered as a vice.

You can clearly understand from the life history of these Nayanars that any one whatever his caste might be, and whatever his service be, could attain the grace of Lord Siva.

Saivas of these times were staunch devotees of Saivism. Ordinary rules of ethics and morality could not be applied to the Nayanars.

Chapter XII
FESTIVALS

LIGHTING FESTIVAL AT ARUNACHALA

Lord Siva assumed the form of a hill at Tiruvannamalai in Tamilnadu. Here, He quelled the pride of Brahma and Vishnu who were quarrelling as to their relative greatness. One day, when Lord Siva was in meditation, Parvati left Him and went to the hill of Arunachala. There she performed penances. She was the guest of the sage Gautama. It was during her penance here that Mahishasura was killed by Durga bidden by Parvati. Parvati saw Lord Siva as Arunachalesvara. She was taken back by Lord Siva to His side and made again Ardhanari, as Apitaku Chamba.

Arunachalesvara is Tejolinga. Arunachala represents the Agni Tattva of the Pancha Bhuta Kshetras.

Arunachalam is another name for Tiruvannamalai. In days of yore, many Siddha Purushas lived in this hill. Idyakadar, Arunagirinathar lived here. This place is famous for its Festival of Lighting (Kartigai Dipam) every year during the month of Kartigai (November), on the day when the full moon falls in the Kartigai Nakshatram. The lighting takes place at about 5 or 5.30 in the evening. A big hollow in a rock is filled with ghee, oil and camphor. A big wick is put in the ghee and lighted. The lighting is seen even at a distance of sixteen miles. It is regarded that he who beholds this light does not take any future birth. The light burns continuously for three months.

A veil is put around the light at the top of the Arunachala hill. The people bring the Isvara Vigraha outside the temple at 5.30 p.m. as soon as Kartigai Nakshatra dawns. Then a Bhana (fire work) is sent towards the light in the hill through the sky. The man who is in charge of the lighting at the hill removes the veil at once. Then the people see the big light and worship the light with folded hands. They repeat loudly 'Harahara, Harohara'.

The esoteric significance is that he who sees the Light of lights that is burning eternally in the chambers of one's heart, through constant meditation, attains immortality. The lighting in the Arunachala brings the message to you that the Atman or Lord Siva is self-effulgent, Jyotis-Svarupa, Light of lights, Sun of suns.

The big light at the hill represents Lord Siva or Paramatman (Supreme Soul). The Bhana is Jiva or the individual soul. The veil represents Avidya that covers the individual soul. The Bhana burns the veil and merges itself in the big light. Even so, if you destroy Avidya by the fire of meditation and Vichara, you can merge yourself in the Supreme Soul or Light of lights.

Kanjivaram, Jambukesvara, Tiruvannamalai, Kalahasti and Chidambaram are the five Bhuta Linga Kshetras. Prithvi Lingam is at Kanjivaram. Apas Lingam is at Jambukesvaram. Tejo-Lingam is at Tiruvannamalai. Vayu-Lingam is at Kalahasti. Akasa-Lingam is at Chidambaram.

These five places represent the apex of five angles of a five-triangled figure which represents the five Bhutas of which the entire world is made up. The Tejas-Tattva is in the middle of the five Bhutas. It forms the way through which the Supreme Soul or Lord Siva can be known or seen or realised by the Jiva. The fire of meditation burns the Avidya of the Jiva and helps him to merge himself in the Supreme Light.

The Vedantin holds that Vak (speech) is Brahman. He proves that Vak is Agni or fire and deduces his doctrine of unity. Agni is the presiding deity of speech. Vak is Agni. Vak is Brahman.

The Panchamurtis or Pancha Tattvas meet at a time which is neither night nor day, when the sun and the moon shine together. The light at the hill is seen at a distance of sixteen miles. This represents the 'Purnakala' or Brahman.

The Yogi beholds that light during meditation at the crown of the head, which represents the top of the Arunachala hill, and merges himself in it during Nirvikalpa Samadhi.

Annihilate the three impurities, Anava, Karma and Maya. Burn the mind, senses and the Vasanas in the fire of knowledge of the Self or Sivajnanam. Attain full illumination and behold the Light of lights which illumines the mind, intellect, sun, stars, lightning and the fire. This is real Kartigai Dipam.

May the Light of lights illumine you all! May Lord Siva bless you with more light! May you merge in this Supreme Light and attain the eternal bliss of Immortality!

VIJAYA DASAMI

The Mother aspect of Godhead is the source of power, prosperity and learning and is worshipped during the Navaratri or Dassera, as Durga, Lakshmi and Sarasvati. Each aspect is worshipped for three nights.

Vijaya Dasami is the tenth day of the bright half of the lunar month of Asvina. It is a great soul-stirring festival which is observed with great éclat throughout the length and breadth of India.

It was on the Vijaya Dasami day that Arjuna, the Pandava hero worshipped the Goddess before starting the fight against the evil-minded Kauravas. It was on that day that Ravana was killed in battle by Sri Rama.

It is the day of victory. Boys are put in the school on this day. 'Hari Om Narayanaya Siddham', 'Om Sri Ganesaya Namah', 'Om Sri Hayagrivaya Namah' are taught to them. Aspirants are initiated on this day.

On this memorable day, the carpenter, the tailor, the mason, the artist, the songster, the typist and all technical workers do Puja for their instruments and implements. This is Ayudha Puja. They behold and recognise the Sakti or power behind these instruments and worship the Devi, for their success, prosperity and peace.

Sri Rama built a united India. Sri Rama gained victory over Ravana who had his capital in Lanka, but whose dominions had been extended over a large part of India. Vijaya Dasami is the day of anniversary of the birth of one united India. It is observed in commemoration of the great victory (Vijaya) of Sri Rama over the Rakshasa king, Ravana. It is the day of triumph of righteousness over unrighteousness.

Angada, Hanuman and others celebrated the victory of Sri Rama over Ravana with great religious ardour, under the leadership of pious Vibhishana, embraced one another in friendship and showed their intense devotion and reverence to Sri Rama. From that day onwards this great victory (Vijaya) has been commemorated year after year by all Hindus.

Sri Rama's victory over Ravana is the victory of spirit over matter, the victory of Sattva over Rajas and Tamas, the victory of soul over mind, sense and body, the victory of idealism over materialism, the victory of goodness over evil, the victory of love and truth over hatred and falsehood, the victory of self-sacrifice and renunciation over selfishness and possession, the victory of the oppressed over the oppressor, the victory of the labour over the capitalists and the imperialists. The memory of this day brings hope and joy to the hearts of the poorest and the most depressed. It humbles the pride of the rich, the strong and the learned, and inspires them to embrace the poor, the weak and the illiterate in love and brotherliness. It awakens a sense of unity among all classes of people.

The Vijaya Dasami has thus become a festival for awakening of universal unity, fraternity, peace and bliss.

The Sakta Puranas interpret this in another way. Rama tried to attain victory through His own valour and prowess but failed. Afterwards, He surrendered His egoism to the Maha Sakti or Devi, and placed Himself as an instrument in Her hands. Thereupon, Devi really fought with Ravana and brought the victory for Sri Rama.

There is an eternal fight going on between Devas and Asuras, between Sattva and Rajas-Tamas, between evil tendencies and virtuous tendencies in man. Gods represent Sattvic forces. The demons or Asuras represent the evil forces. That day on which one kills these evil tendencies, viz., lust, anger, greed, egoism, hatred and attains knowledge of Self or illumination through the grace of the Divine Mother, is the real Vijaya Dasami day or the day of real victory of Self over the non-Self.

May the Devi, Mother Durga teach mankind the way of Dharma and righteousness and bestow peace, bliss and contentment and the final beatitude!

DASSERA

Dassera is the greatest Hindu festival of adoring God as Mother. Hinduism is the only religion in the world which has emphasised much on the Motherhood of God. Mother is the dearest and sweetest of all human relations. Hence, it is proper to look upon God as Mother.

Dassera, Durga Puja and Navaratri are one and the same. Durga is the Sakti of Lord Siva. She is the representation of the power of the Supreme Lord. There is no difference between the Lord and His power. She looks after the affairs of the world. The Divine Mother in Her aspect of Durga is represented as having ten different weapons in Her ten hands. She is sitting on a lion. This indicates that She has control over all forces, even over the brutal force which the lion stands for.

You will find in Devi Sukta of the Rig-Veda Samhita that Vak, the daughter of sage Anbhirna realised her identity with the Divine Mother, the power of the Supreme Lord which manifests throughout the entire universe among the gods, among men and beasts, among the creatures of the deep ocean.

In the Kena Upanishad, you will find that the Divine Mother shed wisdom to Indra and the gods, and said that the gods were able to defeat the demons with the help of the power of the Supreme Lord.

Mahishasura, a great demon, was severely oppressing the gods. The gods invoked the aid of the Divine Mother Durga. She assumed a form with ten hands bearing ten weapons and killed the Asura. Devi fought with Bhandasura and his forces for nine days and nine nights and completed the destruction of all Asuras on the evening of the tenth day, known as the Vijaya Dasami or the day of victory. All the ten days are sacred to Devi.

The Hindus of Bengal worship Goddess Durga on the three days preceding the Vijaya Dasami and perform the immersion ceremony on the Vijaya Dasami day. Durga is also worshipped in March-April during the Vasanta Puja.

The Mother of Durga, wife of the king of Himalayas, longs to see her daughter Durga. Durga is permitted by Lord Siva to visit Her beloved mother only for three days in the year. The festival of Durga Puja is to celebrate this brief visit and it ends with the Vijaya Dasami day when the Goddess Durga leaves for Kailas.

Sri Rama worshipped Durga at the time of the fight with Ravana, to invoke Her aid in the war during the days preceding the Vijaya Dasami day. He fought and won through Her grace.

In Bengal, Durga Puja is a great festival. All who live away from home return home during the Puja days. Mothers meet their distant sons and daughters, wives their husbands.

The potter shows his skill in making the images, the painter in drawing pictures, the songster in playing on his instrument and the priest in reciting the sacred books. The Bengalis save money all the year round only to spend it all during the Puja days. Cloth is distributed.

The Hindu woman of Bengal welcomes the Goddess with a mother's love, and sends away the image on the last day with every ceremony associated with a daughter's departure for her husband's home and with motherly tears in her eyes.

May you all worship Goddess Durga with intense faith and devotion and attain eternal bliss and immortality through Her Grace! Glory to the Divine Mother Durga and Her consort Lord Siva, the joint parents of the universe.

VASANTA NAVARATRI

Devi is worshipped during the Vasanta Navaratri. This occurs during the spring. The worship of Devi is ordained by Her own command. You will find this in the following episode from the Devi Bhagavata.

In days long gone by, Dhruvasindhu, a noble and virtuous king of solar dynasty, ruled over the Kosala country. He had two wives, Manorama and Lilavati. Manorama was the senior queen. Both of them gave birth to beautiful sons. Manorama's son was named Sudarsana and Lilavati's son, Satrujit.

King Dhruvasindhu was killed by a lion when he went out for hunting. Preparations were made to crown the crown-prince Sudarsana. But king Yudhajit of Ujjain, the father of queen Lilavati and king Virasena of Kalinga, the father of queen Manorama were each desirous of securing the, Kosala throne to their respective grandsons. They fought with each other. King Virasena was killed in the battle. Manorama fled to the forest with prince Sudarsana and a eunuch. They took refuge in the Ashrama of Rishi Bharadvaja.

King Yudhajit crowned his grandson, Satrujit, at Ayodhya, the capital of Kosala. He went out to search Manorama and her son in order to put them out of the way, but could not find them. After some time, he came to know that they were in the Ashrama of Rishi Bharadvaja.

He at once started with a big army to the Ashrama. Yudhajit arrogantly demanded of Rishi Bharadvaja the surrender of Manorama and her son. The Rishi said that he would not give up those who had sought protection under him. Yudhajit became very furious. He wanted to attack the Rishi. But his minister told him about the truth of the Rishi's statement. Yudhajit returned to his capital.

FESTIVALS

Fortune began to smile on prince Sudarsana. The son of a hermit called the eunuch by his Sanskrit name 'Kleeba'. The prince caught the first syllable 'Klee' and began to pronounce it as 'Kleem'. This syllable is a powerful, sacred Mantra. It is the Bija Akshara of Parasakti. The prince obtained peace of mind and the grace of the Divine Mother, by the repeated utterings of this syllable. Devi appeared to him, blessed him and gave him divine weapons, and an inexhaustible arrow-case.

The emissaries of the king of Banares passed through the Ashrama of the Rishi, and saw the noble prince Sudarsana and recommended him to princess Sasikala, the daughter of the king of Banares.

A Svayamvara was arranged. Sasikala chose Sudarsana. Yudhajit also was there. Sasikala was wedded to Sudarsana. Yudhajit began to fight with the king of Banares. Devi helped Sudarsana and his father-in-law. Yudhajit mocked at the Devi. Devi reduced Yudhajit and his army to ashes.

Sudarsana and his wife and his father-in-law praised the Devi. She was highly pleased and ordered them to perform Her worship with Homa and other means in all the four Navaratris of the months — Ashadha, Asvina, Magha and Chaitra, beginning with the Sukla Prathama. Then She disappeared.

Thereupon, prince Sudarsana and princess Sasikala came back to the Ashrama of Rishi Bharadvaja. The great Rishi blessed them and crowned Sudarsana as the king of Kosala. Sudarsana and Sasikala and the king of Banares implicitly carried out the commands of the Divine Mother and performed worship in a splendid manner during each of these Navatri days.

Sudarsana's descendants, Sri Rama and Lakshmana, also performed worship of Devi during the Vasanta Navaratri and were blessed with Her assistance in the recovery of Sita.

It is your duty also to perform the worship of Devi for your material and spiritual welfare during the Vasanta Navaratri and follow the noble example set by Sudarsana and Sri Rama. You cannot achieve anything without Mother's blessings. Sing the prayers of the Divine Mother. Repeat Her Mantra and Name. Meditate on Her form. Do Puja. Pray and obtain Her eternal grace and blessings.

GAURI PUJA

Goddess Gauri or Parvati is the consort of Lord Siva. She is the Sakti of Siva. She is recognised as the highest ideal of Indian womanhood. She is a perfect model of feminine virtues. Maidens worship Gauri and invoke Her grace and blessings for securing a suitable bridegroom. She is adored by married women also for securing long life for their husbands.

Certain days are held very sacred to Her memory. Hindu ladies observe fast on these days and worship Goddess Gauri in and through the crescent moon, before breaking the fast.

Chapter XIV

SIVA YOGA MAALA

BOOKS ON SAIVISM

The twenty-eight Saiva Agamas, the hymns (Tevaram and Tiruvasagam) of the Saiva saints form the chief sources of Southern Saivism. The Saiva hymns compiled by Nambi Andar Nambi (A.D. 1000) are collectively called Tirumurai. Tevaram contains the hymns of Sambandhar, Appar and Sundarar. The hymns of Manickavasagar are called Tiruvasagam.

The Agamanta called Saiva Siddhanta is the essence of the 28 Sanskrit Agamas. Agamanta is the inner meaning of the Veda.

Seklar's Periyapuranam (11th century) gives a description of the sixty-three Saiva saints.

Tiruvasagam is a collection of fifty-one poems of unsurpassed spiritual experiences and grandeur. Dr. G.V. Pope has translated this into English.

In the beginning of the 13th century, the great Saiva Siddhanta philosophical movement was inaugurated by Saint Meykandar who is the eminent author of Sivajnana Bodham, the central work of the system. Sivajnana Bodham is regarded as an expansion of twelve verses of the Raurava Agama. This book is the standard exposition of the Saiva Siddhanta views. It contains in a nutshell a systematic expression of the system. It opened the eyes of Tamilians to the supreme excellence of this philosophy. Saint Meykandar taught his philosophy to forty-nine disciples, propagated and popularised the system.

Arulnandi Sivachariar, the first of the forty-nine disciples of Meykandar, is the author of the important work Siva Jnana Siddhiyar. He is also the author of Irupa-Irupathu.

In the thirteenth and fourteenth centuries, there arose fourteen philosophical works, known as standard Saiva Siddhanta Sastras. They are Tiruvundiar, Tirukalitrupadiar, Sivajnana Bodham, Sivajnana Siddhiar, Irupa-Irupathu, Unmai Vilakkam, Sivaprakasam, Tiru Arul Payan, Vinavemba, Partripatirodai, Kodikkavi, Nenju Vidu Thoothu, Unmai Neri Vilakkam and Sangarpaniraharanam.

Sivaprakasam and Tiru Arul Payan are two well-known books written by Umapati Sivachariar (14th century). He is the author of other six Sastras of the group. Tiruvendiar was composed by Saint Uyyavanda-deva-nayanar of Tiruvayalur about the middle of the 12th century. Tirukadavur Uyyavanda-deva-nayanar was the author of the Tirukalitrupadiar.

Unmai Vilakkam is one of the fourteen Sastras written by Manavasagam Kadanthar, another disciple of Meykandar.

Tirumantiram is one of the most authoritative works embodying the Saiva doctrine. The author is Tirumula Nayanar. This work is the foundation upon which the later structure of Saiva Siddhanta philosophy was built. The Saiva doctrine of the Sanskrit Agamas are translated in this book. It is a work of three thousand stanzas composed in the course of three thousand years. It deals with the practical and theoretical aspects of the Saiva religion and philosophy.

Jnanamritam is the earliest treatise which treats of the Siddhanta concepts in the modern scientific manner.

The Saiva Siddhanta rests on the twofold tradition of the Vedas and the Agamas. Nilakantha, who flourished in the 14th century, undertook the systematic reconciliation of the two. He wrote a commentary on the Brahma Sutras. He interpreted it in the light of the Saiva system.

Appayya Dikshita's commentary called Sivarka Mani Dipika is a valuable book.

Siva Purana, Linga Purana, Siva Parakrama, Tiruvilayadal Puranam, Periyapuranam treat of the glory of Lord Siva. These books are translated into Tamil. Bhakta Vilasam is a Sanskrit work. It is a minor Purana upon the Skanda Purana.

The twenty-eight Agamas were written in Sanskrit in the valley of Kashmir. This Agamanta arose in North India long before Jainism came into prominence. It was known there by the name Pratyabhijna Darsanam. Then it spread westwards and southwards. In Western India, it was known by Vira Mahesvara Darsanam, and in South India it was called Suddha Saiva Darsanam. Linga Purana is held in great respect by the Vira Mahesvaras.

CHIDAMBARA RAHASYA

Lord Siva is worshipped in Chidambaram as a formless presence, Akasa Lingam. Chidambaram is an ancient centre of religion and culture. Siva is worshipped at Chidambaram in the dancing aspect as Nataraja. Ardra Darsana, one of the most important festivals of South India, is celebrated every year at Chidambaram, in the month of Margasirsha.

Within the temple is the 'Nritya Sabha' or the 'hall of the dance'. In front of the central shrine is a structure of wood surmounted with tall golden roof known as the 'Kanaka Sabha' or 'the hall of golden dome'. The central temple is dedicated to Nataraja. It is a plain wooden building standing on a stone-pavement, but behind it is an apartment of polished black stone, the roof of which is formed of gold plates. Opposite to the Sivaganga tank, is the 'Raja Sabha' or 'the hall of one thousand columns', with granite pillars. King Varua Chola purified himself by bathing in the tank and attained a golden hue.

The five Prakaras of a Siva temple represent the five Kosas of the body. The three Prakaras of certain temples represent the three bodies of a man. Garbhagriha, Ardhamandap, Mahamandap, Snanamandap, Alankara-mandap, Sabha-mandap represent the six Chakras or the six Adharas of the body.

The Darsanopanishad says: "Chidambaram is in the centre of the heart. Chidambaram is the heart of Virat Purusha". The Mandap with thousand pillars represents the Sahasrara or the thousand-petalled lotus on the crown of the head. Sivaganga represents the pool of nectar, Amritavapi, in Sahasrara. The place where there are Jyotirlinga and Sri Gurumurti, represents Visuddha Chakra. In Tiruchittambalam or Maha Sabha there are five Pithams for Brahma, Vishnu, Rudra, Mahesvara and Sadasiva. The five letters of Panchakshara form the five steps, and the veil represents Avidya or Avarana. The ninety-six Tattvas form the ninety-six windows. The four golden pillars which are in the centre represent the four Vedas. The twenty-eight wooden pillars which surround them represent the twenty-eight Agamas. The space that is within the pillars represents Suddha Vidya. Lord Nataraja has His seat in the Pranavapitham.

There is 'Tiruchittambalam' behind. This is Chidakasa or the famous 'Chidambara Rahasya'. Sivakama Sundari or Parasakti has Her seat in Garbhagriha. Rahasya is Nishkala. Ananda Nataraja Murti is Sakala.

In the East is Brahma. In the South is Vishnu. In the North is Bhairava or Samhara Rudra. There are nine Kalasas in the tower. These represent the nine Saktis. The sixty-four wooden supports in the tower represent the sixty-four Vidyas or Kalas. The twenty-one thousand six hundred copper plates coated with gold, represent the daily twenty-one thousand six hundred breaths of a man. The seventy-two thousand nails represent the seventy-two thousand nerves or the astral tubes in the body.

The eighteen pillars of Kanaka Sabha represent eighteen Puranas. Kanaka Sabha represents the Manipura Chakra. The five Sabhas represent the five Kosas.

If one rightly understands the secrets of Chidambara temple and worships the Lord Nataraja with intense faith, devotion, purity and one-pointedness of mind, he will attain knowledge and eternal bliss. He will be freed from bondage.

Birth in Tiruvarur gives Mukti. Death in Banares gives Mukti. Darsana of Nataraja of Chidambaram gives Mukti.

Adjacent to the Kanaka Sabha is a temple dedicated to Govinda Raja or Vishnu. This teaches a lesson that Siva and Vishnu are essentially one and that a Virasaivite or Vira Vaishnavite should abandon his bigotry and should have a large heart and equal devotion to Lord Siva and Lord Hari and should see his Ishtam in all Murtis.

May Lord Nataraja and Sivakami bless you all and give an understanding heart to comprehend the Chidambara Rahasya!

SIVA AND VISHNU ARE ONE

A Saivite is a devotee of Lord Siva. A Vaishnavite is a devotee of Lord Vishnu. Upasana means worship or sitting near God. Upasaka is one who does Upasana. Upasana or Aradhana leads to realisation of God. A bigoted

Virasaivite entertains hatred towards Lord Vishnu, Vaishnavites and Puranas which treat of Vishnu. He never enters a Vishnu temple. He never drinks water from a Vaishnavite. He never takes food with a Vaishnavite. He never repeats the name of Hari. He speaks ill of Lord Hari, Vaishnavites and Vishnu Purana. He thinks that Lord Siva is superior to Lord Vishnu. He never reads Vishnu Purana. Is this not the height of folly? Is this not extreme ignorance? He has not understood the true nature of Lord Siva. He has no idea of true religion. He is a fanatic, a bigot, a man of little understanding, a narrow sectarian, with a very small constricted heart. He is like a frog in the well which has no idea of the vast ocean.

A bigoted Vira Vaishnavite entertains hatred towards Lord Siva, Saivites and Siva Puranas which treat of Lord Siva. He never enters a Siva temple. He never makes friendship with a Saivite. He never drinks water from the hands of a Saivite. He also behaves exactly like the Virasaivite. The lot of this man is also highly deplorable.

There is a temple in Sankaranarayanar Koil in the Tirunelveli district (Tamilnadu), where the idol has one half of it depicted as Siva and the other half as Vishnu. The inner significance of this is that Lord Siva and Lord Vishnu are one. Sri Sankaracharya also has said in very clear terms that Siva and Vishnu are the one all-pervading Soul.

On one occasion, a Virasaivite entered the temple in Sankaranarayanar Koil to worship the Lord. He offered incense. He plugged the nostrils of Vishnu with the cotton as the fumes were entering His nose also. After that a Vira Vaishnavite entered the temple and he also offered incense. He plugged the nostrils of Siva as the fumes were entering His nose also. Such is the bigotry and narrow-mindedness of sectarians. A devotee should have a large, broad heart. He must see his tutelary deity in all aspects of the Lord and in all forms. He can have intense love for his Ishtam in the beginning, to intensify his devotion for that particular deity (Prema-nishtha), but he should have equal devotion to the other forms of the Lord also.

Siva and Vishnu are one and the same entity. They are essentially one and the same. They are the names given to the different aspects of the all-pervading Supreme Soul or the Absolute. *'Sivasya hridayam vishnur-vishnoscha hridayam sivah* — Vishnu is the heart of Siva and likewise Siva is the heart of Vishnu'.

The sectarian worship is of recent origin. The Saiva Siddhanta of Kantacharya is only five hundred years old. The Vaishnava cults of Madhva and Sri Ramanuja are only six hundred and seven hundred years old respectively. There was no sectarian worship before seven hundred years.

Brahma represents the creative aspect; Vishnu, the preservative aspect; and Siva, the destructive aspect of Paramatman. This is just like your wearing different garbs on different occasions. When you do the function of a judge, you put on one kind of dress. At home you wear another kind of dress. When you do worship in the temple, you wear another kind of dress. You exhibit different kinds of temperament on different occasions. Even so, the Lord does the function of creation when He is associated with Rajas, and He is called Brahma. He preserves the world when He is associated with Sattva Guna, and He is called Vishnu. He destroys the world when He is associated with Tamo-Guna, and He is called Siva or Rudra.

Brahma, Vishnu and Siva have been correlated to the three Avasthas or states of consciousness. During the waking state, Sattva predominates. During the dream state Rajas predominates and during the deep sleep state Tamas predominates. Hence Vishnu, Brahma and Siva are the Murtis of Jagrat, Svapna and Sushupti states of consciousness respectively. The Turiya or the fourth state is Para Brahman. The Turiya state is immediately next to the deep sleep state. Worship of Siva will lead quickly to the attainment of the fourth state.

Vishnu Purana glorifies Vishnu and in some places give, a lower position to Siva. Siva Purana glorifies Siva and gives a lower status to Vishnu. Devi Bhagavata glorifies Devi and gives a lower status to Brahma, Vishnu and Siva. This is only to instil and intensify devotion for the respective deity in the hearts of the devotees. In reality, no deity is superior to another. You must understand the heart of the writer.

May you all realise the oneness of Siva and Vishnu! May you all be endowed with pure subtle intellect and proper understanding!

SIVARATRI MAHIMA

I

Silent adorations to Lord Siva, consort of Parvati, the destructive aspect of Brahman, who is known by the names Sambhu, Sankara, Mahadeva, Sadasiva, Visvanatha, Hara, Tripurari, Gangadhara, Sulapani, Nilakantha, Dakshinamurti, Chandrasekhara, Nilalohita, etc., who is the bestower of auspiciousness, immortality and divine knowledge on His devotees, and who does Tandava Nritya or the Dance of Death at the end of Time or Cosmic Pralaya, and who is the real Regenerator but not the destroyer.

Maha Sivaratri means the great night consecrated to Lord Siva. Maha Sivaratri falls on Trayodasi or the thirteenth day of the dark fortnight of Kumbha month (February-March).

In the Santi Parva of the Mahabharata, Bhishma refers to the observance of the Maha Sivaratri, by king Chitrabhanu, when he was giving the discourse on Dharma, resting on his bed of arrows.

Once upon a time, king Chitrabhanu of the Ikshvaku dynasty, who was ruling over the whole of Jambudvipa, and his wife were observing a fast on the day of Maha Sivaratri. The Sage Ashtavakra came on a visit to the court of the king.

The Sage asked: "O king, why are you observing fast today?" King Chitrabhanu explained the reason for observing a fast on that day. He had the gift of remembering the incidents of his previous birth.

He said to the Sage Ashtavakra: "I was a hunter by name Susvar in my previous birth. I eked out my livelihood by killing and selling birds and animals. One day, I was roaming in a forest in search of animals. I was overtaken by the darkness of night. I was not able to return home and so I climbed up a Bilva tree for shelter. I shot a deer that day but I had no time to take it home. As I was tormented by hunger and thirst, I kept awake throughout the night. I shed profuse tears when I thought of my poor wife and children who were starving and anxiously awaiting my return. I engaged myself in plucking and dropping down the Bilva leaves. There was a Siva Linga at the foot of the Bilva tree. The tears and the leaves fell upon the Siva Linga.

"The day dawned. I returned home and sold the deer. I got food for myself and for my family. I was about to break my fast. A stranger came to me and begged for food. I served him with food first and then I took my food. At the hour of death, I saw two messengers of Lord Siva. They were sent down for the sake of conducting my soul to the abode of Siva. I learnt there for the first time, of the great merit I had earned by the observance of the fast on the day of Maha Sivaratri, though I did it unconsciously by an accident. I lived in the abode of Siva and enjoyed divine bliss for long ages. I am now reborn on this earth as Chitrabhanu."

II

'Sivaratri' means 'night of Lord Siva'. The important features of this religious function are rigid fasting for twenty-four hours and sleepless vigil during the night. Every true devotee of Lord Siva spends the night of Sivaratri in deep meditation, keeps vigil and observes fast.

The worship of Lord Siva consists in offering flowers, Bilva leaves and other gifts on the Linga which is a symbol of Lord Siva, and bathing it with milk, honey, butter, ghee, rose-water, etc.

When creation had been completed, Siva and Parvati had been living on the top of Kailas. Parvati asked: "O venerable Lord, which of the many rituals observed in Thy honour doth please Thee most?" Lord Siva replied: "The thirteenth night of the new moon, Krishna Paksha, in the month of Phalguna (February-March) is known as Sivaratri, My most favourable Tithi. My devotee gives Me greater happiness by mere fasting than by ceremonial baths, and offerings of flowers, sweets, incense, etc.

"The devotee observes strict spiritual discipline in the day and worships Me in four different forms in the four successive Praharas, each made up of three hours of the night. The offering of a few Bilva leaves is more precious to Me than the precious jewels and flowers. He should bathe Me in milk at the first Prahara, in curd at the second, in clarified butter at the third, and in honey at the fourth and last. Next morning, he should feed the Brahmins first and break the fast after the performance of the prescribed ceremonies. There is no ritual, O Parvati, which can compare with this simple routine in sanctity.

Just hear, My Beloved, of an episode which will give you an idea of the glory and power of this ritual.

"Once upon a time, there lived in the town of Varanasi a hunter. He was returning from the forest one evening with the game birds he had killed. He felt tired and sat at the foot of a tree to take some rest. He was overpowered by sleep. When he woke up, it was all thick darkness of night. It was the night of Sivaratri but he did not know it. He climbed up the tree, tied his bundle of dead birds to a branch and sat up waiting for the dawn. The tree happened to be My favourite, the Bilva.

"There was a Linga under that tree. He plucked a few leaves dropped them down. The night-dew trickled down from his body. I was highly pleased with involuntary little gifts of the hunter. The day dawned and the hunter returned to his house.

"In course of time, the hunter fell ill and gave up his last breath. The messengers of Yama arrived at his bedside to carry his soul to Yama. My messengers also went to the spot to take him to My abode. There was a severe fight between Yama's messengers and My messengers. The former were totally defeated. They reported the matter to their Lord. He presented himself in person at the portals of My abode. Nandi gave him an idea of the sanctity of Sivaratri and the love which I had for the hunter. Yama surrendered the hunter to Me and returned to his abode quickly.

"The hunter was able to enter My abode and ward off death by simple fasting and offering of a few Bilva leaves, however involuntary it might be, because it was the night of Sivaratri. Such is the solemnity and sacredness associated with the night".

Parvati was deeply impressed by the speech of Lord Siva on the sanctity and glory of the ritual. She repeated it to Her friends who in their turn passed it on to the ruling princes on earth. Thus was the sanctity of Sivaratri broadcast all over the world.

THE TWELVE JYOTIRLINGAS

सौराष्ट्रे सोमनाथं च श्रीशैले मल्लिकार्जुनम् ।
उज्जयिन्यां महाकालं ओङ्कारममलेश्वरम् ॥१॥

परल्यां वैद्यनाथं च, डाकिन्यां भीमशंकरम् ।
सेतुबन्धे तु रामेशं, नागेशं दारुकावने ॥२॥

वाराणस्यां तु विश्वेशं, त्र्यम्बकं गौतमीतटे ।
हिमालये तु केदारं, घुसृणेशं च शिवालये ॥३॥

एतानि ज्योतिर्लिङ्गानि सायं प्रातःपठेन्नरः ।
सप्त जन्म कृतं पापं, स्मरणेन विनश्यति ॥४॥

॥इति द्वादश ज्योतिर्लिंगानि॥

Saurashtre somanatham cha srisaile mallikarjunam,
Ujjayinyam mahakalam-omkaram-amalesvaram.
Paralyam vaidyanatham cha dakinyam bhimasankaram,
Setubandhe tu ramesam nagesam darukavane.
Varanasyam tu visvesam tryambakam gautamitate,
Himalaye tu kedaram ghusrunesam sivalaye.

Etani jyotirlingani sayam pratah pathennarah,
Saptajanmakritam papam smaranena vinasyati.

He who remembers the twelve Jyotirlingas morning and evening, becomes absolved from sins committed in seven previous births. The twelve Jyotirlingas are:

1. *Somanatha* in Saurashtra (Gujarat), 2. *Mallikarjuna* in Srisaila (Andhra Pradesh), 3. *Mahakala* in Ujjain (Madhya Pradesh), 4. *Omkaresvara* in Amalesvara on the banks of Narmada (Madhya Pradesh), 5. *Vaidyanatha* in Parali (Maharashtra), 6. *Bhimasankara* in Dakini near Pune (Maharashtra), 7. *Ramesvara* in Setubandhana (Tamilnadu), 8. *Nagesa* in Darukavana (Gujarat), 9. *Visvesa* in Varanasi or Banares (Uttar Pradesh), 10. *Tryambaka* on the banks of Godavari in Nasik (Maharashtra), 11. *Kedarnath* in Himalayas (Uttaranchal), and 12. *Ghusrunesa* (Gokarna) in Sivalaya, Karwar District (Karnataka).

In Southern India, there are five famous Siva Lingas which represent the five elements.

1. In Kanjivaram, Chengalput District (Tamilnadu), there is Prithvi Lingam. 2. In Tiruvanai Koil, Trichy District (Tamilnadu), there is Appu Lingam. The Lingam is always in water. Tiruvanai Koil is otherwise known as Jambukesvaram. 3. In Kalahasti, Chittoor District (Andhra Pradesh), there is Vayu Lingam. 4. In Tiruvannamalai (Tamilnadu), there is Tejolingam (Arunachalesvaram). 5. In Chidambaram (Tamilnadu), there is Akasa Lingam.

SIVA NAMA KIRTAN

1. Sivaya Nama Om Sivaya Namah,
   Sivaya Nama Om Namassivaya.
   Siva Siva Siva Siva Sivaya Nama Om
   Hara Hara Hara Hara Namassivaya.
   Siva Siva Siva Siva Sivaya Nama Om
   Bhum Bhum Bhum Bhum Namassivaya.

Sambasadasiva Sambasadasiva
Sambasadasiva Sambasiva.
Om Namassivaya Om Namassivaya
Om Namassivaya Om Namassivaya.
......Sivaya Namah Om Sivaya Namah.....

2. Om Siva Om Siva Omkara Siva
   Umamahesvara Tava Charanam.
   Om Siva Om Siva Omkara Siva
   Paratpara Siva Tava Charanam.
   Namami Sankara Bhavani Sankara
   Girija Sankara Tava Charanam.
   Namami Sankara Bhavani Sankara
   Mridani Sankara Tava Charanam.

3. Hara Hara Siva Siva Sambo
   Hara Hara Siva Siva Sambo
   Hara Hara Siva Siva Hara Hara Sambo
   Hara Hara Siva Siva Sambo
   Hara Hara Siva Siva Sambo.

4. Namaste Namaste Vibho Visvamurte
   Namaste Namaste Chidanandamurte
   Namaste Namaste Tapoyogagamya
   Namaste Namaste Srutijnanagamya.

5. Sankarane Sankarane Sambho Gangadharane,
   Sankarane Sankarane Sambho Gangadharane.

6. Kasivisvanatha Sadasiva,
   Bhum Bolo Kailasapati Bhum Bolo Kailasapati.

7. Hara Hara Mahadeva Sambho Kasivisvanatha Gange
   Visvanatha Gange Kasi Visvanatha Gange.

8. Om Siva Hara Hara Gange Hara Hara,
   Om Siva Hara Hara Gange Hara Hara
   Om Siva Hara Hara Om Siva Hara Hara,
   Bhum Bhum Hara Hara Om Siva Hara Hara.

9. Mahadeva Siva Sankara Sambho
    Umakanta Hara Tripurare
   Mrityunjaya Vrishabhadhvaja Sulin
    Gangadhara Mrida Madanare
   Jaya Sambho Jaya Sambho
    Siva Gauri Sankara Jaya Sambho
   Jaya Sambho Jaya Sambho
    Jaya Gauri Sankara Jaya Sambho
   Rudram Pasupatim Isanam
    Kalaye Kasipurinatham
   Hara Siva Sankara Gaurisam
    Vande Gangadharamisam.

10. Jaya Siva Sankara Hara Tripurare
     Pahi Pasupati Pinakadharin.

11. Chandrasekhara Chandrasekhara
     Chandrasekhara Pahi Mam
    Chandrasekhara Chandrasekhara
     Chandrasekhara Raksha Mam.

12. Agad Bhum Agad Bhum Bhaje Damaru,
    Nache Sadasiva Jagadguru
    Nache Brahma Nache Vishnu Nache Mahadeva,
    Kappar Leke Kaali Nache Nache Adideva.
                              (Agad Bhum...)

13. Nataraja Nataraja Nartana Sundara Nataraja
    Sivaraja Sivaraja Sivakami Priya Sivaraja.

14. Bol Sankar Bol Sankar Sankar Sankar Bol
    Hara Hara Hara Hara Mahadeva Sambho Sankar Bol
    Siva Siva Siva Siva Sadasiva Sambho Sankar Bol.

15. Jaya Jagad-Janani Sankata-harani
    Tribhuvana Tarini Mahesvari.

16. Jaya Gange Jaya Gange Rani
    Jaya Gange Jaya Hara Gange.

17. Devi Bhajo Durga-Bhavani
    Devi Bhajo Durga
    Jagad-Janani Mahishasura-Mardini
    Devi Bhajo Durga.

18. Radhe Govinda Bhajo Radhe Gopal
    Radhe Govinda Bhajo Radhe Gopal.

19. Bruhi Mukundeti Rasane   (Bruhi)
    Kesava Madhava Govindeti
    Krishnananda Sadanandeti   (Bruhi)
    Radha Ramana Hare Rameti
    Rajivaksha Ghana Syameti   (Bruhi).

20. Gauri Ramana Karunabharana
    Pahi Kripa-Purna Sarana
    Nilakantha-Dhara Gaura Sarira
    Natha Jana-Subhakara Mandara   (Gauri)
    Balachandra-Dhara Punya-Sarira
    Suma-Sara-Mada-Hara Sankara   (Gauri).

21. Piba Re Rama Rasam Rasane
    Piba Re Rama Rasam
    Durikrita-Pataka-Samsargam
    Purita Nana Vidha Phala Vargam   (Piba Re)
    Janana-Marana-Bhaya-Soka Viduram
    Sakala Sastra-Nigamagama-Saram   (Piba Re)
    Paripalita-Sarasija-Garbhandam
    Parama Pavitrikrita Pashandam   (Piba Re)
    Suddha-Paramahamsasrama-Gitam
    Suka-Saunaka-Kausika-Mukha Pitam (Piba Re).

22. Sivoham Sivoham Sivoham Soham
    Sivoham Sivoham Sivoham Soham
    Satchidananda Svarupoham.

23. Chidanandarupah Sivoham Sivoham
    Chidanandarupah Sivoham Sivoham.

24. Arunachala Siva Arunachala Siva
    Arunachala Siva Aruna Siva,
    Arunachala Siva Arunachala Siva
    Arunachala Siva Aruna Siva.

शिवस्तोत्रम्
श्री शिव-अष्टोत्तरशत-नामावली

१. ॐ शिवाय नमः
२. ॐ महेश्वराय नमः
३. ॐ शम्भवे नमः
४. ॐ पिनाकिने नमः
५. ॐ शशिशेखराय नमः
६. ॐ वामदेवाय नमः
७. ॐ विरूपाक्षाय नमः
८. ॐ कर्दिने नमः
९. ॐ नीललोहिताय नमः
१०. ॐ शङ्कराय नमः
११. ॐ शूलपाणये नमः
१२. ॐ खट्वाङ्गिने नमः
१३. ॐ विष्णुवल्लभाय नमः
१४. ॐ शिपिविष्टाय नमः
१५. ॐ अम्बिकानाथाय नमः
१६. ॐ श्रीकण्ठाय नमः
१७. ॐ भक्तवत्सलाय नमः
१८. ॐ भवाय नमः
१९. ॐ शर्वाय नमः
२०. ॐ त्रिलोकेशाय नमः
२१. ॐ शितिकण्ठाय नमः
२२. ॐ शिवाप्रियाय नमः
२३. ॐ उग्राय नमः
२४. ॐ कपालिने नमः
२५. ॐ कामारये नमः
२६. ॐ अन्धकासुरसूदनाय नमः
२७. ॐ गङ्गाधराय नमः
२८. ॐ ललाटाक्षाय नमः
२९. ॐ कालकालाय नमः
३०. ॐ कृपानिधये नमः
३१. ॐ भीमाय नमः
३२. ॐ परशुहस्ताय नमः
३३. ॐ मृगपाणये नमः
३४. ॐ जटाधराय नमः
३५. ॐ कैलासवासिने नमः
३६. ॐ कवचिने नमः
३७. ॐ कठोराय नमः
३८. ॐ त्रिपुरान्तकाय नमः
३९. ॐ वृषाङ्काय नमः
४०. ॐ वृषभारूढाय नमः
४१. ॐ भस्मोद्धूलितविग्रहाय नमः
४२. ॐ सामप्रियाय नमः
४३. ॐ स्वरमयाय नमः
४४. ॐ त्रयीमूर्तये नमः
४५. ॐ अनीश्वराय नमः
४६. ॐ सर्वज्ञाय नमः
४७. ॐ परमात्मने नमः
४८. ॐ सोमसूर्याग्निलोचनाय नमः
४९. ॐ हविषे नमः
५०. ॐ यज्ञमयाय नमः
५१. ॐ सोमाय नमः
५२. ॐ पञ्चवक्त्राय नमः
५३. ॐ सदाशिवाय नमः
५४. ॐ विश्वेश्वराय नमः

५५.	ॐ वीरभद्राय नमः	५६.	ॐ गणनाथाय नमः
५७.	ॐ प्रजापतये नमः	५८.	ॐ हिरण्यरेतसे नमः
५९.	ॐ दुर्धर्षाय नमः	६०.	ॐ गिरीशाय नमः
६१.	ॐ गिरिशाय नमः	६२.	ॐ अनघाय नमः
६३.	ॐ भुजङ्गभूषणाय नमः	६४.	ॐ भर्गाय नमः
६५.	ॐ गिरिधन्वने नमः	६६.	ॐ गिरिप्रियाय नमः
६७.	ॐ कृत्तिवाससे नमः	६८.	ॐ पुरारातये नमः
६९.	ॐ भगवते नमः	७०.	ॐ प्रमथाधिपाय नमः
७१.	ॐ मृत्युञ्जयाय नमः	७२.	ॐ सूक्ष्मतनवे नमः
७३.	ॐ जगद्व्यापिने नमः	७४.	ॐ जगद्गुरवे नमः
७५.	ॐ व्योमकेशाय नमः	७६.	ॐ महासेनजनकाय नमः
७७.	ॐ चारुविक्रमाय नमः	७८.	ॐ रुद्राय नमः
७९.	ॐ भूतपतये नमः	८०.	ॐ स्थाणवे नमः
८१.	ॐ अहिर्बुध्न्याय नमः	८२.	ॐ दिगम्बराय नमः
८३.	ॐ अष्टमूर्तये नमः	८४.	ॐ अनेकात्मने नमः
८५.	ॐ सात्त्विकाय नमः	८६.	ॐ शुद्धविग्रहाय नमः
८७.	ॐ शाश्वताय नमः	८८.	ॐ खण्डपरशवे नमः
८९.	ॐ अजाय नमः	९०.	ॐ पाशविमोचनाय नमः
९१.	ॐ मृडाय नमः	९२.	ॐ पशुपतये नमः
९३.	ॐ देवाय नमः	९४.	ॐ महादेवाय नमः
९५.	ॐ अव्ययाय नमः	९६.	ॐ हरये नमः
९७.	ॐ पूषदन्तभिदे नमः	९८.	ॐ अव्यग्राय नमः
९९.	ॐ दक्षध्वरहराय नमः	१००.	ॐ हराय नमः
१०१.	ॐ भगनेत्रभिदे नमः	१०२.	ॐ अव्यक्ताय नमः
१०३.	ॐ सहस्राक्षाय नमः	१०४.	ॐ सहस्रपदे नमः
१०५.	ॐ अपवर्गप्रदाय नमः	१०६.	ॐ अनन्ताय नमः
१०७.	ॐ तारकाय नमः	१०८.	ॐ परमेश्वराय नमः

||इति श्री शिव-अष्टोत्तरशत-नामावली ||

श्रीदेव्यष्टोत्तरशतनामावलिः

१. ॐ आदिशक्त्यै नमः
२. ॐ महादेव्यै नमः
३. ॐ अम्बिकायै नमः
४. ॐ परमेश्वर्यै नमः
५. ॐ ईश्वर्यै नमः
६. ॐ अनीश्वर्यै नमः
७. ॐ योगिन्यै नमः
८. ॐ सर्वभूतेश्वर्यै नमः
९. ॐ जयायै नमः
१०. ॐ विजयायै नमः
११. ॐ जयन्त्यै नमः
१२. ॐ शाम्भव्यै नमः
१३. ॐ शान्त्यै नमः
१४. ॐ ब्राह्म्यै नमः
१५. ॐ ब्रह्माण्डधारिण्यै नमः
१६. ॐ महारूपायै नमः
१७. ॐ महामायायै नमः
१८. ॐ माहेश्वर्यै नमः
१९. ॐ लोकरक्षिण्यै नमः
२०. ॐ दुर्गायै नमः
२१. ॐ दुर्गपारायै नमः
२२. ॐ भक्तचिन्तामण्यै नमः
२३. ॐ मृत्यै नमः
२४. ॐ सिद्ध्यै नमः
२५. ॐ मूर्त्यै नमः
२६. ॐ सर्वसिद्धिप्रदायै नमः
२७. ॐ मन्त्रमूर्त्यै नमः
२८. ॐ महाकाल्यै नमः
२९. ॐ सर्वमूर्तिस्वरूपिण्यै नमः
३०. ॐ वेदमूर्त्यै नमः
३१. ॐ वेदभूत्यै नमः
३२. ॐ वेदान्तायै नमः
३३. ॐ व्यवहारिण्यै नमः
३४. ॐ अनघायै नमः
३५. ॐ भगवत्यै नमः
३६. ॐ रौद्रायै नमः
३७. ॐ रुद्रस्वरूपिण्यै नमः
३८. ॐ नारायण्यै नमः
३९. ॐ नारसिंह्यै नमः
४०. ॐ नागयज्ञोपवीतिन्यै नमः
४१. ॐ शङ्खचक्रगदाधारिण्यै नमः
४२. ॐ जटामुकुटशोभिन्यै नमः
४३. ॐ अप्रमाणायै नमः
४४. ॐ प्रमाणायै नमः
४५. ॐ आदिमध्यावसानायै नमः
४६. ॐ पुण्यदायै नमः
४७. ॐ पुण्योपचारिण्यै नमः
४८. ॐ पुण्यकीर्त्यै नमः
४९. ॐ स्तुतायै नमः
५०. ॐ विशालाक्ष्यै नमः
५१. ॐ गम्भीरायै नमः
५२. ॐ रूपान्वितायै नमः
५३. ॐ कालरात्र्यै नमः
५४. ॐ अनल्पसिद्ध्यै नमः
५५. ॐ कमलायै नमः
५६. ॐ पद्मवासिन्यै नमः

५७. ॐ महासरस्वत्यै नमः ५८. ॐ मनःसिद्धायै नमः
५९. ॐ मनोयोगिन्यै नमः ६०. ॐ मातङ्गिन्यै नमः
६१. ॐ चण्डमुण्डचारिण्यै नमः ६२. ॐ दैत्यदानवनाशिन्यै नमः
६३. ॐ मेषज्योतिषायै नमः ६४. ॐ परंज्योतिषायै नमः
६५. ॐ आत्मज्योतिषायै नमः ६६. ॐ सर्वज्योतिस्वरूपिण्यै नमः
६७. ॐ सहस्त्रमूर्त्यै नमः ६८. ॐ शर्वाण्यै नमः
६९. ॐ सूर्यमूर्तिस्वरूपिण्यै नमः ७०. ॐ आयुर्लक्ष्म्यै नमः
७१. ॐ विद्यालक्ष्म्यै नमः ७२. ॐ सर्वलक्ष्मीप्रदायै नमः
७३. ॐ विचक्षणायै नमः ७४. ॐ क्षीरार्णववासिन्यै नमः
७५. ॐ वागीश्वर्यै नमः ७६. ॐ वाक्सिद्ध्यै नमः
७७. ॐ अज्ञानज्ञानगोचरायै नमः ७८. ॐ बलायै नमः
७९. ॐ परमकल्याण्यै नमः ८०. ॐ भानुमण्डलवासिन्यै नमः
८१. ॐ अव्यक्तायै नमः ८२. ॐ व्यक्तरूपायै नमः
८३. ॐ अव्यक्तरूपायै नमः ८४. ॐ अनन्तायै नमः
८५. ॐ चन्द्रायै नमः ८६. ॐ चन्द्रमण्डलवासिन्यै नमः
८७. ॐ चन्द्रमण्डलमण्डितायै नमः ८८. ॐ भैरव्यै नमः
८९. ॐ परमानन्दायै नमः ९०. ॐ शिवायै नमः
९१. ॐ अपराजितायै नमः ९२. ॐ ज्ञानप्राप्त्यै नमः
९३. ॐ ज्ञानवत्यै नमः ९४. ॐ ज्ञानमूर्त्यै नमः
९५. ॐ कलावत्यै नमः ९६. ॐ श्मशानवासिन्यै नमः
९७. ॐ मात्रे नमः ९८. ॐ परमकल्पिन्यै नमः
९९. ॐ घोषवत्यै नमः १००. ॐ दारिद्र्यहारिण्यै नमः
१०१. ॐ शिवतेजोमुख्यै नमः १०२. ॐ विष्णुवल्लभायै नमः
१०३. ॐ केशविभूषितायै नमः १०४. ॐ कूर्मायै नमः
१०५. ॐ महिषासुरघातिन्यै नमः १०६. ॐ सर्वरक्षायै नमः
१०७. ॐ महाकाल्यै नमः १०८. ॐ महालक्ष्म्यै नमः

इति श्रीदेव्यष्टोत्तरशतनामावलिः ।

अथ शिवनीराजनम्

हरि ॐ नमोऽस्त्वनन्ताय सहस्रमूर्तये सहस्रपादाक्षिशिरोरुबाहवे । सहस्रनाम्ने पुरुषाय शाश्वते सहस्रकोटियुगधारिणे नमः ॥१॥

ॐ जय गङ्गाधर हर शिव जय गिरिजाधीश, शिव जय गौरीनाथ । त्वं मां पालय नित्यं त्वं मां पालय शम्भो कृपया जगदीश । ॐ हर हर हर महादेव ॥२॥

कैलासे गिरिशिखरे कल्पद्रुमविपिने शिव कल्पद्रुमविपिने गुञ्जति मधुकरपुञ्जे गुञ्जति मधुकरपुञ्जे कुञ्जवने गहने । कोकिल कूजति खेलति हंसावलिललिता शिव हंसावलिललिता रचयतिकलाकलापं रचयति-कलाकलापं नृत्यति मुदसहिता । ॐ हर हर हर महादेव ॥३॥

तस्मिँल्ललितसुदेशे शालामणिरचिता, शिव शालामणिरचिता, तन्मध्ये हरनिकटे तन्मध्ये हरनिकटे गौरी मुदसहिता । क्रीडां रचयति भूषां रञ्जितनिजमीशं, शिव रञ्जितनिजमीशं, इन्द्रादिकसुरसेवित ब्रह्मादिकसुर-सेवित प्रणमति ते शीर्षम् । ॐ हर हर हर महादेव ॥४॥

विबुधवधूर्बहु नृत्यति हृदये मृदसहिता, शिव हृदये मृदसहिता, किन्नरगानं कुरुते किन्नरगानं कुरुते सप्तस्वरसहिता । धिनकत थै थै धिनकत मृदंग वादयते, शिव मृदंग वादयते, क्वणक्वणललिता वेणुं क्वणक्वणललिता वेणुं मधुरं नादयते । ॐ हर हर हर महादेव ॥५॥

कण कण-चरणे रचयति नूपुरमुज्ज्वलितं, शिव नूपुरमुज्ज्वलितं, चक्राकारं भ्रमयति चक्राकारं भ्रमयति कुरुते तां धिकताम् । तां तां लुप-चुप तालं नादयते, शिव तालं नादयते, अङ्गुष्ठाङ्गुलिनादं अङ्गुष्ठाङ्गुलिनादं लास्यकतां कुरुते । ॐ हर हर हर महादेव ॥६॥

कर्पूरद्युतिगौरं पञ्चाननसहितं, शिव पञ्चाननसहितं, त्रिनयन शशि-धरमौले त्रिनयन शशिधरमौले विषधर कण्ठयुतं ॥ सुन्दरजटाकलापं पावकयुतफालं, शिव पावकयुतफालं, डमरुत्रिशूलपिनाकं डमरुत्रिशूल-पिनाकं करधृतनृकपालम् । ॐ हर हर हर महादेव ॥७॥

शङ्खुनिनादं कृत्वा झल्लरि नादयते, शिव झल्लरि नादयते, नीराजयते ब्रह्मा नीराजयते विष्णुर्वेद-ऋचं पठते । इति मृदुचरणसरोजं हृदि कमले धृत्वा, शिव हृदि कमले धृत्वा, अवलोकयति महेशं शिवलोकयति सुरेशं, ईशं अभिनत्वा । ॐ हर हर हर महादेव ॥८॥

रुण्डै रचयति मालां पन्नगमुपवीतं, शिव पन्नगमुपवीतं, वामविभागे गिरिजा वामविभागे गौरी रूपं अतिललितम् । सुन्दरसकलशरीरे कृतभस्माभरणं शिव कृतभस्माभरणं इति वृषभध्वजरूपं हर-शिव-शङ्कर-रूपं तापत्रयहरणम् । ॐ हर हर हर महादेव ॥९॥

ध्यानं आरतिसमये हृदये इति कृत्वा शिव हृदये इति कृत्वा रामं त्रिजटानाथं शम्भुं त्रिजटानाथं ईशं अभिनत्वा । संगीतमेवं प्रतिदिन पठनं यः कुरुते शिव पठनं यः कुरुते शिवसायुज्यं गच्छति हरसायुज्यं गच्छति भक्त्या यः शृणुते । ॐ हर हर हर महादेव ॥१०॥

जय गङ्गाधर हर शिव जय गिरिजाधीश, शिव जय गौरीनाथ । त्वं मां पालय नित्यं त्वं मां पालय शम्भो कृपया जगदीश । ॐ हर हर हर महादेव ॥११॥

इति श्री शिवनीराजनं सम्पूर्णम् ।

अथ शिवध्यानावलिः

ॐ वन्दे देवमुमापतिं सुरगुरुं वन्दे जगत्कारणं,
वन्दे पन्नगभूषणं मृगधरं वन्दे पशूनां पतिम् ।
वन्दे सूर्यशशाङ्कवह्निनयनं वन्दे मुकुन्दप्रियं,
वन्दे भक्तजनाश्रयं च वरदं वन्दे शिवं शङ्करम् ॥१

शान्तं पद्मासनस्थं शशिधरमुकुटं पञ्चवक्त्रं त्रिनेत्रं,
शूलं वज्रं च खड्गं परशुमभयदं दक्षिणाङ्गे वहन्तम् ।
नागं पाशं च घण्टां डमरुकसहितं चांकुशं वामभागे,
नानालङ्कारदीप्तं स्फटिकमणिनिभं पार्वतीशं नमामि ॥२

कर्पूरगौरं करुणावतारं संसारसारं भुजगेन्द्रहारम् ।
सदावसन्तं हृदयारविन्दे भवं भवानीसहितं नमामि ॥३॥

असितगिरिसमं स्यात् कज्जलं सिन्धुपात्रे
सुरतरुवरशाखा लेखनी पत्रमुर्वी ।
लिखति यदि गृहीत्वा शारदा सर्वकालं
तदपि तव गुणानामीश पारं न याति ॥४॥

त्वमेव माता च पिता त्वमेव त्वमेव बन्धुश्च सखा त्वमेव ।
त्वमेव विद्याद्रविणं त्वमेव त्वमेव सर्वं मम देव देव ॥५॥

करचरणकृतं वाक्कायजं कर्मजं वा
श्रवणनयनजं वा मानसंवाऽपराधम् ।
विहितमविहितं वा सर्वमेतत् क्षमस्व
जय जय करुणाब्धे श्री महादेव शम्भो ॥६॥

चन्द्रोद्भासितशेखरे स्मरहरे गङ्गाधरे शङ्करे
सर्पैर्भूषितकण्ठकर्णविवरे नेत्रोत्थवैश्वानरे ।

दन्तित्वक्कृतसुन्दरांबरधरे त्रैलोक्यसारे हरे
मोक्षार्थं कुरु चित्तवृत्तिमचलामन्यैस्तु किं कर्मभिः ॥७॥

इति शिवध्यानावलिः सम्पूर्णा ॥

अथ शिवपुष्पाञ्जलिः

हरि ॐ यज्ञेन यज्ञमयजन्त देवाः तानि धर्माणि प्रथमा न्यासन्। ते ह नाकं महिमानः सचन्ते यत्र पूर्वे साध्याः सन्ति देवाः ॥

ॐ राजाधिराजाय प्रसह्य साहिने। नमो वयं वैश्रवणाय कुर्महे। स मे कामान् कामकामाय मह्यं। कामेश्वरो वैश्रवणो ददातु। कुबेराय वैश्रवणाय महाराजाय नमः ॥

ॐ विश्वतश्चक्षुरुत विश्वतो मुखं विश्वतो बाहुरुत विश्वतस्पात्। संबाहुभ्यां धमति सम्पतत्रैर्द्यावाभूमी जनयन्देव एकः ॥

ॐ तत्पुरुषाय विद्महे महादेवाय धीमहि। तन्नो रुद्रः प्रचोदयात् ॥
नानासुगन्धपुष्पाणि यथाकालोद्भवानि च।
मयाऽऽहृतानि दिव्यानि गृहाण परमेश्वर ॥

इति शिवपुष्पाञ्जलिः सम्पूर्णा ॥

बिल्वाष्टकम्

त्रिदलं त्रिगुणाकारं त्रिनेत्रं च त्रियायुधम्।
त्रिजन्मपाप-संहारमेकबिल्वं शिवार्पणम् ॥१

त्रिशाखैर्बिल्वपत्रैश्च ह्यच्छिद्रैः कोमलैः शुभैः।
शिवपूजां करिष्यामि ह्येकबिल्वं शिवार्पणम् ॥२

अखण्डबिल्वपत्रेण पूजिते नन्दिकेश्वरे।
शुद्ध्यन्ति सर्वपापेभ्यो ह्येकबिल्वं शिवार्पणम् ॥३

शालिग्रामशिलामेकां विप्राणां जातु अर्पयेत्।
सोमयज्ञ-महापुण्यमेकबिल्वं शिवार्पणम्॥४

दन्तिकोटिसहस्राणि वाजपेयशतानि च।
कोटिकन्या-महादानमेकबिल्वं शिवार्पणम्॥५

लक्ष्म्याः स्तनत उत्पन्नं महादेवस्य च प्रियम्।
बिल्ववृक्षं प्रयच्छामि ह्येकबिल्वं शिवार्पणम्॥६

दर्शनं बिल्ववृक्षस्य स्पर्शनं पापनाशनम्।
अघोरपापसंहारमेकबिल्वं शिवार्पणम्॥७

मूलतो ब्रह्मरूपाय मध्यतो विष्णुरूपिणे।
अग्रतः शिवरूपाय ह्येकबिल्वं शिवार्पणम्॥८

बिल्वाष्टकमिदं पुण्यं यः पठेच्छिवसन्निधौ।
सर्वपापविनिर्मुक्तः शिवलोकमवाप्नुयात्॥९

॥इति बिल्वाष्टकं सम्पूर्णम्॥

शिवमहिम्नः स्तोत्रम्

ॐ श्रीगणेशाय नमः

हरि ॐ गजाननं भूतगणाधिसेवितं
कपित्थजम्बूफलसारभक्षणम्।
उमासुतं शोकविनाशकारणं
नमामि विघ्नेश्वरपादपंकजम्॥

महिम्नः पारं ते परमविदुषो यद्सदृशी
स्तुतिर्ब्रह्मादीनामपि तदवसन्नास्त्वयि गिरः।

अथाऽवाच्यः सर्वः स्वमतिपरिणामावधि गृणन्
ममाप्येषः स्तोत्रे हर निरपवादः परिकरः ॥१॥

अतीतः पन्थानं तव च महिमा वाङ्मनसयो-
रतद्व्यावृत्या यं चकितमभिदत्ते श्रुतिरपि ।
स कस्य स्तोतव्यः कतिविधगुणः कस्य विषयः
पदे त्वर्वाचीने पतति न मनः कस्य न वचः ॥२॥

मधुस्फीता वाचः परममृतं निर्मितवत-
स्तव ब्रह्मन् किं वागपि सुरगुरोर्विस्मयपदम् ।
मम त्वेतां वाणीं गुणकथनपुण्येन भवतः
पुनामीत्यर्थेऽस्मिन्पुरमथन बुद्धिर्व्यवसिता ॥३॥

तवैश्वर्यं यत्तज्जगदुदयरक्षाप्रलयकृत्
त्रयीवस्तु व्यस्तं तिसृषु गुणभिन्नासु तनुषु ।
अभव्यानामस्मिन्वरद रमणीयामरमणीं
विहन्तुं व्याक्रोशीं विदधत इहैके जडधियः ॥४॥

किमीहः किं कायः स खलु किमुपायस्त्रिभुवनं
किमाधारो धाता सृजति किमुपादान इति च ।
अतर्क्यैश्वर्ये त्वय्यनवसरदुःस्थो हतधियः
कुतर्कोऽयं कांश्चिन्मुखरयति मोहाय जगतः ॥५॥

अजन्मानो लोकाः किमवयववन्तोऽपि जगता-
मधिष्ठातारं किं भवविधिरनादृत्य भवति ।
अनीशो वा कुर्याद्भुवनजनने कः परिकरो
यतो मन्दास्त्वां प्रत्यमरवर संशेरत इमे ॥६॥

256 LORD SIVA AND HIS WORSHIP

त्रयी सांख्यं योगः पशुपतिमतं वैष्णवमिति
प्रभिन्ने प्रस्थाने परमिदमदः पथ्यमिति च ।
रुचीनां वैचित्र्यादृजुकुटिलनानापथजुषां
नृणामेको गम्यस्त्वमसि पयसामर्णव इव ॥७॥

महोक्षः खट्वाङ्गं परशुरजिनं भस्म फणिनः
कपालं चेतीयत्तव वरद तन्त्रोपकरणम् ।
सुरास्तां तामृद्धिं दधति तु भवद्भूप्रणिहितां
न हि स्वात्मारामं विषयमृगतृष्णा भ्रमयति ॥८॥

ध्रुवं कश्चित्सर्वं सकलमपरस्त्वध्रुवमिदं
परो ध्रौव्याध्रौव्ये जगति गदति व्यस्तविषये ।
समस्तेऽप्येतस्मिन्पुरमथन तैर्विस्मित इव
स्तुवञ्जिह्रेमि त्वां न खलु ननु धृष्टा मुखरतः ॥९॥

तवैश्वर्यं यत्नाद्यदुपरि विरिञ्चिर्हरिरधः
परिच्छेत्तुं यातावनलमनलस्कन्धवपुषः ।
ततो भक्तिश्रद्धाभरगुरुगृणद्भ्यां गिरिश यत्
स्वयं तस्थे ताभ्यां तव किमनुवृत्तिर्न फलति ॥१०॥

अयत्नादापाद्य त्रिभुवनमवैरव्यतिकरं
दशास्यो यद्बाहूनभृत रणकण्डूपरवशान् ।
शिरःपद्मश्रेणीरचितचरणाम्भोरुहबलेः
स्थिरायास्त्वद्भक्तेस्त्रिपुरहर विस्फूर्जितमिदम् ॥११॥

अमुष्य त्वत्सेवासमधिगतसारं भुजवनं
बलात्कैलासेऽपि त्वदधिवसतौ विक्रमयतः ।

SIVA STOTRAS 257

अलभ्या पातालेऽप्यलसचलितांगुष्ठशिरसि
प्रतिष्ठा त्वय्यासीद्ध्रुवमुपचितो मुह्यति खलः ॥१२॥

यदृद्धिं सुत्राम्णो वरद परमोच्चैरपि सती-
मधश्चक्रे बाणः परिजनविधेयस्त्रिभुवनः ।
न तच्चित्रं तस्मिन्वरिवसितरि त्वच्चरणयो-
र्न कस्या उन्नत्यै भवति शिरसस्त्वय्यवनतिः ॥१३॥

अकाण्डब्रह्माण्डक्षयचकितदेवासुरकृपा-
विधेयस्यासीद्यस्त्रिनयन विषं संहृतवतः ।
स कल्माषः कण्ठे तव न कुरुते न श्रियमहो
विकारोऽपि श्लाघ्यो भुवनभयभङ्गव्यसनिनः ॥१४॥

असिद्धार्था नैव क्वचिदपि सदेवासुरनरे
निवर्तन्ते नित्यं जगति जयिनो यस्य विशिखाः ।
स पश्यन्नीश त्वामितरसुरसाधारणमभूत्-
स्मरः स्मर्तव्यात्मा न हि वशिषु पथ्यः परिभवः ॥१५॥

मही पादाघाताद्व्रजति सहसा संशयपदं
पदं विष्णोर्भ्राम्यद्भुजपरिघरुग्णग्रहगणम् ।
मुहुर्द्यौर्दौस्थ्यं यात्यनिभृतजटाताडिततटा
जगद्रक्षायै त्वं नटसि ननु वामैव विभुता ॥१६॥

वियद्व्यापी तारागणगुणितफेनोद्गमरुचिः
प्रवाहो वारां यः पृषतलघुदृष्टः शिरसि ते ।
जगद्द्वीपाकारं जलधिवलयं तेन कृतमि-
त्यनेनैवोन्नेयं धृतमहिम दिव्यं तव वपुः ॥१७॥

रथः क्षोणी यन्ता शतधृतिरगेन्द्रो धनुरथो
रथाङ्गे चन्द्राकौं रथचरणपाणिः शर इति ।
दिधक्षोस्ते कोऽयं त्रिपुरतृणमाडम्बरविधि-
र्विधेयैः क्रीडन्त्यो न खलु परतन्त्राः प्रभुधियः ॥१८॥

हरिस्ते साहस्रं कमलबलिमाधाय पदयो-
र्यदेकोने तस्मिन्निजमुदहरन्नेत्रकमलम् ।
गतो भक्त्युद्रेकः परिणतिमसौ चक्रवपुषा
त्रयाणां रक्षायै त्रिपुरहर जागर्ति जगताम् ॥१९॥

क्रतौ सुप्ते जाग्रत्त्वमसि फलयोगे क्रतुमतां
क्व कर्म प्रध्वस्तं फलति पुरुषाराधनमृते ।
अतस्त्वां संप्रेक्ष्य क्रतुषु फलदानप्रतिभुवं
श्रुतौ श्रद्धां बद्ध्वा दृढपरिकरः कर्मसु जनः ॥२०॥

क्रियादक्षो दक्षः क्रतुपतिरधीशस्तनुभृता-
मृषीणामार्त्विज्यं शरणद सदस्याः सुरगणाः ।
क्रतुभ्रंशस्त्वत्तः क्रतुफलविधानव्यसनिनो
ध्रुवं कर्तुः श्रद्धाविधुरमभिचाराय हि मखाः ॥२१॥

प्रजानाथं नाथ प्रसभमभिकं स्वां दुहितरं
गतं रोहिद्भूतां रिरमयिषुमृष्यस्य वपुषा ।
धनुष्पाणेर्यातं दिवमपि सपत्राकृतममुं
त्रसन्तं तेऽद्यापि त्यजति न मृगव्याधरभसः ॥२२॥

स्वलावण्याशंसा धृतधनुषमह्नाय तृणवत्
पुरः प्लुष्टं दृष्ट्वा पुरमथन पुष्पायुधमपि ।

SIVA STOTRAS

259

यदि स्त्रैणं दैवी यर्मानरत देहार्धघटना-
दवैति त्वामद्धा बत वरद मुग्धा युवतयः ॥२३॥

श्मशानेष्वाक्रीडा स्मरहर पिशाचाः सहचरा-
श्चिताभस्मालेपः स्रगपि नृकरोटीपरिकरः ।
अमङ्गल्यं शीलं तव भवतु नामैवमखिलं
तथापिस्मर्तॄणां वरद परमं मङ्गलमसि ॥२४॥

मनः प्रत्यक्चित्ते सविधमवधायात्तमरुतः
प्रहृष्यद्रोमाणः प्रमदसलिलोत्संगितदृशः ।
यदालोक्याह्लादं ह्रद इव निमज्यामृतमये
दधत्यन्तस्तत्त्वं किमपि यमिनस्तत्किल भवान् ॥२५॥

त्वमर्कस्त्वं सोमस्त्वमसि पवनस्त्वं हुतवह-
स्त्वमापस्त्वं व्योम त्वमु धरणिरात्मा त्वमिति च ।
परिच्छिन्नामेवं त्वयि परिणता बिभ्रतु गिरं
न विद्मस्तत्त्वं वयमिह तु यत्त्वं न भवसि ॥२६॥

त्रयीं तिस्रो वृत्तीस्त्रिभुवनमथो त्रीनपि सुरान्
अकाराद्यैर्वर्णैस्त्रिभिरभिदधत्तीर्णविकृति ।
तुरीयं ते धाम ध्वनिभिरवरुन्धानमणुभिः
समस्तं व्यस्तं त्वां शरणद गृणात्योमिति पदम् ॥२७॥

भवः शर्वो रुद्रः पशुपतिरथोग्रः सहमहां-
स्तथा भीमेशानाविति यदभिधानाष्टकमिदम् ।
अमुष्मिन्नत्येकं प्रविरचति देव श्रुतिरपि
प्रियायास्मै धाम्ने प्रणिहितनमस्योऽस्मि भवते ॥२८॥

नमो नेदिष्ठाय प्रियदव दविष्ठाय च नमो
नमः क्षोदिष्ठाय स्मरहर महिष्ठाय च नमः ।
नमो वर्षिष्ठाय त्रिनयन यविष्ठाय च नमो
नमः सर्वस्मै ते तदिदमिति सर्वाय च नमः ॥२९॥

बहुलरजसे विश्वोत्पत्तौ भवाय नमो नमः
प्रबलतमसे तत्संहारे हराय नमो नमः ।
जनसुखकृते सत्वोद्रिक्तौ मृडाय नमो नमः
प्रमहसि पदे निस्त्रैगुण्ये शिवाय नमो नमः ॥३०॥

कृशपरिणति चेतः क्लेशवश्यं क्व चेदं
क्व च तव गुणसीमोल्लङ्घिनी शश्वदृद्धिः ।
इति चकितममन्दीकृत्य मां भक्तिराधाद्-
वरद चरणयोस्ते वाक्यपुष्पोपहारम् ॥३१॥

असितगिरिसमं स्यात् कज्जलं सिन्धुपात्रे
सुरतरुवरशाखा लेखनी पत्रमुर्वी ।
लिखति यदि गृहीत्वा शारदा सर्वकालं
तदपि तव गुणानामीश पारं न याति ॥३२॥

असुरसुरमुनीन्द्रैरर्चितस्येन्दुमौले-
र्ग्रथितगुणमहिम्नो निर्गुणस्येश्वरस्य ।
सकलगणवरिष्ठः पुष्पदन्ताभिधानो
रुचिरमलघुवृत्तैः स्तोत्रमेतच्चकार ॥३३॥

अहरहरनवद्यं धूर्जटेः स्तोत्रमेतत्
पठति परमभक्त्या शुद्धचित्तः पुमान् यः ।

SIVA STOTRAS 261

स भवति शिवलोके रुद्रतुल्यस्तथाऽत्र
प्रचुरतरधनायुः पुत्रवान् कीर्तिमांश्च ॥३४॥

दीक्षा दानं तपस्तीर्थं ज्ञानं यागादिकाः क्रियाः ।
महिम्नःस्तवपाठस्य कलां नार्हन्ति षोडशीम् ॥३५॥

आसमाप्तमिदं स्तोत्रं पुण्यं गन्धर्वभाषितं ।
अनौपम्यं मनोहारि शिवमीश्वरवर्णनम् ॥३६॥

महेशान्नपरो देवो महिम्नो नापरा स्तुतिः ।
अघोरान्नपरो मन्त्रो नास्ति तत्त्वं गुरोः परम् ॥३७॥

कुसुमदशननामा सर्वगन्धर्वराजः
शशिधरवरमौलेर्देवदेवस्य दासः ।
स खलु निज महिम्नो भ्रष्ट एवास्य रोषात्-
स्तवनमिदमकार्षीद्दिव्यदिव्यं महिम्नः ॥३८॥

सुरवरमुनिपूज्यं स्वर्गमोक्षैकहेतुं
पठति यदि मनुष्यः प्राञ्जलिर्नान्य चेताः ।
व्रजति शिवसमीपं किन्नरैः स्तूयमानः
स्तवनमिदममोघं पुष्पदन्तप्रणीतम् ॥३९॥

श्रीपुष्पदन्तमुखपङ्कजनिर्गतेन
स्तोत्रेण किल्बिषहरेण हरप्रियेण ।
कण्ठस्थितेन पठितेन समाहितेन
सुप्रीणितो भवति भूतपतिर्महेशः ॥४०॥

इत्येषा वाङ्मयी पूजा श्रीमच्छङ्करपादयोः ।
अर्पिता तेन देवेशः प्रीयतां मे सदाशिवः ॥४१॥

यदस्तं पदं भ्रष्टं मात्राहीनं च यद्भवेत्।
तत्सर्वं क्षम्यतां देव प्रसीद परमेश्वर ॥४२॥

इति श्रीपुष्पदन्ताचार्यविरचितं शिवमहिम्नः स्तोत्रं सम्पूर्णम्।

अथ शिवस्तुतिः

ॐ महादेव शिव शङ्कर शम्भो उमाकान्त हर त्रिपुरारे
मृत्युञ्जय वृषभध्वज शूलिन् गङ्गाधर मृड मदनारे।
हर शिव शङ्कर गौरीशं वन्दे गङ्गाधरमीशं
रुद्रं पशुपतिमीशानं कलये काशीपुरिनाथम् ॥१॥

जय शम्भो जय शम्भो शिव गौरीशङ्कर जय शम्भो।
जय शम्भो जय शम्भो शिव गौरीशङ्कर जय शम्भो ॥२॥

ॐ नमः पार्वतीपतये हर हर महादेव॥

वेदसार-शिवस्तवः

पशूनां पतिं पापनाशं परेशं
    गजेन्द्रस्य कृत्तिं वसानं वरेण्यम्।
जटाजूटमध्ये स्फुरद्गांगवारिं
    महादेवमेकं स्मरामि स्मरारिम् ॥१॥

महेशं सुरेशं सुरारार्तिनाशं
    विभुं विश्वनाथं विभूत्यंगभूषम्।
विरूपाक्षमिन्द्रर्कवह्नित्रिनेत्रं
    सदानन्दमीडे प्रभुं पञ्चवक्त्रम् ॥२॥

गिरीशं गणेशं गले नीलवर्णं
    गवेन्द्राधिरूढं गुणातीतरूपम्।

भवं भास्वरं भस्मना भूषिताङ्गं
    भवानीकलत्रं भजे पञ्चवक्त्रम् ॥३॥

शिवाकान्त शम्भो शशाङ्कार्धमौले
    महेशान शूलिन् जटाजूटधारिन् ।
त्वमेको जगद्व्यापको विश्वरूप
    प्रसीद प्रसीद प्रभो पूर्णरूप ॥४॥

परात्मानमेकं जगद्बीजमाद्यं
    निरीहं निराकारमोङ्कारवेद्यं ।
यतो जायते पाल्यते येन विश्वं
    तमीशं भजे लीयते यत्र विश्वम् ॥५॥

न भूमिर्न चापो न वह्निर्न वायु-
    र्न चाकाशमास्ते न तन्द्रा न निद्रा ।
न ग्रीष्मो न शीतं न देशो न वेषो
    न यस्यास्ति मूर्तिस्त्रिमूर्तिं तमीडे ॥६॥

अजं शाश्वतं कारणं कारणानां
    शिवं केवलं भासकं भासकानाम् ।
तुरीयं तमःपारमाद्यन्तहीनं
    प्रपद्ये परं पावनं द्वैतहीनम् ॥७॥

नमस्ते नमस्ते विभो विश्वमूर्ते
    नमस्ते नमस्ते चिदानन्दमूर्ते ।
नमस्ते नमस्ते तपोयोगगम्य
    नमस्ते नमस्ते श्रुतिज्ञानगम्य ॥८॥

प्रभो शूलपाणे विभो विश्वनाथ
    महादेव शम्भो महेश त्रिनेत्र ।

शिवाकान्त शान्त स्मरारे पुरारे
त्वदन्यो वरेण्यो न मान्यो न गण्यः ॥९॥

शम्भो महेश करुणामय शूलपाणे
गौरीपते पशुपते पशुपाशनाशिन् ।
काशीपते करुणया जगदेतदेक-
स्त्वं हंसि पासि विदधासि महेश्वरोऽसि ॥१०॥

त्वत्तो जगद्भवति देव भव स्मरारे
त्वय्येव तिष्ठति जगन्मृड विश्वनाथ ।
त्वय्येव गच्छति लयं जगदेतदीश
लिङ्गात्मकं हर चराचर विश्वरूपिन् ॥११॥

इति श्रीमच्छंकराचार्यविरचितं वेदसारशिवस्तोत्रं सम्पूर्णम् ।

श्री शिवमानसपूजा

ॐ श्रीगणेशाय नमः

१. रत्नैः कल्पितमासनं हिमजलैः स्नानं च दिव्याम्बरम् ।
नानारत्नविभूषितं मृगमदामोदाङ्कितं चन्दनम् ।
जातीचम्पकबिल्वपत्ररचितं पुष्पं च धूपं तथा ।
दीपं देव दयानिधे पशुपते हृत्कल्पितं गृह्यताम् ॥

२. सौवर्णे मणिखण्डरत्नरचिते पात्रे घृतं पायसम् ।
भक्ष्यं पञ्चविधं पयोदधियुतं रम्भाफलं पानकम् ।
शाकानामयुतं जलं रुचिकरं कर्पूरखण्डोज्ज्वलम् ।
ताम्बूलं मनसा मया विरचितं भक्त्या प्रभो स्वीकुरु ॥

३. छत्रं चामरयोर्युगं व्यजनकं चादर्शकं निर्मलम् ।
वीणा भेरिमृदङ्गकाहलकलागीतं च नृत्यं तथा ।

साष्टाङ्गं प्रणतिः स्तुतिर्बहुविधा ह्येतत्समस्तं मया ।
संकल्पेन समर्पितं तव विभो पूजां गृहाण प्रभो ॥

४. आत्मा त्वं गिरिजा मतिः सहचराः प्राणाः शरीरं गृहम् ।
पूजा ते विषयोपभोगरचना निद्रा समाधिस्थितिः ।
संचारः पदयोः प्रदक्षिणविधिः स्तोत्राणि सर्वा गिरो ।
यद्यत्कर्म करोमि तत्तदखिलं शम्भो तवाराधनम् ॥

५. इत्येवं हरपूजनं प्रतिदिनं यो वा त्रिसन्ध्यं पठेत् ।
सेवाश्लोकचतुष्टयं प्रतिदिनं पूजा हरेर्मानसि ।
सोऽयं सौख्यमवाप्नुयाद् द्युतिधरं साक्षाद्धरेर्दर्शनम् ।
व्यासस्तेन महावसानसमये कैलासलोकं गतः ॥

६. करचरणकृतं वाक्कायजं कर्मजं वा ।
श्रवणनयनजं वा मानसं वापराधम् ।
विहितमविहितं वा सर्वमेतत्क्षमस्व ।
जय जय करुणाब्धे श्रीमहादेव शम्भो ॥

॥ इति श्रीशिवमानसपूजा समाप्तम् ॥

॥ रुद्रं चमकं च ॥

ॐ अस्य श्रीरुद्राध्यायप्रश्नमहामन्त्रस्य, अघोर ऋषिः, अनुष्टुप् छन्दः, संकर्षणमूर्तिस्वरूपो योऽसावादित्यः, परमपुरुषः स एष रुद्रो देवता । नमः शिवायेति बीजम् । शिवतरायेति शक्तिः । महादेवायेति कीलकम् । श्रीसाम्बसदाशिवप्रसादसिद्ध्यर्थे जपे विनियोगः ॥

ॐ अग्निहोत्रात्मने अङ्गुष्ठाभ्यां नमः । ॐ दर्शपूर्णमासात्मने तर्जनीभ्यां नमः । ॐ चातुर्मास्यात्मने मध्यमाभ्यां नमः । ॐ निरूढपशुबन्धात्मने अनामिकाभ्यां नमः । ॐ ज्योतिष्टोमात्मने कनिष्ठिकाभ्यां नमः । ॐ सर्वक्रत्वात्मने करतलकरपृष्ठाभ्यां नमः ।

ॐ अग्निहोत्रात्मने हृदयाय नमः । ॐ दर्शपूर्णमासात्मने शिरसे स्वाहा । ॐ चातुर्मास्यात्मने शिखायै वषट् । ॐ निरूढ-पशुबन्धात्मने कवचाय हुं । ॐ ज्योतिष्टोमात्मने नेत्रत्रयाय वौषट् । ॐ सर्वक्रत्वात्मने अस्त्राय फट् । भूर्भुवस्सुवरोमिति दिग्बन्धः ॥

ध्यानम्—

आपाताळनभःस्थलान्तभुवनब्रह्माण्डमाविस्फुर-
ज्ज्योतिःस्फाटिकलिङ्गमौळिविलसत्पूर्णेदुवान्तामृतैः ।
अस्तोकाप्लुतमेकमीशमनिशं रुद्रानुवाकाञ्जपन्
ध्यायेदीप्सितसिद्धये ध्रुवपदं विप्रोऽभिषिञ्चेच्छिवम् ॥

ब्रह्माण्डव्याप्तदेहा भसितहिमरुचा भासमाना भुजङ्गैः
कण्ठेकालाः कपर्दाकलितशशिकलाऽचण्डकोदण्डहस्ताः ।
त्र्यक्षा रुद्राक्षमालाप्रकटितविभवाः शाम्भवा मूर्तिभेदाः
रुद्राः श्रीरुद्रसूक्तप्रकटितविभवा नः प्रयच्छन्तु सौख्यम् ॥

ॐ गणानां त्वा गणपतिᳪ॑ हवामहे कविं कवीनामुपमश्रवस्त-मम् । ज्येष्ठराजं ब्रह्मणां ब्रह्मणस्पत आनःशृण्वन्नूतिभिस्सीद-सादनम् ॥ ॐ श्रीमहागणाधिपतये नमः ॥

शं च मे मयश्च मे प्रियं च मेऽनुकामश्च मे कामश्च मे सौमनसश्च मे भद्रं च मे श्रेयश्च मे वस्यश्च मे यशश्च मे भगश्च मे द्रविणं च मे यन्ता च मे धर्ता च मे क्षेमश्च मे धृतिश्च मे विश्वं च ॥१॥ मे महश्च मे सँविश्च मे ज्ञात्रं च मे सूश्च मे प्रसूश्च मे सीरं च मे लयश्च म ऋतं च मेऽमृतं च मेऽयक्ष्मं च मेऽनामयच्च मे जीवातुश्च मे दीर्घायुत्वं च मेऽनमित्रं च मेऽभयं च मे सुगं च मे शयनं च मे सूषा च मे सुदिनं च मे ॥

ॐ शान्तिः शान्तिः शान्तिः ॥

॥ श्रीरुद्रप्रश्नः ॥

॥ प्रथमोऽनुवाकः ॥

ॐ नमो भगवते रुद्राय ॥

ॐ नमस्ते रुद्र मन्यव उतोत इषवे नमः । नमस्ते अस्तु धन्वने बाहुभ्यामुत ते नमः । या त इषुः शिवतमा शिवं बभूव ते धनुः । शिवा शरव्या या तव तया नो रुद्र मृडय । या ते रुद्र शिवा तनूरघोराऽपापकाशिनी । तया नस्तनुवा शन्तमया गिरिशंता-भिचाकशीहि । यामिषुं गिरिशंत हस्ते ॥१॥ बिभर्ष्यस्तवे । शिवां गिरित्र तां कुरु मा हि ँ सीः पुरुषं जगत् । शिवेन वचसा त्वा गिरिशाच्छावदामसि । यथा नः सर्वमिज्जगदयक्ष्म ँ सुमना असत् । अध्यवोचदधिवक्ता प्रथमो दैव्यो भिषक् । अही ँ श्च सर्वा-ञ्जभयन्त्सर्वाश्च या तु धान्यः । असौ यस्ताम्रो अरुण उत बभ्रुः सुमङ्गलः । ये चे मा ँ रुद्रा अभितो दिक्षु ॥२॥ श्रिताः सहस्रशो-ऽवैषा ँ हेड ईमहे । असौ योऽवसर्पति नीलग्रीवो विलोहितः । उतैनं गोपा अदृशन्नदृशन्नुदहार्यः । उतैनं विश्वाभूतानि स दृष्टो मृडयाति नः । नमो अस्तु नीलग्रीवाय सहस्राक्षाय मीढुषे । अथो ये अस्य सत्वानोऽहं तेभ्योऽकरन्नमः । प्रमुञ्च धन्वनस्त्वमुभयोरार्त्नि-योर्ज्याम् । याश्च ते हस्त इषवः ॥३॥ परा ता भगवो वप । अवतत्य धनुस्त्व ँ सहस्राक्ष शतेषुधे । निशीर्य शल्यानां मुखा

शिवो नः सुमना भव। विज्यं धनुः कपर्दिनो विशल्यो बाणवाँ उत। अनेशन्नस्येषव आभुरस्य निषङ्गतिः। या ते हेतिर्मीढुष्टम हस्ते बभूव ते धनुः। तयाऽस्मान्विश्वतस्त्वमयक्ष्मया परिब्भुज। नमस्ते अस्त्वायुधायानाततताय धृष्णवे। उभाभ्यामुत ते नमो बाहुभ्यां तव धन्वने। परिते धन्वनो हेतिरस्मान्वृणक्तु विश्वतः। अथो य इषुधिस्तवारे अस्मन्निधेहि तम् ॥४॥ शम्भवे नमः ॥

नमस्ते अस्तु भगवन्विश्वेश्वराय महादेवाय त्र्यम्बकाय त्रिपुरान्तकाय त्रिकालाग्निकालाय कालाग्निरुद्राय नीलकण्ठाय मृत्युंजयाय सर्वेश्वराय सदाशिवाय श्रीमन्महादेवाय नमः ॥

द्वितीयोऽनुवाकः ॥

नमो हिरण्यबाहवे सेनान्ये दिशां च पतये नमो नमो वृक्ष्येभ्यो हरिकेशेभ्यः पशूनां पतये नमो नमः सस्पिञ्जराय त्विषीमते पथीनां पतये नमो नमो बभ्लुशाय विव्याधिनेऽन्नानां पतये नमो नमो हरिकेशायोपवीतिने पुष्टानां पतये नमो नमो भवस्य हेत्यै जगतां पतये नमो नमो रुद्रायाततविने क्षेत्राणां पतये नमो नमः सूतायाहन्त्याय वनानां पतये नमो नमः ॥५॥ रोहिताय स्थपतये वृक्षाणां पतये नमो नमो मन्त्रिणे वाणिजाय कक्षाणां पतये नमो नमो भुवंतये वारिवस्कृतायौषधीनां पतये नमो नम उच्चैर्घोषायाक्रन्दयते पत्तीनां पतये नमो नमः कृत्स्नवीताय धावते सत्त्वनां पतये नमः ॥६॥

तृतीयोऽनुवाकः ॥

नमः सहमानाय निव्याधिन आव्याधिनीनां पतये नमो नमः ककुभाय निषङ्गिणे स्तेनानां पतये नमो नमो निषङ्गिण इषुधिमते तस्कराणां पतये नमो नमो वञ्चते परिवञ्चते स्तायूनां पतये नमो नमो निचेरवे परिचरायारण्यानां पतये नमः सृकाविभ्यो जिघाँ सद्भ्यो मुष्णतां पतये नमो नमोऽसिमद्भ्यो नक्तंचरद्भ्यः प्रकृन्तानां पतये नमो नम उष्णीषिणे गिरिचराय कुलुञ्चानां पतये नमो नमः ॥७॥ इषुमद्भ्यो धन्वाविभ्यश्च वो नमो नम आतन्वानेभ्यः प्रतिदधानेभ्यश्च वो नमो नम आयच्छद्भ्यो विसृजद्भ्यश्च वो नमो नम आसीनेभ्यः शयानेभ्यश्च वो नमो नमः स्वपद्भ्यो जाग्रद्भ्यश्च वो नमो नमस्तिष्ठद्भ्यो धावद्भ्यश्च वो नमो नमः सभाभ्यः सभापतिभ्यश्च वो नमो नमो अश्वेभ्योऽश्वपतिभ्यश्च वो नमो नमः ॥८॥

चतुर्थोऽनुवाकः ॥

नम आव्याधिनीभ्यो विविध्यन्तीभ्यश्च वो नमो नम उगणाभ्यस्तृंहतीभ्यश्च वो नमो नमो गृत्सेभ्यो गृत्सपतिभ्यश्च वो नमो नमो व्रातेभ्यो व्रातपतिभ्यश्च वो नमो नमो गणेभ्यो गणपतिभ्यश्च वो नमो नमो विरूपेभ्यो विश्वरूपेभ्यश्च वो नमो नमो महद्भ्यः क्षुल्लकेभ्यश्च वो नमो नमो रथिभ्योऽरथेभ्यश्च वो नमो नमो रथेभ्यः ॥९॥ रथपतिभ्यश्च वो नमो नमः सेनाभ्यः सेनानिभ्यश्च वो नमो नमः क्षत्तृभ्यः संग्रहीतृभ्यश्च वो नमो नमस्तक्षभ्योरथकारेभ्यश्च वो नमो नमः कुलालेभ्यः कमारिभ्यश्च वो नमो नमः पुञ्जिष्टेभ्यो

निषादेभ्यश्च वो नमो नम इषुकृद्भ्यो धन्वकृद्भ्यश्च वो नमो नमो मृगयुभ्यः श्वनिभ्यश्च वो नमो नमः श्वभ्यः श्वपतिभ्यश्च वो नमः ॥ १० ॥

पञ्चमोऽनुवाक: ॥

नमो भवाय च रुद्राय च नमः शर्वाय च पशुपतये नमो नीलग्रीवाय च शितिकण्ठाय च नमः कपर्दिने च व्युप्तकेशाय नमः सहस्राक्षाय च शतधन्वने च नमो गिरिशाय च शिपिविष्टाय च नमो मीढुष्टमाय चेषुमते च नमो ह्रस्वाय च वामनाय च नमो बृहते च वर्षीयसे च नमो वृद्धाय च संवृध्वने च ॥११॥ नमो अग्रियाय च प्रथमाय च नम आशवे चाजिराय च नमः शीघ्रियाय च शीभ्याय च नम ऊर्म्याय चावस्वन्याय च नमः स्रोतस्याय च द्वीप्याय च ॥१२॥

षष्ठोऽनुवाक: ॥

नमो ज्येष्ठाय च कनिष्ठाय च नमः पूर्वजाय चापरजाय च नमो मध्यमाय चापगल्भाय च नमो जघन्याय च बुध्नियाय च नमः सोभ्याय च प्रतिसर्याय च नमो याम्याय च क्षेम्याय च नम उर्वर्याय च खल्याय च नमः श्लोक्याय चावसान्याय च नमो वन्याय च कक्ष्याय च नमः श्रवाय च प्रतिश्रवाय च ॥१३॥ नम आशुषेणाय चाशुरथाय च नमः शूराय चावभिन्दते च नमो वर्मिणे च वरूथिने च नमो बिल्मिने च कवचिने च नमः श्रुताय च श्रुतसेनाय च ॥१४॥

सप्तमोऽनुवाकः ॥

नमो दुन्दुभ्याय चाहनन्याय च नमो धृष्णवे च प्रमृशाय च नमो दूताय च प्रहिताय च नमो निषङ्गिणे चेषुधिमते च नमस्तीक्ष्णेषवे चायुधिने च नमः स्वायुधाय च सुधन्वने च नमः स्रुत्याय च पथ्याय च नमः काट्याय च नीप्याय च नमः सूद्याय च सरस्याय च नमो नाद्याय च वैशन्ताय च ॥१५॥ नमः कूप्याय चावट्याय च नमो वर्ष्याय चावर्ष्याय च नमो मेघ्याय च विद्युत्याय च नम ईध्रियाय चातप्याय च नमो वात्याय च रेष्मियाय च नमो वास्तव्याय च वास्तुपाय च ॥१६॥

अष्टमोऽनुवाकः ॥

नमः सोमाय च रुद्राय च नमस्ताम्राय चारुणाय च नमः शङ्गाय च पशुपतये च नम उग्राय च भीमाय च नमो अग्रेवधाय च दूरेवधाय च नमो हन्त्रे च हनीयसे च नमो वृक्षेभ्यो हरिकेशेभ्यो नमस्ताराय नमश्शंभवे च मयोभवे च नमः शंकराय च मयस्कराय च नमः शिवाय च शिवतराय च ॥१७॥ नमस्तीर्थ्याय च कूल्याय च नमः पार्याय चावार्याय च नमः प्रतरणाय चोत्तरणाय च नम आतार्याय चालाद्याय च नमः शष्प्याय च फेन्याय च नमः सिकत्याय च प्रवाह्याय च ॥१८॥

नवमोऽनुवाकः ॥

नम इरिण्याय च प्रपथ्याय च नमः किँशिलाय च क्षयणाय च नमः कपर्दिने च पुलस्तये च नमो गोष्ठ्याय च गृह्याय च

नमस्तल्प्याय च गेह्याय च नमः काट्याय च गह्वरेष्ठाय च नमो हृदय्याय च निवेष्प्याय च नमः पाँसव्याय च रजस्याय च नमः शुष्क्याय च हरित्याय च नमो लोप्याय चोलप्याय च ॥१९॥ नम ऊर्व्याय च सूर्म्याय च नमः पर्ण्याय च पर्णशद्याय च नमोऽपगुरमाणाय चाभिघ्नते च नम आख्खिदते च प्रख्खिदते च नमो वः किरिकेभ्यो देवानाँ हृदयेभ्यो नमो विक्षीणकेभ्यो नमो विचिन्वत्केभ्यो नम आनिहतेभ्यो नम आमीवत्केभ्यः ॥२०॥

दशमोऽनुवाकः ॥

द्रापे अन्धसस्पते दरिद्रन्नीललोहित। एषां पुरुषाणामेषां पशूनां मा भेर्माऽरो मो एषां किं चनाममत्। या ते रुद्र शिवा तनूशिवा विश्वाहभेषजी। शिवा रुद्रस्य भेषजी तया नो मृड जीवसे ॥ इमाँ रुद्राय तवसे कपर्दिने क्षयद्वीराय प्रभरामहे मतिम्। यथा नः शमसद्द्विपदे चतुष्पदे विश्वं पुष्टं ग्रामे अस्मिन् ॥२१॥ अनातुरम्। मृडा नो रुद्रोत नो मयस्कृधि क्षयद्वीराय नमसा विधेम ते। यच्छं च योश्च मनुरायजे पिता तदश्याम तव रुद्र प्रणीतौ। मा नो महान्तमुत मा नो अर्भकं मा न उक्षन्तमुत मा न उक्षितम्। मा नोऽवधीः पितरं मोत मातरं प्रिया मा नस्तनुवः ॥२२॥ रुद्ररीरिषः। मा नस्तोके तनये मा न आयुषि मानो गोषु मा नो अश्वेषु रीरिषः। वीरान्मा नो रुद्र भामितोऽवधीर्हविष्मन्तो नमसा विधेम ते। आरात्ते गोघ्न उत पूरुषघ्ने क्षयद्वीराय सुम्नमस्मे ते अस्तु। रक्षा च नो अधि च देव ब्रूह्यथा च नः शर्म यच्छद्विबर्हाः। स्तुहि ॥२३॥ श्रुतं गर्तसदं युवानं मृगन्न भीममुपहत्नुमुग्रम्। मृडा

जरित्रे रुद्र स्तवानो अन्यन्ते अस्मन्निवपन्तु सेनाः । परिणो रुद्रस्य हेतिर्वृणक्तु परि त्वेषस्य दुर्मतिरघायोः । अव स्थिरा मघवद्भ्यस्तनुष्व मीढ्वस्तोकाय तनयाय मृडय । मीढुष्टम शिवतम शिवो नः सुमना भव । परमे वृक्ष आयुधन्निधाय कृत्तिं वसान आचर पिनाकम् ॥२४॥ बिभ्रदागहि । विकिरिद विलोहित नमस्ते अस्तु भगवः । यास्ते सहस्त्रꣳ हेतयोन्यमस्मन्निवपन्तु ताः । सहस्त्राणि सहस्त्रधा बाहुवोस्तव हेतयः । तासामीशानो भगवः पराचीना मुखा कृधि ॥२५॥

एकादशोऽनुवाकः ॥

सहस्त्राणि सहस्त्रशो ये रुद्रा अधि भूम्याम् । तेषाꣳ सहस्त्रयोजनेऽवधन्वानि तन्मसि । अस्मिन् महत्यर्णवेऽन्तरिक्षे भवा अधि । नीलग्रीवाशिशतिकण्ठाः शर्वा अधः क्षमाचराः । नीलग्रीवाशिशतिकण्ठा दिवꣳ रुद्रा उपश्रिताः । ये वृक्षेषु सस्पिञ्जरा नीलग्रीवा विलोहिताः । ये भूतानामधिपतयो विशिखासः कपर्दिनः । ये अन्नेषु विविध्यन्ति पात्रेषु पिबतो जनान् । ये पथां पथिरक्षय ऐलबृदा यव्युधः । ये तीर्थानि ॥२६॥ प्रचरन्ति सृकावन्तो निषङ्गिणः । य एतावन्तश्च भूयाꣳसश्च दिशो रुद्रा वितस्थिरे । तेषाꣳ सहस्त्रयोजनेऽवधन्वानि तन्मसि । नमो रुद्रेभ्यो ये पृथिव्यां येऽन्तरिक्षे ये दिवि येषामन्नं वातो वर्षमिषवस्तेभ्यो दश प्राचीर्दश दक्षिणा दश प्रतीचीर्दशोदीचीर्दशोर्ध्वास्तेभ्यो नमस्ते नो मृडयन्तु ते यं द्विष्मो यश्च नो द्वेष्टि तं वो जम्भे दधामि ॥२७॥

275

ॐ त्र्यम्बकं यजामहे सुगन्धि पुष्टिवर्धनम्। उर्वारुकमिव बन्धनान्मृत्योर्मुक्षीय माऽमृतात्। यो रुद्रो अग्नौ यो अप्सु य ओषधीषु यो रुद्रो विश्वा भुवनाविवेश तस्मै रुद्राय नमो अस्तु। तमु ष्टुहि यः स्विषुः सुधन्वा यो विश्वस्य क्षयति भेषजस्य। यक्ष्वामहे सौ मनसाय रुद्रं नमोभिर्देवमसुरं दुवस्य। अयं मे हस्तो भगवानयं मे भगवत्तरः। अयं मे विश्वभेषजोऽयँ शिवाभिमर्शनः। ये ते सहस्रमयुतं पाशा मृत्यो मर्त्याय हन्तवे। तान्यज्ञस्य मायया सर्वानव यजामहे। मृत्यवे स्वाहा मृत्यवे स्वाहाँ। ॐ नमो भगवते रुद्राय विष्णवे मृत्युर्मे पाहि। प्राणानां ग्रन्थिरसि रुद्रो मा विशान्तकः। तेनान्नेनाप्यायस्व॥

ॐ शान्तिः शान्तिः शान्तिः॥

॥चमकम्॥

प्रथमोऽनुवाक: ॥

ॐ अग्नाविष्णू सजोषसे मा वर्धन्तु वां गिर: । द्युम्नैर्वाजे-भिरागतम् । वाजश्च मे प्रसवश्च मे प्रयतिश्च मे प्रसितिश्च मे धीतिश्च मे क्रतुश्च मे स्वरश्च मे श्लोकश्च मे श्रावश्च मे श्रुतिश्च मे ज्योतिश्च मे सुवश्च मे प्राणश्च मेऽपान: ॥१॥ च मे व्यानश्च मेऽसुश्च मे चित्तं च म आधीतं च मे वाक्च मे मनश्च मे चक्षुश्च मे श्रोत्रं च मे दक्षश्च मे बलं चम ओजश्च मे सहश्च म आयुश्च मे जरा च म आत्मा च मे तनूश्च मे शर्म च मे वर्म च मेऽङ्गानि च मेऽस्थानि च मे परूँषि च मे शरीराणि च मे ।

द्वितीयोऽनुवाक: ॥

ज्यैष्ठ्यं च म आधिपत्यं च मे मन्युश्च मे भामश्च मेऽमश्च मेऽम्भश्च मे जेमा च मे महिमा च मे वरिमा च मे प्रथिमा च मे वर्ष्मा च मे द्राघुया च मे वृद्धं च मे वृद्धिश्च मे सत्यं च मे श्रद्धा च मे जगच्च ॥३॥ मे धनं च मे वशश्च मे त्विषिश्च मे क्रीडा च मे मोदश्च मे जातं च मे जनिष्यमाणं च मे सूक्तं च मे सुकृतं च मे वित्तं च मे वेद्यं च मे भूतं च मे भविष्यच्च मे सुगं च मे सुपथं च म ऋद्धं च म ऋद्धिश्च मे क्लृप्तं च मे क्लृप्तिश्च मे मतिश्च मे सुमतिश्च मे ॥४॥

तृतीयोऽनुवाकः ॥

शं च मे मयश्च मे प्रियं च मेऽनुकामश्च मे कामश्च मे सौमनसश्च मे भद्रं च मे श्रेयश्च मे वस्यश्च मे यशश्च मे भगश्च मे द्रविणं च मे यन्ता च मे धर्ता च मे क्षेमश्च मे धृतिश्च मे विश्वं च ॥५॥ मे महश्च मे सँविश्च मे ज्ञात्रं च मे सूश्च मे प्रसूश्च मे सीरं च मे लयश्च म ऋतं च मेऽमृतं च मेऽयक्ष्मं च मेऽनामयच्च मे जीवातुश्च मे दीर्घायुत्वं च मेऽनमित्रं च मेऽभयं च मे सुगं च मे शयनं च मे सूषा च मे सुदिनं च मे ॥६॥

चतुर्थोऽनुवाकः ॥

ऊर्क्च मे सूनृता च मे पयश्च मे रसश्च मे घृतं च मे मधु च मे सग्धिश्च मे सपीतिश्च मे कृषिश्च मे वृष्टिश्च मे जैत्रं च म औद्भिद्यं च मे रयिश्च मे रायश्च मे पुष्टं च मे पुष्टिश्च मे विभु च ॥७॥ मे प्रभु च मे बहु च मे भूयश्च मे पूर्णं च मे पूर्णतरं च मेऽक्षितिश्च मे कूयवाश्च मेऽत्रं च मेऽक्षुच्च मे व्रीहयश्च मे यवाश्च मे माषाश्च मे तिलाश्च मे मुद्गाश्च मे खल्वाश्च मे गोधूमाश्च मे मसुराश्च मे प्रियंगवश्च मेऽणवश्च मे श्यामाकाश्च मे नीवाराश्च मे ॥८॥

पञ्चमोऽनुवाकः ॥

अश्मा च मे मृत्तिका च मे गिरयश्च मे पर्वताश्च मे सिकताश्च मे वनस्पतयश्च मे हिरण्यं च मेऽयश्च मे सीसं च मे त्रपुरच मे श्यामं च मे लोहं च मेऽग्निश्च म आपश्च मे वीरुधश्च म ओषधयश्च मे कृष्टपच्यं च ॥९॥ मेऽकृष्टपच्यं च मे ग्राम्याश्च

मे पशव आरण्याश्च यज्ञेन कल्पन्तां वित्तं च मे वित्तिश्च मे भूतं च मे भूतिश्च मे वसु च मे वसतिश्च मे कर्म च मे शक्तिश्च मेऽर्थश्च म एमश्च म इतिश्च मे गतिश्च मे ॥१०॥

षष्ठोऽनुवाक: ॥

अग्निश्च म इन्द्रश्च मे सोमश्च म इन्द्रश्च मे सविता च म इन्द्रश्च मे सरस्वती च म इन्द्रश्च मे पूषा च म इन्द्रश्च मे बृहस्पतिश्च म इन्द्रश्च मे मित्रश्च म इन्द्रश्च मे वरुणश्च म इन्द्रश्च मे त्वष्टा च ॥११॥ म इन्द्रश्च मे धाता च म इन्द्रश्च मे विष्णुश्च म इन्द्रश्च मेऽश्विनौ च म इन्द्रश्च मे मरुतश्च म इन्द्रश्च मे विश्वे च मे देवा इन्द्रश्च मे पृथिवी च म इन्द्रश्च मेऽन्तरिक्षं च म इन्द्रश्च मे द्यौश्च म इन्द्रश्च मे दिशश्च म इन्द्रश्च मे मूर्धा च म इन्द्रश्च मे प्रजापतिश्च म इन्द्रश्च मे ॥१२॥

सप्तमोऽनुवाक: ॥

अँशुश्च मे रश्मिश्च मेऽदाभ्यश्च मेऽधिपतिश्च म उपाँशुश्च मेऽन्तर्यामश्च म ऐन्द्रवायवश्च मे मैत्रावरुणश्च म आश्विनश्च मे प्रतिप्रस्थानश्च मे शुक्रश्च मे मन्थी च म आग्रयणश्च मे वैश्वदेवश्च मे ध्रुवश्च मे वैश्वानरश्च म ऋतुग्रहाश्च ॥१३॥ मेऽतिग्रह्याश्च म ऐन्द्राग्नश्च मे वैश्वदेवश्च मे मरुत्वतीयाश्च मे माहेन्द्रश्च म आदित्यश्च मे सावित्रश्च मे सारस्वतश्च मे पौष्णश्च मे पात्नीवतश्च मे हारियोजनश्च मे ॥१४॥

अष्टमोऽनुवाक: ॥

इध्मश्च मे बर्हिश्च मे वेदिश्च मे धिष्णियाश्च मे स्रुचश्च मे चमसाश्च मे ग्रावाणश्च मे स्वरवश्च म उपरवाश्च मेऽधिषवणे च मे द्रोणकलशश्च मे वायव्यानि च मे पूतभृच्च म आधवनीयश्च म आग्नीध्रं च मे हविर्धानं च मे गृहाश्च मे सदश्च मे पुरोडाशाश्च मे पचताश्च मेऽवभृथश्च मे स्वगाकारश्च मे ॥१५॥

नवमोऽनुवाक: ॥

अग्निश्च मे घर्मश्च मेऽर्कश्च मे सूर्यश्च मे प्राणश्च मेऽश्वमेधश्च मे पृथिवी च मेऽदितिश्च मे दितिश्च मे द्यौश्च मे शक्वरीरङ्गुलयो दिशश्च मे यज्ञेन कल्पन्तामृक्च मे साम च मे स्तोमश्च मे यजुश्च मे दीक्षा च मे तपश्च म ऋतुश्च मे व्रतं च मेऽहोरात्रयोर्वृष्ट्या बृहद्रन्थरे च मे यज्ञेन कल्पेताम् ॥१६॥

दशमोऽनुवाक: ॥

गर्भाश्च मे वत्साश्च मे त्यविश्च मे त्र्यवी च मे दित्यवाट् च मे दित्यौही च मे पञ्चाविश्च मे पञ्चावी च मे त्रिवत्सश्च मे त्रिवत्सा च मे तुर्यवाट् च मे तुर्यौही च मे पष्ठवाट् च मे पष्ठौही च म उक्षा च मे वशा च म ऋषभश्च ॥१७॥ मे वेहच्च मेऽनड्वाञ्च मे धेनुश्च म आयुर्यज्ञेन कल्पतां प्राणो यज्ञेन कल्पतामपानो यज्ञेन कल्पतां व्यानो यज्ञेन कल्पतां चक्षुर्यज्ञेन कल्पतां श्रोत्रं यज्ञेन

कल्पतां मनो यज्ञेन कल्पतां वाग्यज्ञेन कल्पतामात्मा यज्ञेन कल्पतां यज्ञो यज्ञेन कल्पताम् ॥१८॥

एकादशोऽनुवाकः ॥

एका च मे तिस्रश्च मे पञ्च च मे सप्त च मे नव च म एकादश च मे त्रयोदश च मे पञ्चदश च मे सप्तदश च मे नवदश च म एकविँ॒शतिश्च मे त्रयोविँ॒शतिश्च मे पञ्चविँ॒शतिश्च मे सप्तविँ॒शतिश्च मे नवविँ॒शतिश्च म एकत्रिँ॒शच्च मे त्रयस्त्रिँ॒शच्च मे चतस्रश्च ॥१९॥ मेऽष्टौ च मे द्वादश च मे षोडश च मे विँ॒शतिश्च मे चतुर्विँ॒शतिश्च मेऽष्टाविँ॒शतिश्च मे द्वात्रिँ॒शच्च मे षट्त्रिँ॒शच्च मे चत्वारिँ॒शच्च मे चतुरचत्वारिँ॒शच्च मेऽष्टाचत्वारिँ॒शच्च मे वाजश्च प्रसवश्चापिजश्च क्रतुश्च सुवश्च मूर्धा च व्यश्नियश्चान्त्यायनश्चान्त्यश्च भौवनश्च भुवनश्चाधिपतिश्च ॥२०॥

इडा देवहूर्मनुर्यज्ञनीर्बृहस्पतिरुक्थामदा निशँ॒सिषद्विश्वे देवाः सूक्तवाचः पृथिवि मातर्मा मा हिँ॒सीर्मधु मनिष्ये मधु जनिष्ये मधु वक्ष्यामि मधु वदिष्यामि मधुमतीं देवेभ्यो वाचमुद्यासँ॒शुश्रूषेण्यां मनुष्येभ्यस्तं मा देवा अवन्तु शोभायै पितरोऽनुमदन्तु ॥

ॐ शान्तिः शान्तिः शान्तिः ॥

ॐ भवाय देवाय नमः।   ॐ भवस्य देवस्य पत्नै नमः।
ॐ शर्वाय देवाय नमः।   ॐ शर्वस्य देवस्य पत्नै नमः।
ॐ ईशानाय देवाय नमः।   ॐ ईशानस्य देवस्य पत्नै नमः।
ॐ पशुपतये देवाय नमः।   ॐ पशुपतेर्देवस्य पत्नै नमः।
ॐ रुद्राय देवाय नमः।   ॐ रुद्रस्य देवस्य पत्नै नमः।
ॐ उग्राय देवाय नमः।   ॐ उग्रस्य देवस्य पत्नै नमः।
ॐ भीमाय देवाय नमः।   ॐ भीमस्य देवस्य पत्नै नमः।
ॐ महते देवाय नमः।   ॐ महतोर्देवस्य पत्नै नमः।

ॐ निधनपतये नमः   ॐ निधनपतान्तिकाय नमः।
ॐ ऊर्ध्वाय नमः   ॐ ऊर्ध्वलिङ्गाय नमः।
ॐ हिरण्याय नमः   ॐ हिरण्यलिङ्गाय नमः।
ॐ सुवर्णाय नमः   ॐ सुवर्णलिङ्गाय नमः।
ॐ दिव्याय नमः   ॐ दिव्यलिङ्गाय नमः।
ॐ भवाय नमः   ॐ भवलिङ्गाय नमः।
ॐ शर्वाय नमः   ॐ शर्वलिङ्गाय नमः।
ॐ शिवाय नमः   ॐ शिवलिङ्गाय नमः।
ॐ ज्वलाय नमः   ॐ ज्वललिङ्गाय नमः।
ॐ आत्माय नमः   ॐ आत्मलिङ्गाय नमः।
ॐ परमाय नमः   ॐ परमलिङ्गाय नमः।

एतत् सोमस्य सूर्यस्य सर्वलिङ्ग ँ स्थापयति पाणिमन्त्रं पवित्रम् ॥

हरिः ॐ सद्यो जातं प्रपद्यामि सद्यो जाताय वै नमो नमः। भवे भवे नाति भवे भवस्य मां भवोद्भवाय नमः। वामदेवाय नमो, ज्येष्ठाय नमः श्रेष्ठाय नमो, रुद्राय नमः कालाय नमः

कलविकरणाय नमो बलविकरणाय नमो बलाय नमो बलप्रमथनाय नमः सर्वभूतदमनाय नमो मनोन्मनाय नमः ॥

अघोरेभ्योऽथ घोरेभ्यो घोरघोरतरेभ्यः ।
सर्वेभ्यः सर्वशर्वेभ्यो नमस्ते अस्तु रुद्ररूपेभ्यः ॥

ॐ तत्पुरुषाय विद्महे महादेवाय धीमहि ।
तन्नो रुद्रः प्रचोदयात् ॥

ईशानः सर्वविद्यानामीश्वरः सर्वभूतानां ब्रह्माधिपतिर्ब्रह्मणोधि-पतिर्ब्रह्मा शिवो मे अस्तु सदा शिवोम् ॥

ॐ नमो हिरण्यबाहवे हिरण्यवर्णाय हिरण्यरूपाय हिरण्य-पतयेऽम्बिकापतये उमापतये पशुपतये नमो नमः ॥

ॐ तच्छंयोरावृणीमहे । गातुं यज्ञाय । गातुं यज्ञपतये । दैवीस्वस्तिरस्तुनः । स्वस्तिर्मानुषेभ्यः । ऊर्ध्वं जिगातु भेषजम् । शं नो अस्तु द्विपदे । शं चतुष्पदे ॥

ॐ शान्तिः शान्तिः शान्तिः ॥

जगदीश-आरती

ॐ जय जगदीश हरे, स्वामी जय जगदीश हरे।
भक्त जनन के सङ्कट, क्षण में दूर करे॥ ॐ जय...

जो ध्यावे फल पावे, दुख विनसे मन का,
स्वामी दुख विनसे मन का।
सुख सम्पति घर आवे, कष्ट मिटे तन का॥ ॐ जय...

मातु पिता तुम मेरे, शरण गहूँ किसकी,
स्वामी शरण गहूँ किसकी।
तुम बिन और न दूजा, आस करूँ किसकी॥ ॐ जय...

तुम पूरण परमात्मा, तुम अन्तर्यामी, स्वामी तुम अन्तर्यामी।
पारब्रह्म परमेश्वर, तुम सबके स्वामी॥ ॐ जय...

तुम करुणा के सागर, तुम पालन-कर्ता
स्वामी तुम पालन-कर्ता।
मैं मूरख खल कामी, कृपा करो भर्ता॥ ॐ जय...

तुम हो एक अगोचर, सबके प्राणपती,
स्वामी सबके प्राणपती।
किस विधि मिलूँ दयामय, तुम से मैं कुमती॥ ॐ जय...

दीनबन्धु दुखहर्ता, तुम रक्षक मेरे, स्वामी तुम रक्षक मेरे।
अपने हाथ उठाओ, द्वार पड़ा तेरे॥ ॐ जय...

विषय विकार मिटाओ, पाप हरो देवा, स्वामी पाप हरो देवा।
श्रद्धा भक्ति बढ़ाओ, सन्तन की सेवा॥ ॐ जय...

शिव आरती

जय शिव ओङ्कारा, हर जय शिव ओङ्कारा।
ब्रह्मा विष्णु सदाशिव अर्धांङ्गी धारा॥

जय शिव...

एकानन चतुरानन, पञ्चानन राजै, शिव पञ्चानन राजै।
हंसासन गरुड़ासन, हंसासन गरुड़ासन, वृषभासन साजै॥

जय शिव...

दो भुज चार चतुर्भुज, दशभुज ते सोहै, शिव दशभुज ते सोहै।
तीनों रूप निरखता, तीनों रूप निरखता, त्रिभुवन जन मोहै॥

जय शिव...

अक्षमाला वनमाला, रुण्डमालाधारी, शिव रुण्डमालाधारी।
चन्दनमृगमद चन्दा, चन्दनमृगमद चन्दा, भाले शुभकारी॥

जय शिव...

श्वेताम्बर पीताम्बर, बाघम्बर अङ्गे, शिव बाघम्बर अङ्गे।
सनकादिक प्रभुतादिक, सनकादिक प्रभुतादिक, भूतादिक सङ्गे॥

जय शिव...

कर मध्ये करमण्डल चक्र त्रिशूल धर्ता, शिव चक्र त्रिशूल धर्ता।
जगकर्ता जगभर्ता, जगकर्ता जगभर्ता, जग का संहर्ता॥

जय शिव...

ब्रह्मा विष्णु सदाशिव जानत अविवेका, शिव जानत अविवेका।
प्रणव अक्षरनु मध्ये, प्रणव अक्षरनु मध्ये, ये तीनों एका॥

जय शिव...

त्रिगुण स्वामी जी की आरती जो कोई नरगावे,
शिव जो कोई नर गावै ।
कहत शिवानन्द स्वामी, कहत शिवानन्द स्वामी,
मनवाञ्छित फल पावे ॥
जय शिव. . .